D1086540

BATTLES
OF
WORLD
WAR II

MARTIN MARIX EVANS

Airlife

Copyright © 2002 Airlife Publishing Ltd

First published in the UK in 2002
by Airlife Publishing Ltd

Text written by Martin Marix Evans
Maps created by Peter Harper

British Library Cataloguing-in-Publication Data
  A catalogue record for this book
  is available from the British Library

ISBN 1 84037 387 3

All rights reserved. No part of this book may be reproduced
or transmitted in any form or by any means, electronic or
mechanical including photocopying, recording or by any
information storage and retrieval system, without permission
from the Publisher in writing.

Printed in Hong Kong

*Contact us for a free catalogue that describes the complete
range of Vital Guides and other Airlife books.*

Airlife Publishing Ltd
101 Longden Road, Shrewsbury, SY3 9EB, England
E-mail: sales@airlifebooks.com
Website: www.airlifebooks.com

Contents

The Battles of Narvik

On 9 April 1940 the Germans invaded Denmark and Norway in a move that caught the Allies entirely unprepared. Paratroops seized Stavanger and landed near Oslo, and almost the entire German Navy carried five army groups to key locations, from north to south: Group I to Narvik, Group II to Trondheim, Group III to Bergen, Group IV to Kristiansand and Group V to Oslo. German naval losses comprised the heavy cruiser *Blücher* to Norwegian coastal artillery in Oslo Fjord, the light cruiser *Königsberg* to artillery and Royal Navy aircraft off Bergen, the cruiser *Karlsruhe* to the British submarine *Truant* off Kristiansand, and the pocket battleship *Lützow* was severely damaged by torpedoes from the submarine *Spearfish* south of Oslo Fjord.

On land the Allied response to the invasion was slow. The Norwegians, under Major-General Otto Ruge, staged a fighting retreat, withdrawing northwards, while the British concentrated on the warm-water port of Narvik in the far north because it was the route by which Swedish iron ore was exported and thus a key consideration for the German armaments industry. Here ten destroyers had landed a large German force, and at 04.30 hours on 10 April a flotilla of five British destroyers under Captain B. Warburton-Lee entered Ofot Fjord. They sank the German ships *Wilhelm Heidkamp* and *Anton Schmidt* and six merchant vessels, as well as damaging three more enemy destroyers. As they

withdrew, *Zenker*, *Geise* and *Koeliner* emerged from Herjans Fjord to the north-east and *Georg Thiele* and *Bernard Von Arnim* from a bay to the south-west. HMS *Hunter* was hit and began to sink, while Warburton-Lee's command, *Hardy*, was severely damaged and had to be beached, her captain killed. A shell hit the bridge of *Hotspur*, and out of control she ran into *Hunter*, finally sinking her. The surviving destroyers, *Hostile* and *Havoc*, returned to help *Hotspur* escape.

On 13 April the British struck again. The battleship HMS *Warspite*, in company with nine destroyers, entered the fjord at 13.00 hours. The 15-inch guns of the capital ship smashed the gallant resistance of the remaining eight German destroyers and a Swordfish aircraft accounted for the submarine *U-64* by torpedo.

The land battle for Narvik was a long time in coming. The expeditionary force for Norway had been embarked from the Clyde in Scotland on 11 April for a number of destinations, but it was poorly organized and the Narvik force was under the command of an elderly major-general, P.J. Mackesy. He set up a base at Harstad, offshore in the Lofoten Islands, and resisted efforts by Admiral Whitworth to persuade him to attack Narvik at once with the Royal Marines and Guards Brigade at his disposal. Mackesy feared that naval bombardment of the town would result in unacceptable civilian casualties, but the delay gave the defending German

British soldiers and a lone civilian crowd the quay of a fishing port during the withdrawal from Norway. (Taylor Library)

RAF Coastal Command attack on shipping in a Norwegian fjord. (Taylor Library)

Germans were advancing northwards, and the 24th Guards Brigade was deployed to oppose them.

The third battle of Narvik began on the night of 13/14 May, just as yet another commander-in-chief, Lieutenant-General Claude Auchinleck took over. Three battalions of Chasseurs Alpins, two of the French Foreign Legion, four of Polish troops and some 3,500 Norwegians under the command of the French general M.E. Béthouart established themselves north of the town, and by 28 May all German resistance had ceased. However, in France, the offensive begun by the Germans on 10 May was fast approaching a climax. The decision was taken to abandon the Norwegian campaign in order to oppose the Germans closer to England. By 8 June the entire Allied force of about 24,000 men had been evacuated. As they sailed away, the German battlecruisers *Scharnhorst* and *Gneisenau*, in company with the cruiser *Hipper*, intercepted the British aircraft-carrier *Glorious*. The carrier had taken on board the RAF Hurricanes and Gladiators that had been flying in Norway. In spite of the bravery with which the escorting destroyers made smoke, *Glorious* was fatally damaged and the destroyer *Ardent* was sunk. The second escort ship, *Acasta*, attacked and hit *Scharnhorst* with a torpedo before herself being sunk. Forty-five men survived, while 1,474 Royal Navy and 41 RAF men were lost.

The conquest of Norway cost the German Navy not only ship losses that would cripple her future surface operations, but also some 5,500 men as casualties. Further, a garrison of 350,000 men was needed to retain Norway against possible Allied invasion. What was gained was a base from which aircraft and naval vessels could do damage to Allied shipping.

commander, Major-General Eduard Dietl, time to reinforce the place. Admiral the Earl of Cork and Orrery was sent with further reinforcements and instructions to assume overall command. He ordered a bombardment on 24 April, but it did not bring the benefits hoped for. Meanwhile the

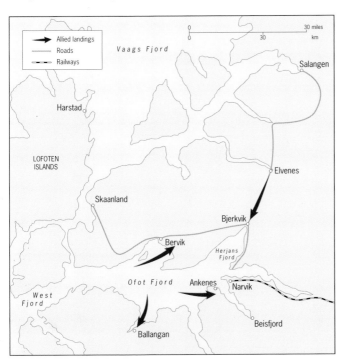

Casualties

German: 5,500

British: 4,500 (1,500 in the naval action, 8 June)

Norwegian: 1,800

French and Polish: 500

After the fall of Poland in 1939, a period known as the Phoney War, a time of inactivity other than preparation for war, followed during the harsh winter. Allied plans assumed an attack would be made through Belgium, and Plan D, an advance into Belgium once attack forced her to abandon her neutrality, was adopted. On the German side a plan was eventually evolved for the attack by Army Group B through Belgium and the Netherlands to be a feint, while the major thrust was to be through the forested region of the Ardennes, over the River Meuse and across the plains of northern France to the Channel. The operation was called *Sichelschnitt* – Sickle-stroke.

On Friday 10 May the German assault began, and the Allies, including the British Expeditionary Force (BEF), moved to a north–south line east of Brussels. While the French opposed 3rd and 4th Panzer in Belgium, the bulk of the German Panzers were making their way along the forest roads of the Ardennes further south, facing only light resistance, a few felled trees and no air attack. By Sunday evening they were on the Meuse, Rommel's 7th Panzer at Dinant, Reinhardt's XLI Panzer Corps at Monthermé and Guderian's XIX Panzer Corps at Sedan.

It was the view of Allied commanders that, as in the First World War, a river crossing could not be made without massive artillery support, and the arrival of the tanks on the riverside appeared to be no cause for great alarm. What they had not recognized was that aircraft could be used instead, and the 1,000-plane attack spearheaded by Junkers Ju 87Bs, Stuka dive-bombers, of the *Luftwaffe*'s Eighth Flying Corps on the French Second Army at 11 a.m. on Monday 13 May was devastating. By early afternoon 1st Panzer had crossed at Glaire and 10th Panzer at Wadelincourt, and by dark they had gained the hills south of the river, allowing 2nd Panzer to overcome the tough resistance at Donchery.

At Monthermé, at the confluence of the Meuse and the Semois rivers north of Sedan, Reinhardt's XLI Panzer were heroically opposed by machine-gunners of the French Colonial Infantry, and it was not until Wednesday 15 May that 6th Panzer broke through.

Rommel's 7th Panzer was at Dinant on Sunday 12 May, in time to see the Belgian Engineers blow the bridges there, and at Houx and Yvoir later in the afternoon. The French were hurrying men into the sector and had gained some time, but in the night a small German party crossed the footbridge to the island at Houx, and from there, at 05.30 hours on Monday, attacked over the lock gates to gain a precarious bridgehead on the western bank. At Bouvignes, nearer Dinant, a group who had crossed in rubber boats and were meeting fierce resistance were supported by Panzers firing from the riverside road to the east. Rommel's engineers were building pontoon bridges at Houx and tanks were passing over them the next day. French reinforcements were yet to arrive, and French armour was being deployed in small groups rather than a concentrated mass, and with refuelling support lacking. On Wednesday 15 May Rommel cut past the French armour at Flavion, leaving his artillery and infantry to engage it, and drove west as fast as he could. Corap's army had been penetrated and bypassed. At 05.15 hours on Friday the Germans were at Le Câteau, having come 30 miles (50 km) in twenty-four hours.

South of Sedan Guderian left 10th Panzer and the Grossdeutschland Regiment to attack the French at Stonne while he turned his main force westwards. The partially formed French 4th Armoured Division, under the command of Colonel Charles de

The island at Houx, north of Dinant on the Meuse, used by Rommel's troops to establish a bridgehead on the west bank.

(Author)

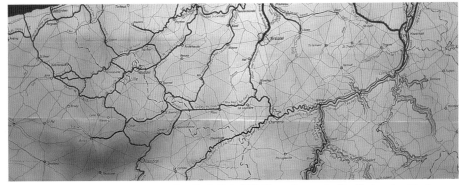

German map of river and canal obstacles produced in Berlin in 1939. The southern route offers the fewest problems.
(Author's collection)

Gaulle since 11 May, attempted to cut off the German advance at Montcornet on Friday 17 May, but Guderian scarcely mentions it in his memoirs. He was in dispute with Kleist, who wanted to halt the advance and allow the rest of the Army to catch up. Guderian managed to get permission to continue a 'reconnaissance in force', ceased to use radio communication and, apparently leaving his HQ stationary, pushed on. De Gaulle's second attack two days later at Crécy-sur-Serre was equally ineffective. On the night of 20/21 May Spitta Battalion of 2nd Panzer reached the sea at Noyelles on the Somme estuary. They had come 200 miles (320 km) in ten days.

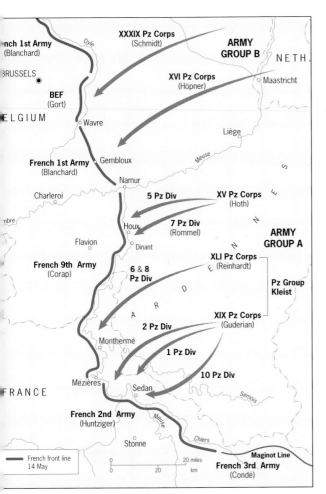

Forces opposed on the Meuse front:

French:
9th Army, General André Corap
2nd Army, General Charles Huntziger

German:
Army Group A, Colonel-General Gerd von Rundstedt
From 4th Army, Colonel-General Gunther von Kluge,
XV Panzer Corps, General Hermann Hoth
(5th Panzer and 7th Panzer, General-major Erwin Rommel)
From 12th Army, Colonel-General Wilhelm List, and
16th Army, Colonel-General Ernst Busch,
Panzer Group Kleist, General Ewald von Kleist,
XLI Panzer Corps, General Georg-Hans Reinhardt (6th and 8th Panzer)
XIX Panzer Corps, General Heinz Guderian (1st, 2nd and 10th Panzer and Grossdeutschland Regiment)

Operation Dynamo, Dunkirk

The breakthrough by the Germans was caused by, and added to, the disarray of the French High Command, and faith was placed in a new Commander-in-Chief, the 73-year-old General Weygand, who rushed home from Syria on 19 May and had to rest before he could take up his duties on Tuesday 21 May. The arrangements to meet General Lord Gort were botched, so that the Englishman missed the meeting and only General Billotte gained full knowledge of Weygand's intentions. Billotte was fatally injured in a car crash that evening and died two days later. First Army Group was leaderless for three days. Gort undertook an armoured strike west of Arras on Tuesday 21 May which Rommel reported was made by five divisions. 'Frankforce' under Major-General Harold Franklyn actually comprised three infantry battalions (6th, 7th and 8th Durham Light Infantry), two tank battalions (4th and 7th Royal Tank Regiment) and a motor-cycle battalion of 4th Royal Northumberland Fusiliers, and the French 3rd Light Mechanized Division formed the right wing. Although Rommel was given a set-back, the Allies had to withdraw, and it became clear to Gort that his task was now to preserve the BEF as best he could.

Uncertainty in the German High Command helped. Von Rundstedt and Adolf Hitler both worried about the vulnerable flanks of the lines of advance of the Panzers, and now the Arras attack had confirmed their fears. They were also worried about using tanks on boggy terrain, for their maps showed in a blue tint large tracts of clay familiar from the Ypres battles of the previous war and, in purple, areas of soft ground crossed by drainage ditches. They decided to use the Panzers as an anvil along the line of the canalized River Aa and the infantry of Army Group B and the *Luftwaffe* as the hammer to break the Allies. The 'Halt Order' remained in force from Friday 24 May until the evening of Sunday 26 May, preventing any advance by the Panzers, and on Tuesday 28 May it rained, causing Guderian to report the terrain more suitable for infantry than tanks. This combination of circumstances allowed the British on the south and east and the French on the south and west to form a defensive perimeter from Nieuport to Dunkirk.

By chance the Royal Navy, in need of small vessels for coastal and harbour duties, had appealed on 14 May to boat owners to volunteer their craft. On 19 May Vice-Admiral Bertram Ramsay was appointed to plan a possible evacuation of the BEF, and he was to make use of more than 370 of these small craft in Operation Dynamo. It soon became clear that only Dunkirk and the beaches immediately east of that harbour would be available, as Guderian's XIX Panzer Corps enveloped Boulogne and Calais. Offshore sandbanks parallel with the coast would force ships to run close inshore both approaching and departing from evacuation points, bringing them under enemy guns.

Operation Dynamo began on Sunday 26 May, just

British troops queue until neck-deep before being taken off the beaches of Dunkirk. *(Taylor Library)*

as the Halt Order was lifted. The British were now, technically, under the command of Admiral Jean Abrial, who was responsible for Dunkirk and whom Weygand had ordered to preserve a French enclave as a base for a counter-attack. The British, on the other hand were determined to evacuate as many men as possible and to destroy everything they could not take home – a source of friction with their allies. In spite of this they did co-operate to get increasing numbers of men away, and improved organization on the beaches and at the eastern breakwater of the harbour, the 'mole', followed the arrival of Rear-Admiral W.F. Wake-Walker on Thursday 30 May. The air atttacks were serious but limited by RAF sorties planned in the light of radar data acquired by installations in England and by adverse weather on Tuesday and Thursday. Lord Gort was ordered home on Friday 31 May, and at the same time the order was given from London that French and British troops should now evacuate in equal numbers. On that day the weather improved, the German air raids resumed and increasing numbers of ships operated only by night.

German pressure increased with an attack by four divisions on the Bergues–Furnes canal and at La Panne on Saturday 1 June. Weygand ordered the dissolution of 1st Army Group, and General Blanchard was evacuated, leaving some 25,000 French troops to maintain the perimeter. By Monday 3 June the Germans had advanced to the Dunkirk–Furnes canal, on the outskirts of the town,

A British destroyer, crowded with escaping soldiers, speeds away from Dunkirk. (Taylor Library)

and that night the last men were embarked and blockships were sunk in Dunkirk harbour. At 08.00 hours on 4 June the commanders of the French 60th and 68th Infantry Divisions made contact with the Germans, and shortly afterwards they and the 32nd Infantry Division surrendered. The Germans reported taking in all, both combat troops and wounded, about 40,000 men prisoner. Of 861 vessels, 693 of them British, recorded as taking part in Operation Dynamo, 243 were sunk, including twenty warships.

The war in France was not over; it now turned southwards. In the west the 51st Highland Division was surrounded at St-Valery-en-Caux, and, an evacuation attempt having failed, was obliged to surrender on 12 June. The last organized British unit to leave was 159 (Lloyds) Battery, 53rd City of London Regiment, from Marseilles on 20 June. An armistice was signed the following day when Hitler compelled the French to humble themselves at Compiègne, where Germany had conceded in the previous war.

Allied Forces and Commanders:
French Land Forces, C-in-C: General Maurice-Gustave Gamelin to 19 May 1940; General Maxime Weygand thereafter.
French Forces, North-East Front, C-in-C: General Joseph Georges.
1st Army Group, General Gaston Billotte, injured 21 May, died 23 May. From 24 May, General Georges Blanchard.
from north to south of the line 10 May
French Seventh Army, General Henri Giraud
British Expeditionary Force, General the Viscount Gort to 31 May, Major-General Harold Alexander thereafter.
French First Army, General Blanchard to 24 May, General René Prioux thereafter.
French Ninth Army, General André Corap to 16 May, General Giraud thereafter.
French Second Army, General Charles Huntziger

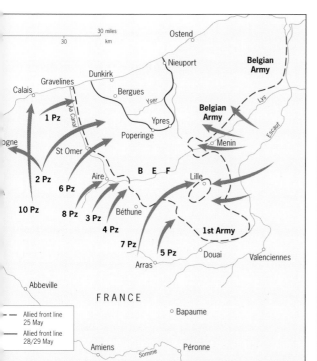

British and Allied Troops Landed in England (Admiralty figures)

Date	From Beaches	From Harbour	Total
27 May	0	7,669	7,669
28 May	5,930	11,874	17,804
29 May	13,752	33,558	47,310
30 May	29,512	24,311	53,823
31 May	22,942	45,072	68,014
1 June	17,348	47,081	64,429
2 June	6,695	19,561	26,256
3 June	1,870	24,876	26,746
4 June	622	25,553	26,175
Total	**98,671**	**239,555**	**338,226**

Of whom the British troops numbered 198,315 (59 %)

The French and other Allies numbered 139,911 (41 %)

Spitfires taking off from an airfield near London, 1 October 1940. (Taylor Library)

After the fall of France Hitler gave orders for the invasion of England in an operation codenamed Sealion. In preparation for this, the German airforce, the *Luftwaffe*, was given the task of destroying the Royal Air Force.

Fear of air attack had been widespread in forecasts of what would happen in a mid-twentieth-century war, but preparations in Britain did not receive full attention before the appointment of Dowding to Fighter Command in 1936. Radar (Radio Detection and Ranging) was shown to be viable by Robert Watson-Watt on 26 February 1935, and it was developed under the codename of Radio Direction Finding (RDF). By September 1939 eighteen Chain Home stations, as the early-warning system was known, had been built and connected to Dowding's HQ at Stanmore, and more were under construction. Together with the visual recognition and radio intercept posts of the Royal Observer Corps and the command and control systems of the Operations Rooms, radar would give the RAF the opportunity to counter *Luftwaffe* attacks. However, it took about fifteen minutes for a German force to fly from France to RAF airfields just south of London with Me 109 cover at 26,000 feet (7,900 m) and seventeen minutes for radar information to reach a squadron and get a Spitfire to 20,000 feet (6,100 m). In theory the attackers still had a slight advantage.

The first phase of the Battle of Britain began on 12 August, with attacks on RAF fighter airfields. At the same time the Chain Home station at Ventnor on the Isle of Wight was destroyed, but the Germans failed to appreciate how important it was to bomb the others. In the following week raids continued, reducing, as the Germans believed, the RAF to about two hundred operational fighters, whereas the true figure was about six hundred. In the process, *Luftflotte* 5, flying from Scandinavia, lost 75 aircraft in twenty-four hours to 12 and 13 Groups. On 14 August the American Olympic Gold Medal bobsleigh driver, Billy Fiske, was killed flying a Hurricane. He had joined the RAF as a Canadian. Bad weather on 19 August forced a pause.

German bomber performance had been unimpressive. The Ju 87 Stuka dive-bomber, now meeting serious opposition from modern fighters, proved too slow and cumbersome in air battle. The level bombers were too light to carry sufficient loads to inflict severe damage on airfields. Thinking he could destroy what he considered was the small remnant of Dowding's force in the air, Göring changed tactics, sending small bomber forces to attack sensitive airfield targets and large fighter forces to kill off the fighters that were bound to hurry to their defence, while other bombers switched to night operations. The new approach came perilously close to success, in spite of the unforeseen strength of the RAF, and precipitated a fierce dispute between Park and Leigh-Mallory

10

about tactics. The latter favoured 'Big Wing' formations to concentrate on shooting down German bombers, and resented having to protect Park's airfields while his aircraft were in combat. The time interval associated with radar warnings had widened in favour of the British as their operatives increased in skill, thus making Big Wing organization feasible, but the argument was not put to the test under the conditions of the second phase: circumstances changed again.

On 25 August stray German bombers dropped their loads on London. In retaliation, the RAF flew raids on Berlin. It is possible, but not certain, that these events caused Hitler to target London. For whatever reason, the bombing of London, known as the Blitz, began on 7 September in a daylight raid of 300 bombers, escorted by 600 fighters. The RAF was taken by surprise and was poised to continue its defence of airfields. The huge fires in London guided 180 night bombers to continue the attack. There were more than 2,000 casualties, 430 of them fatal. On 8 September the Duxford wing left the airfields to fend for themselves and went for the German bombers, with significant success. In developing their attacks on London the Germans dispensed with feints at other targets. This allowed Park to intercept with doubled-up squadrons as far from London as Canterbury on 15 September, and also helped 12 Group's Big Wing catch raiders over the Thames. A second wave on the same day met the same fate. Winston Churchill, visiting 11 Group's HQ at Uxbridge that day, asked Park about the strength of his reserves, only to be told there were none. The Germans lost sixty aircraft on 15 September (not the 185 claimed by the RAF),

bringing the total to 175 in a week. It was the turning point, and Göring was forced to admit that he had failed to destroy the RAF; the emphasis now changed to bombing raids on cities.

London was not alone in being bombed; Birmingham and Liverpool had already suffered, and other cities in the south of England and Wales would also be hit in the coming months. The defence of London took time to build, but within days anti-aircraft guns and searchlights were in evidence, even if largely ineffectual. On 15 October a 400-bomber night raid on London did massive damage, while the RAF shot down only one enemy aircraft. In November raids were made on Coventry, Birmingham and major sea-ports, and the ports became the prime targets from February to May 1941.

Two factors brought the Blitz to an end. First, the planned attack on the USSR, Operation Barbarossa, drew the *Luftwaffe* away from England in May 1941. Second, British technical competence increased with radar control of searchlights and anti-aircraft guns and with the introduction of the AI Mk IV radar-equipped Bristol Beaufighter, the first success of which was over Oxfordshire on the night of 19 November 1940.

The plotting table in the Operations Room at Duxford, now a part of the Imperial War Museum. (Author)

Allied Forces and Commanders
RAF Fighter Command, Air Chief Marshal Sir Hugh Dowding to 24 November 1940, Air Marshal Sir William Sholto Douglas thereafter.
    10 Group, Air Vice-Marshal Sir Quintin Brand.
    11 Group, Air Vice-Marshal Sir Keith Park.
    12 Group, Air Vice-Marshal Sir Trafford Leigh-Mallory.
    13 Group, Air Vice-Marshal Richard Saul.
Anti-Aircraft Command, General Frederick Pile.
German Forces and Commanders
    Luftwaffe, *Reichsmarschall* Hermann Göring.
    Luftflotte 2, *Feldmarschall* Albert Kesselring.
    Luftflotte 3, *Feldmarschall* Hugo Sperrle.
    Luftflotte 5, General Hans-Jurgen Stummpf.

The memory of the Blitz was evoked in a German propaganda sheet dropped to British troops in Italy in 1944. (Tom Roe Collection)

RAF Fighter Aircraft and Pilots

Vickers-Supermarine Spitfire, 19 squadrons at July 1940.

Hawker Hurricane, 31 squadrons at September 1939.

Number available for operations on 3 August 1940:	708
Losses, July to October 1940:	
Total losses	1,140
Severe damage	710
Total	1,850
Fighters built, July to October 1940:	
Hurricanes	1,134
Spitfires	731
Total	1,865
Casualties, Pilots killed, missing or POW:	481
Pilots wounded:	422

Luftwaffe Aircraft

Estimated operational against Britain August 1940:	
Bombers (Heinkel 111, Dornier 17 and	
Junkers 88)	998
Dive-bombers (Ju 87)	261
Single-engine fighters (Me 109)	805
Twin-engine fighters (Me 110)	224
Other	262
Losses July to October 1940:	
Claimed by RAF	2,692
Admitted by Germany	896
Total losses	1,733
Severe damage	643
Losses in the Blitz	*c.*600
Civilian Casualties in the Blitz	
Killed	43,000
Injured	139,000

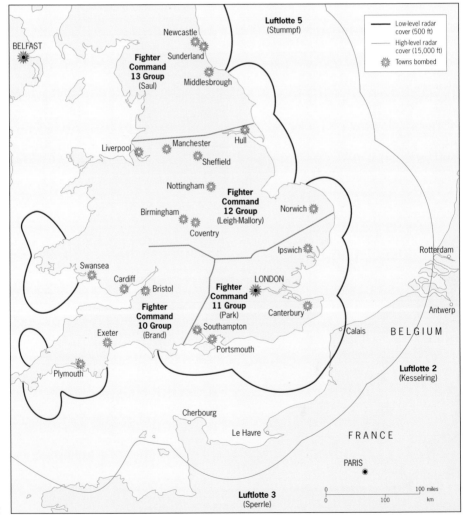

At the outbreak of the war, the *Kriegsmarine*, the German Navy, was seriously deficient in men and ships, but the few it had were formidable. The fall of Norway and of France provided forward naval bases from which they could operate, but before that the pocket battleships *Deutschland* (to be renamed *Lützow* in 1940) and *Admiral Graf Spee* were in operation in the North and South Atlantic respectively. The *Graf Spee* had sailed from Wilhelmshaven on 21 August 1939 and operated from the start of the war on 3 September principally off the south-western shores of Africa. She destroyed nine ships but was hunted down by twenty-two British warships organized in eight groups, one of which (the cruisers HMS *Exeter*, HMS *Ajax* and HMS *Achilles*), under the command of Commodore Henry Harwood, was positioned off the estuary of the River Plate in South America. The German ship was sighted on 13 December 1939, and action was joined, but the 9-inch (229 mm) guns of *Exeter*, the most heavily armed of the cruisers, were ill-matched with the 11-inch guns of *Graf Spee* and she was severely damaged. The light cruisers were also damaged but scored hits on their adversary, which was making for the port of Montevideo. Now short of ammunition and in the belief that overwhelming British forces were gathering, Captain Hans Langsdorff took his ship to sea and blew her up on 17 December.

In the North Atlantic the losses sustained in the Norwegian campaign limited what the Germans could attempt. The battle-cruisers *Scharnhorst* and *Gneisenau* made a successful foray into the Atlantic early in 1941, sinking twenty-two ships, before entering the French port of Brest. They broke out of there in February 1942 and managed to run the length of the English Channel under British attack to gain their home ports. The pocket battleship *Admiral Scheer* was withdrawn from operations in the South Atlantic and Indian Oceans, where she accounted for sixteen ships, to join the force threatening convoys to the USSR in 1942. This was to be the principal function of the German surface Navy for the rest of the war.

The surface War of the Atlantic had, however, come to an end in May 1941. The formidable modern battleship *Bismarck* and the heavy cruiser *Prinz Eugen* sailed from Gdynia (Danzig) on 18 May and were observed by RAF aircraft in Bergen on 21 May. They put to sea heading for the Denmark Strait, between Iceland and Greenland, to take station to attack shipping in mid-Atlantic. They were seen by the British cruisers HMS *Suffolk* and HMS *Norfolk* on 23 May, and the battle-cruiser HMS *Hood* and the battleship HMS *Prince of Wales*, the latter still with workmen aboard and not fully ready for service, moved to intercept. The German ships concentrated their fire on *Hood*, and a chance shell hit her magazine, blowing her up with the loss of all but three of her crew. The *Prince of Wales* was also hit and forced to withdraw. The German ships were themselves damaged, and *Bismarck* was then, on 24 May, hit by a torpedo launched by a Swordfish aircraft from the carrier HMS *Victorious*. Leaking fuel, she turned for Brest while *Prinz Eugen* sailed south before, eventually, making for France as well.

The pursuing British ships lost contact and, until

Swordfish torpedo-bombers huddled on the deck of HMS Victorious *before their attack on* Bismarck. *(Taylor Library)* 13

In the distance smoke rises from the doomed **Bismarck**, *under fire from* **HMS** Rodney. *(Taylor Library)*

radio silence was breached, had no idea where their enemy was. Even then errors on handling the data led to the battleship HMS *King George V* sailing in the wrong direction for a while. On 26 May, at 10.30 hours, an RAF Coastal Command Catalina (PBY-5) piloted by a US Navy officer saw *Bismarck*, and attacks were launched by Swordfish from the carrier HMS *Ark Royal*, part of Force 'H' in company with the battle-cruiser HMS *Renown* and the cruiser HMS *Sheffield,* approaching from Gibraltar. The first wave of torpedo-bombers, relying on radar in the foul weather, mistook *Sheffield* for *Bismarck*, but fortunately scored no hits. The second wave, commanded by Lieutenant-Commander Tim Coode, took off at 19.15 hours and lost cloud cover at two miles' range and 700 feet of altitude. The battleship avoided most of the torpedoes, but at least one damaged her steering gear. The battleships *King George V* and *Rodney* were able to close on the helpless ship, and she was finally sunk by torpedoes from the cruiser HMS *Dorsetshire*. Only 115 of her crew of 2,222 survived. Recent underwater investigation has shown that she had not, as was alleged, been scuttled.

The surface war then moved to the battles off the shores of Norway rather than the main British supply routes across the Atlantic. The USSR was desperate for supplies in the fight on the Eastern Front, and ships sailed in the most evil of conditions for the White Sea ports of Archangel and Molotovsk, open in summer, and the ice-free port of Murmansk.

The Arctic Convoys, as they were known, demanded outstanding courage of the Allied seamen. Their routes took them as far from the aircraft and warship bases in Norway as ice conditions permitted. In March 1942 Convoy PQ12 was threatened by *Bismarck*'s sister ship *Tirpitz*, and the presence of this huge battleship in Trondheim led to a series of attacks on her by the British, some from the air and some from the sea by human torpedoes (October 1942) and by midget submarines (September 1943). On 20 March 1942 Convoy PQ13 lost five ships. Air attack then became more severe, and PQ16 lost seven ships in May. On 27 June PQ17 sailed from Iceland. On 4 July Ultra intelligence reported that *Tirpitz, Admiral Hipper, Admiral Scheer, Lützow* and a force of destroyers were at Altenfjord to attack the convoy. The convoy was ordered to scatter, and the waiting U-boats and aircraft sank twenty-six of its thirty-seven ships. The needs of Operation Torch in North Africa caused convoys to be suspended until the end of the year, when JW51B was attacked by a force including *Admiral Hipper* and *Lützow* in what became known as the Battle of the Barents Sea. The Germans were, at a price, driven off and Hitler lost faith in the use of large surface vessels. After another pause in the sending of convoys to the USSR when the anti-submarine war reached its height, Convoy JU55B was the target of *Scharnhorst* in December 1943. Forewarned by Ultra, the British 10th Cruiser Squadron was sent to prevent the attack. In the Battle of North Cape *Scharnhorst* was driven back and intercepted by a heavy squadron under Admiral Sir Bruce Fraser and sunk.

Tirpitz was moved to Tromsø to become, in effect, a defensive artillery battery, and was subjected to various bomb atacks until finally destroyed by 'Tallboy' bombs dropped by 617 Squadron, RAF Bomber Command, the unit that had attacked the Ruhr dams and earned the nickname of the Dam Busters.

German Surface Raiders

Battle-cruisers
Scharnhorst: launched December 1936, 31,000 tons, nine 11-inch (279 mm) guns, twelve 5.9-inch (150 mm) guns and fourteen 4.1-inch (100 mm) guns.
Gneisenau: launched October 1936, armament as *Scharnhorst*.
Heavy Cruisers
Admiral Hipper: launched February 1937, 12,000 tons, eight 8-inch (203 mm) guns, twelve 4.1-inch guns and twelve torpedo tubes.
Prinz Eugen: launched August 1937, 14,600 tons, armament as *Admiral Hipper*.
Pocket Battleships
Lützow (formerly *Deutschland*): launched May 1931, 12,000 tons, six 11-inch, eight 5.9-inch and six 4.1-inch guns.

Admiral Graf Spee: launched June 1934, 12,000 tons, six 11-inch, eight 5.9-inch, six 4.1-inch guns and eight torpedo tubes.
Admiral Scheer: launched April 1933, 12,000 tons, armament as *Graf Spee*.
Battleship
Bismarck: launched April 1939, 42,000 tons, eight 15-inch (381 mm), twelve 5.9-inch and sixteen 4.1-inch guns.

Arctic Convoys: 21 August 1941 to 16 April 1945

4.43 million tons of cargo shipped.
7% of cargo lost.
7.8% of eastbound ships lost.
3.8% of westbound ships lost.

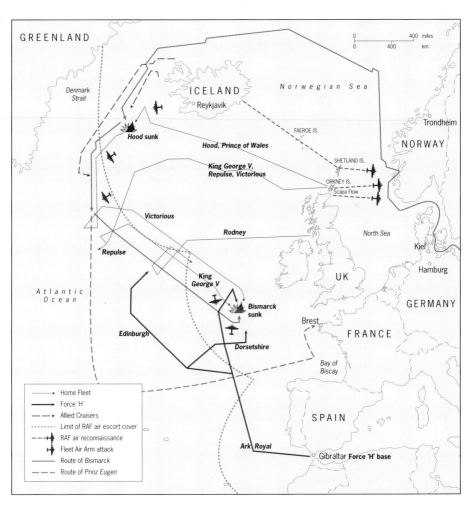

A Grumman Avenger of No. 819 Squadron, Fleet Air Arm, flying from the escort carrier HMS Tracker, attacks German submarine U-288 while defending Arctic Convoy RA58 on 3 April 1944. (Taylor Library)

The liner *Athenia* was torpedoed by a German U-boat commanded by *Kapitänleutnant* Fritz-Julius Lemp on 1 September 1939, the first victim of the submarine war. The U-boat offensive was under the command of Admiral Karl Dönitz, who thought that, given a sufficient number of vessels, he could win the war for Germany. He required 300, but in August 1940 had a mere twenty-seven, of which only thirteen were on station.

The British tactics were informed by their experience in the previous war, and they were of the opinion that U-boats could only operate effectively close inshore. The anti-submarine cover for convoys, sparse as it was with few corvettes and destroyers available, was therefore limited to a line at 12° West, with heavier ships to counter surface attacks employed further out into the Atlantic. The principal weapon employed against the submerged enemy was the depth-charge (D/C), a cylinder packed with explosive and fitted with a detonator operated by water pressure to go off at a given depth. The underwater target was located by Asdic, or Sonar, which had serious limitations. A submarine on the surface could be engaged with gunfire.

In order to overcome the hit-and-miss risks of allowing individual submarines lurking off ports in the hope of seeing a target, Dönitz built up his fleet of sea-going U-boats and devised the tactic of the wolf-pack to attack Allied convoys. Far out in mid-Atlantic a line of U-boats stood guard at right angles to the route of a convoy which intelligence suggested was due to pass. When one of the waiting boats located the target, a high-frequency radio message was sent to HQ and a medium-frequency homing signal was then broadcast to concentrate the U-boats to attack. The strike usually took place at night, with the U-boats moving swiftly on the surface to penetrate the escort screen and fire their torpedoes as quickly as possible before withdrawing, or, if seen by an escort vessel, crash-diving before bobbing and weaving to escape detection. The system worked exceedingly well.

The antidote was in the restriction of the packs' freedom of movement, but lacking appropriate radar

at this stage of the war, the emphasis was on air observation and attack and the extension of escort by anti-submarine ships. These ships did little to combat tactics that Dönitz had designed to evade them. In April 1941 flying commenced from Iceland, and in June the Royal Canadian Navy started escorting convoys from Newfoundland. It was, however, a departure from normal conduct that made the greatest contribution to the anti-U-boat war. On 9 May 1941 Convoy OB318 was attacked south of Iceland by a number of U-boats, including *U-110* commanded by *Kapitänleutnant* Lemp, who sank two of the convoy's ships. He in turn was attacked by the destroyers *Bulldog*, *Broadway* and *Aubretia*. Depth-charge damage was so severe that Lemp was forced to surface and abandon ship. The destroyers began an intense fire to sink their enemy, but Commander A.J. Baker Cresswell of *Bulldog*, recalling the capture of ciphers from the German ship *Magdeburg* in 1914, ordered a cease-fire and sent a boarding party to the U-boat to see what they might find. Lemp and another German swam back to their boat to defend it, but were shot, and the boarding went ahead to discover a mass of classified documents, charts showing minefields, codes and an Enigma machine in perfect order. The Enigma coding/decoding device enabled the British to understand the German naval messages vital to organizing the U-boat wolf-packs up to February 1942. At that point the Germans put extra rotors into their Enigma machines. HMS *Petard* acquired one of the new machines from *U-559* in the Mediterranean in November.

In August 1941 the British Prime Minister Winston Churchill and the American President Franklin D. Roosevelt agreed that the western half of the Atlantic Ocean, including Iceland, should become, in practice, an American protectorate in which ships would enjoy escort by US Navy vessels, releasing the British to concentrate on waters closer to Europe. This, coupled with particular efficiency and parsimony in the consumption of supplies in Britain, rendered the German effort to starve England ineffective. There was still a serious gap in the air cover of the ocean, leaving a vulnerable hour-glass-shaped area, narrow between Greenland and Labrador, wide between Spain and Florida, closing to total cover between Brazil and Ascension Island and widening again in the South Atlantic.

The entry of the USA into the war after the attack on Pearl Harbor in December 1941 gave the U-boats a renewed period of destructive success. The Americans failed to institute a system of coastal convoys, and relied on regular patrols to search for and destroy U-boats. Sinkings became commonplace for a while, but the extension of aircraft reconnaissance and the organization of convoys along British and Canadian lines steadily reduced the losses.

Other factors contributing to the increasing effectiveness of the Allied campaign were the more effective air cover given to convoys by auxiliary aircraft carriers and very-long-range (VLR) aircraft flying from the shore. The auxiliary HMS *Audacity*, a converted merchant vessel, sailed with Convoy OG74 to Gibraltar on 13 September 1941, providing cover with her Martlet fighters flying ahead and to the side of the convoy to sight U-boats before they could become a threat. The Leigh Light, proved in action by Jeaffreson Greswell in June 1942, illuminated submarines moving on the surface by night. The introduction of the VLR Liberator (PB4Y-1) aircraft in August 1942 narrowed the mid-Atlantic gap. The new 10 cm radar with a 360° sweep enabled escort ships to maintain surveillance in the dark, and high-frequency direction-finding equipment (HF/DF, or Huff-Duff) permitted a fix to be taken on U-boat radio transmissions. The problems arose when specialist ships were needed for other operations or where under-equipped and inexperienced crews were involved. The acoustic torpedo, first used on 12 May 1943 by RAF pilot John Wright, homed on submarines.

By early 1943 Dönitz was in command of the *Kriegsmarine*, the German Navy, and also of more

than 400 U-boats. Another change in the Enigma machine broke the Allied access to intelligence in March, and merchant ship losses increased alarmingly. Convoys were given priority in escort ships and aircraft cover. VLR Liberators were numerous by May, and more escort carriers were put into service. U-boat losses increased intolerably, twenty-seven in May alone, bringing the total to a hundred that year. The wolf-packs were withdrawn and Allied shipping losses levelled off. The war in the Atlantic continued, but could now be sustained.

Asdic/Sonar

In 1917 the Allied Submarine Detection Investigation Committee, a joint French and British working party, was set up to look into a system of detecting submarines by using sound. A pulse of noise was reflected from a submarine's hull and by analysis of the time elapsed, distance could be calculated. Asdic, as it became known to the British, could determine distance and direction, but not depth. It was therefore necessary for an attacking ship to drop a pattern of depth-charges set for differing depths to try to rupture a U-boat's hull. As the noise of the pulse was also heard within the submarine, evasive action could be taken. In the USA Sound-Navigation, Ranging (Sonar) was developed in the 1930s, and the name was adopted by the Royal Navy in 1943.

The Consolidated Vultee Model 32 Liberator

The B-24 (US Army Air Force designation), PB4Y (US Navy) or Liberator (British) was put into production in 1940. The version used for long-range reconnaissance, the GRV, had four Pratt & Whitney engines and sacrificed armour to increase fuel capacity. It carried a .303 or 50-calibre gun in the nose, a 50-calibre in the upper turret, four .303 or two 50-calibres in the waist and four .303s in a Boulton Paul tail turret. The payload of depth-charges was 5,400 pounds (2,450 kg).

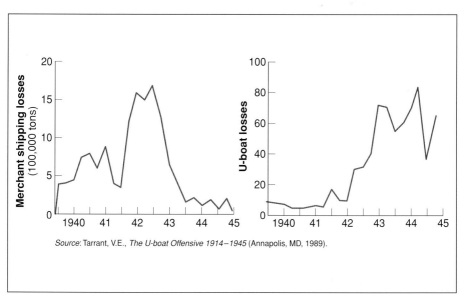

Source: Tarrant, V.E., *The U-boat Offensive 1914–1945* (Annapolis, MD, 1989).

The Battles of the Mediterranean Sea

With the fall of France in June 1940 and the entry of Italy into the conflict on the German side, Britain faced Germany in the Battle of Britain, and Italy in North and East Africa. Further, the French forces were an unknown quantity in the power equation. There were French troops in the mandated territory of Syria and more troops in her province of Algeria and protectorate of Tunisia. The British held the key naval bases of Gibraltar and Malta on the route to Egypt, an ally since 1936, and the Suez Canal, a crucial route to India and to the oil-rich Persian Gulf – a long and vulnerable line of communication.

Admiral François Darlan had given his undertaking to Winston Churchill, the British Prime Minister, that the French fleet would never be allowed to fall into the hands of the Germans or the Italians. With the formation of the Vichy government in what remained of France, a government to which Darlan was apparently loyal, the question arose in earnest, for at Mers-el-Kebir, the port of Oran in Algeria, there were two battleships, two battle-cruisers, *Dunkerque* and *Strasbourg*, of capability similar to *Scharnhorst*, an aircraft-carrier, three light cruisers, ten destroyers and eight submarines, as well as a large number of lesser craft. A little further to the east there were another three cruisers, nine destroyers and more than twenty submarines. The possible threat to the British Navy in the Mediterranean was immense.

Vice-Admiral James Somerville was ordered to take Force H and issue an ultimatum to the French, requiring them to remove their ships to a neutral or non-threatening port, scuttle them, or face destruction. The force, including three battleships, the carrier *Ark Royal*, two cruisers and eleven destroyers, served this notice on Admiral Gensoul on 3 July, the same day as French ships in British ports were taken over. The Admiral refused to meet the British, and replied to a letter that the ships would not be surrendered to anyone. He was, perhaps, truthful, but at 17.54 hours the British, lacking the required response, opened fire. The *Strasbourg* got away and managed to reach Toulon, as did the cruisers from Algiers, but the French battleships were sunk or beached and the *Dunkerque* ran aground. The loss of life was considerable and the attack was a source of lasting bitterness on the part of the French. The French squadron in Alexandria, a battleship, three heavy and one light cruiser and three destroyers, agreed to immobilize itself. Only the substantial Italian Navy remained.

The sinking Italian submarine Cobalto, *rammed by, and damaged by gunnery from, the destroyer HMS* Ithuriel *on convoy escort duty in the Mediterranean. (Taylor Library)*

As the land war in the Balkans and North Africa evolved, the importance of supply routes through the Mediterranean led to successive encounters between the navies. In July 1940 Admiral Sir Andrew Cunningham was in command of a convoy that had to fight off an Italian attack, and on 18 July HMAS *Sydney* sank an Italian cruiser. The threat to British convoys was removed in dramatic fashion.

The principal Italian naval base was at Taranto, in the northern corner of the gulf that divides the 'heel' from the 'toe' of Italy. On 11 November 1940 the port was raided from the air. Aerial photographic reconnaissance had shown that, shortly before the planned date of the raid, barrage balloons and torpedo nets had been deployed in the outer harbour, the Mar Grande. With this intelligence the success of the raid could be guaranteed, provided the aircraft got through the other defences. Surprise and darkness were the key. That night twenty-one Swordfish biplane torpedo bombers flew from the carrier *Illustrious* in two waves an hour apart. The first approached from the west and the leading aircraft dropped flares before attacking the cruisers in the inner harbour, thus drawing the anti-aircraft fire from their comrades who were launching their torpedoes on targets in the outer harbour. The second wave came from the north-west to avoid the torpedo nets and balloons. Only two British aircraft were shot down, and three battleships and a cruiser were hit. Even more important was the withdrawal of the Italian ships to ports further north and west, increasing the range of any attack they might plan on British convoys. The success of the attack was closely studied by the Japanese, but not by the Americans, as the events at Pearl Harbor would show.

In November 1940 the Italian *Duce* (leader), Benito Mussolini, began an attempt to invade Greece, and in early 1941 his fleet moved towards the straits between Cape Matapan, at the southern extreme of Greece, and the island of Crete to oppose British efforts to lend support to the Greeks. On 25 March the British code-breakers at Bletchley Park, who had broken the Italian C38M machine cipher, reported the Italian intention. On 27 March air reconnaissance revealed that three Italian cruisers were moving east, and Admiral Cunningham sailed from Alexandria with three battleships, the aircraft-carrier *Formidable* and nine destroyers to rendezvous with Vice-Admiral H.D. Pridham-Wippel's force of four cruisers and four destroyers south of Crete. Further observation from the air showed that there were three Italian formations, one including the battleship *Vittorio Veneto*, and that they, too, were south of Crete.

Air strikes from *Formidable* on 28 March scored small success, although one torpedo did the battleship slight damage. One Swordfish of No. 815 Squadron flew from Crete to join in the action, and its pilot, Lieutenant Michael Torrens-Spence, saw the carrier-borne aircraft attack through the Italian smoke-screen as the ships moved to the west. Then, taking advantage of a break in the smoke, he launched a torpedo on the cruiser *Pola*. He saw no hit, but the *Pola* sustained such severe damage that, at 21.00 hours, Admiral Angelo Iachino ordered the cruisers *Zara* and *Fiume* back to her assistance. With the advantage of his radar, Cunningham was able to carry out a night attack, and at about 22.30 hours, to sink all three of the heavy cruisers and two of their destroyer escorts. The *Vittorio Veneto* succeeded in returning to Taranto and the cruisers *Garibaldi* and *Abruzzi* made it to Brindisi. It was a major blow to Italian sea power. For the British it would mean that the reverses to come in Greece and Crete could, to some extent, be mitigated by the evacuation of a proportion of her troops.

Military operations in the Mediterranean were intensely interdependent, action at sea, surface, submarine and aerial, linking closely with land campaigns. The British supply lines to the Middle East and Egypt ran either round the Cape of Good Hope, the extreme southern tip of Africa, or, three weeks shorter in sailing time, across the Mediterranean Sea. This quick route was exposed to attack by air and sea from the north, and at its centre was the fortress island of Malta, a mere sixty miles (95 km) from Sicily.

The Italians launched their first air raid on the island on 11 June 1940. The governor, Lieutenant-General William Dobbie, had only four aircraft at his disposal, and one of those was irretrievably damaged. The defence had to be conducted by Gloster Gladiator biplanes named *Faith*, *Hope* and *Charity*, which were found in crates aboard the carrier *Glorious*. Immediate efforts to reinforce Malta were put in hand, but only just sufficient to resist German attacks from Sicily which started in January 1941. German distraction with the invasion of the USSR in June gave some respite, but from December 1941 pressure grew inexorably.

Between January and late July 1942 there was just one day on which Malta was not subjected to air attack. In January alone there were 262 raids. Attacks were also made by submarine and surface vessels and by aircraft on the convoys attempting to supply the island. Of the eighty-six cargo vessels that tried to get through, in convoy or independently, thirty-one were sunk. Even when they made harbour their troubles were not at an end. In June 1942 two convoys tried to convene on Malta, one from the west and one from the east. The latter was forced to turn back with nine merchant ships left of the eleven that set out, while the other got through with two of the six that began the voyage. These two were bombed as they unloaded their cargo, and of the 26,000 tons carried by the six vessels only 5,000 tons were delivered. The civilians took to an appalling underground existence which brought disease to add to their sufferings. By

the end of the siege 1,493 would be dead and a further 3,764 wounded.

Supplies and reinforcements also arrived by other means. In March 1942 the carrier HMS *Eagle* succeeded in flying two formations of sixteen Spitfires each into Malta from from 600 miles (965 km) away, but in April problems with her steering gear kept her in port. Churchill appealed to Roosevelt for help, and the American carrier *Wasp* was sent to pick up fighters in the Clyde, Scotland, to help the now seaworthy *Eagle* deliver 126 Spitfires in April and May. Supplies were also carried by submarine. The minelayers *Rorqual* and *Cachalot* were used from mid 1941 onwards. *Rorqual*'s first cargo consisted of two tons of medical supplies, sixty-two tons of aviation fuel, forty-five tons of kerosene for cooking, nearly a hundred and fifty bags of mail and twenty-five passengers.

Malta's gallantry in resisting the Axis was recognized in April 1942 with the unprecedented award of Britain's highest civilian decoration for bravery, the George Cross. By that time the strain was telling on General Dobbie, and he was relieved, by General Lord Gort. On 10 May the German Commander-in-Chief South, Field Marshal Albrecht Kesselring, declared that Malta had been neutralized, and that the threat to German supply lines to North Africa was over as Rommel approached, and was obviously going to take, Egypt, and so German aircraft were held to combat attempts at relief. Although the verdict was mistaken and the easing of air attack welcome, the situation on the island was desperate and became yet more so with the failure of the convoys from east and west in June.

A convoy on an entirely new scale was planned to bring relief. With fourteen merchant vessels as cargo carriers, the escort would comprise four aircraft-carriers, one of which, HMS *Furious*, would fly in fighters from a distance, while *Victorious*, *Indomitable* and *Eagle* would provide air cover as far as the Tunisian coast. There would be two battleships, *Nelson* and *Rodney*, seven cruisers and twenty-four destroyers. Altogether there would be thirty-seven warships for fourteen merchantmen. The undertaking was code-named Operation Pedestal.

Vice-Admiral Sir Neville Syfret took his convoy through the Straits of Gibraltar in fog on 10 August. *Furious* flew off her thirty-eight Spitfires the next day and turned for Gibraltar, but later that day, about seventy miles (112 km) north of Algiers, *Eagle* was torpedoed by the German submarine *U-73* and sank, taking her Hurricane fighters with her. That evening a force of thirty-six Junkers Ju 88 and Heinkel He 111 bombers made a rather feeble attack, while their bases were hit in turn by RAF Bristol Beaufighters from Malta. The intensity of the attacks mounted steeply on 12 August as about eighty torpedo- and dive-bombers

The surviving Gloster Gladiator, Faith, *wingless, awaits restoration before being installed in Malta's Aviation Museum. (Nigel Cave)*

June 1942: heavy anti-aircraft guns open fire on enemy aircraft over Malta. (Taylor Library)

scored slight damage on the carrier *Victorious* and seriously damaged one of the merchant ships, which was later sunk. Then *Indomitable* had her flight deck so badly damaged that she had to turn back and one of the destoyers was sunk. By early evening the convoy was off Bizerte, on the Tunisian coast, the point at which the major vessels had to turn back, leaving four cruisers and twelve destoyers to complete the escort task, Rear-Admiral H.M. Burrough in command.

As they approached the Tunisian coast, along which they planned to creep towards Malta, the Italian submarine *Axum* torpedoed Burrough's flagship, the cruiser *Nigeria*, and the anti-aircraft cruiser *Cairo*. *Nigeria* was forced to attempt the return trip to Gibraltar, in which she succeeded, but *Cairo* was too badly damaged and had to be sunk. The two cargo vessels were lost and the cruiser *Kenya* was hit by a torpedo, though the damage was slight. On they went, round the north-eastern extremity of Tunisia, Cape Bon, and down the coast where the minesweepers would, with luck, prevent further loss. The danger, when it came, was from coastal craft, motor torpedo boats. By morning four more merchantmen and another cruiser had gone.

Some respite was provided by Axis mistakes. The Italian Navy put to sea to try to repeat their success of the previous June against the convoy from Alexandria, but their German allies insisted that the

Luftwaffe could and should finish the job. As the Italians returned to port the British submarine *Unbroken* torpedoed two cruisers, *Bolzano* and *Attendolo*, near the Strait of Messina.

The morning of 13 August brought fresh attacks, sinking one merchant vessel and damaging three more, including the American oil tanker *Ohio*. The remaining three cargo vessels, *Melbourne Star*, *Port Chalmers* and *Rochester Castle*, were sent with all speed and under cover of Malta-based aircraft to make port that afternoon, while the damaged ships were nursed along by the remaining destroyers. Another air attack accounted for *Dorset*, but *Brisbane Star* and *Ohio* made it, the latter kept afloat by a destroyer lashed alongside and with a crashed German dive-bomber lodged in her deck. Of the fourteen merchant ships that had started the voyage, five survived and only two were unscathed. Four warships had been lost and three damaged. The threat of starvation and the inevitable consequence, the surrender of Malta, had been averted.

Kesselring renewed his efforts in October, but once again the island held out. November brought the final relief. In North Africa the Second Battle of El Alamein deprived the Germans of air bases, and the arrival of the convoy from Alexandria in Operation Stonehenge brought crucial supplies when food was down to twelve days' rations and aviation fuel to five.

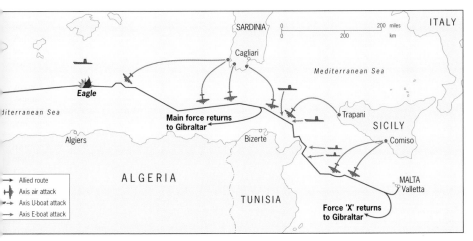

The Bomber Campaign against Germany

The Avro Lancaster served with 65 squadrons in the RAF. Their heavy night bombers dropped a total of over 600,000 tons of bombs and flew 156,000 sorties during the war. (Martin Bowman)

At the outbreak of the war there was no substantial previous experience to draw upon in planning a strategic bombing campaign or predicting its outcome. The belief that the bomber would always get through led to the policy of mounting a massive counter-bombing campaign rather than defensive measures. For Britain the drawback was that the German air force was larger, and that, until Germany struck at Britain with bombers, Britain would leave Germany alone. Before the late summer of 1940, therefore, tactical bombing of military targets in the field was the principal activity. When Germany began to bomb London on 25 August 1940, which might well have been an operational error, RAF Bomber Command retaliated with a raid on Berlin.

The problem with daylight raids, as the attacks by the *Luftwaffe* on England in the Battle of Britain demonstrated, was that bombers were excessively vulnerable unless given substantial fighter protection. Britain therefore carried out bombing raids by night. The inevitable consequence was that precision bombing was out of the question. An analysis by D.M. Butt, an official of the British war cabinet secretariat, of 100 raids made between early June and late July 1941 showed that of 6,103 sorties only 4,065 in fact attacked the assigned target, and of these only one in three dropped its bombs within five miles (8 km) of the target. A policy of area bombing was thus the only one possible if strategic bombing was to be carried out at all, and in 1941 bombing was virtually the only means of striking back at the enemy.

Air Marshal Arthur Harris became AOC-in-C of Bomber Command in February 1942 and energetically pursued the area bombing policy, mounting raids on Lübeck and Rostock, and in May the first 1,000-bomber raid was directed against Cologne (Köln). Immense damage was done, but the raids on Essen, two nights later, and Bremen, on 25 June, were less productive from the bombers' point of view and too costly in aircraft lost. It was concluded that such large raids yielded too small a dividend. Increased reliance was placed on technical developments in navigation and bomb aiming. Research done in Britain by Solly Zuckerman and J.D. Bernal into the effect of German bombing showed, in February 1942, that loss of industrial production was caused by direct damage to factories and that incendiary bombs did the most harm to them. It further showed that morale was not significantly depressed by bombing. These conclusions were ignored by Churchill's scientific adviser, Lord Cherwell, who advocated the area bombing policy.

In March 1942 the Ruhr was attacked with success, and in July 1943 Hamburg was bombed with such intensity that 40,000 civilians were killed. In November that year the emphasis shifted to Berlin, and by the following March over 9,000 sorties had been made, with a loss rate of over ten per cent. An even greater number of missions were flown over other cities, with similarly unsustainable losses. Nor was the campaign hitting German output. Tank production rose from 760 a month in early 1943 to 1,229 by the end of the year. Aircraft output increased from 15,288 in 1942 to 25,094 in 1943 and 39,275 in 1944. The German night-fighter and anti-aircraft defences were proving that, even if the bomber got through, the cost was intolerable.

General Henry Arnold, commander of the United States Army Air Force (USAAF), was, in the case of Europe but not of Japan, an advocate of strategic bombing of specific targets rather than the area bombing favoured by Harris. At the Casablanca Conference of January 1943 it was agreed that both policies were to be employed, and the Eighth USAAF was tasked with hitting such targets as aircraft and ball-bearing factories in the Combined Bombing Offensive (CBO). The CBO had been advocated by Lieutenant-General Ira C. Eaker, commander of the Eighth USAAF, and provided that the British would continue their night raids while the Americans would operate by day. The precision required dictated that the raids must be made by daylight, and the USAAF put its faith in the self-defensive capabilities of its B-17 Flying Fortress aircraft. The British warned of the danger from high-performance fighters, but early experience over France, where fighter cover was available, increased American confidence. In January 1943 the first raid beyond supporting fighter range was carried out and the expensive campaign continued until the autumn.

On 17 August the Americans attacked the towns of Schweinfurt, east of Frankfurt-am-Main, and Regensburg, south-east of Nürnberg, with a force of 376 B-17s. Sixty aircraft were shot down. However, Schweinfurt's production met nearly forty per cent of Germany's ball-bearing needs and was considered a mandatory target. Increased armament of both B-17s and B-24s (Liberators) and tight formation flying were, it was hoped, to prove adequate defence. On 14 October 360 B-17s in two task forces and 60 B-24s in another were to carry out the attack. The Germans had developed tactics to counter the American use of large, tight formations, using *Schwarm* (four aircraft) and *Staffel* (squadron, twelve aircraft) formations to break up the large bomber masses and finish off the damaged, separated individuals. Their fighters, Messerschmitt Me 109Gs and Focke-Wulf Fw 190As, were nearly twice as fast as the bombers.

In the event the weather prevented more than twenty-nine B-24s of 2nd Bombardment Division getting together, and they could only make a feint towards the Frisian Islands. The B-17s, beyond friendly fighter support range, met the *Luftwaffe* fighters between Aachen and Frankfurt. For three hours more than three hundred aircraft mauled the American formations, breaking them up with rocket attacks and picking off the dispersed aircraft with gunfire. Of the first wave, 1st Bombardment Division, 40th Combat Bombardment Wing lost twenty-seven bombers on the journey to the target. The second group, 3rd Bombardment Division, took a more southerly route and got through with the loss of a single aircraft. The bombing itself was successful. The 228 B-17s dropped nearly 400 tons of high explosive and 88 tons of incendiaries on or close to the three factories. The return journey was even more heavily attacked by German fighters, and the total losses for the mission were forty-five from the 1st Division and fifteen from the 2nd, with a further twelve severely damaged and 121 needing repairs. The German losses were thirty-eight fighters shot down and twenty damaged. Although some two-thirds of the production capacity of the ball-bearing factories had been destroyed, the USAAF would remember the day as Black Thursday.

The solution to the vulnerability of the bombers came with the re-engining of a fighter the Americans had rejected but the British had bought – the P-51 Mustang, with an engine derived from the Rolls-Royce Merlin and built by Packard. With a range of over 600 miles, this fighter could provide the protection which daylight bombers required. The use of fighters in this way was something that the British Air Chief Marshal Sir Charles Portal had expressly rejected earlier in the war, and the American experience showed him to have been mistaken.

The Boeing B-17 Flying Fortress was flown by the USAAF on daylight raids over occupied Europe. Before the introduction of long-range fighters, they suffered greatly from the Luftwaffe's defending fighters.

With the invasion of France in June 1944, bombing policy was revised once more. In the period of the invasion itself the emphasis was on disruption of German transport likely to bring support to the areas attacked by the Allies. Once this requirement had passed, the argument was how to proceed. Three schools of thought existed. US General Carl Spaatz, supported by Portal, favoured targeting German fuel production plants; without fuel the transport and armoured fighting vehicles would come to a halt. Air Marshal Sir Arthur Tedder advocated the destruction of the German transport system. Harris adhered to area bombing, and in the last three months of 1944 more than half Bomber Command's attacks were on cities.

As the Allies advanced into Germany from east and west, and as the Russians were pushing the Germans back from Breslau (Wroclaw) in Poland, it was proposed in London that the cites on the line of retreat from, or reinforcement of, that place should be bombed in addition to Berlin. This brought Dresden, Chemnitz and Leipzig into danger. Harris was doubtful about it, given the distance and the small intelligence possessed about the city of Dresden in particular, but the orders were clear, the support of the Soviet armies being considered essential. On the night of 13/14 February 1945 805 aircraft of Bomber Command, in two waves, dropped 2,659 tons of high-explosive and incendiary bombs on Dresden, and the USAAF followed up on 14 and 15 February with forces totalling 600 bombers. The best figures available for casualties suggest that 50,000 people were killed.

Given the proved ability of bombers at that time to carry out precision raids, and the collapse of the *Luftwaffe* after the Ardennes campaign, the need for area bombing appears, at the least, questionable, much as the raid may have seemed necessary at the time.

Approximate figures for the weight of bombs dropped in the war against Germany are, by the RAF, 955,044 and, by the USAAF, 621,877: over one and a half million tons.

Strategic Air Offensive, Germany

RAF Bomber Command and Eighth USAAF sorties (missions) flown, aircraft lost and, in brackets, losses from causes other than enemy gunfire, between September 1939 and May 1945.

	RAF		USAAF	
	Flown	Lost	Flown	Lost
1939	333	41 (8)		
1940	20,809	652 (158)		
1941	30,608	1,272 (359)		
1942	35,050	1,716 (316)	1,453	42 (5)
1943	64,528	2,671 (357)	27,362	1,036 (108)
1944	157,448	2,932 (359)	210,544	3,497 (394)
1945	64,758	838 (239)	94,186	973 (150)
	373,514	10,123 (1,796)	332,904	5,548 (657)

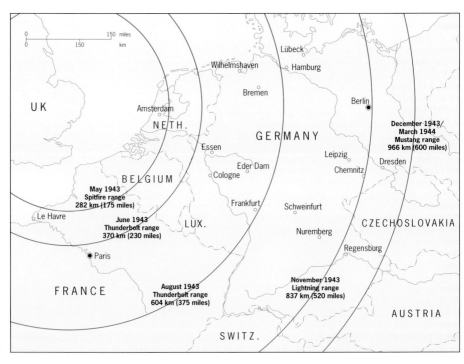

The Siege of Tobruk

An Australian soldier watches Italian prisoners being trucked into Tobruk, December 1940. (Taylor Library)

On 10 June 1940, when it became clear that the Germans were winning in France, Mussolini declared war. On 13 September the commander of the Italian forces in Libya, Marshal Rodolfo Graziani, who had succeeded Marshal Italo Balbo when he was shot down by his own anti-aircraft guns, received orders to attack the British in Egypt. His Tenth Army advanced to Sidi Barrani but halted to await supplies. In Operation Compass General Archibald Wavell launched the Western Desert Force under General Richard O'Connor against the numerically superior Italians, rolling them back as far as Beda Fomm, 400 miles (640 km) to the west, and taking 130,000 prisoners. This final coup was achieved by the 7th Armoured Divison cutting across the broad peninsula of Cyrenaica to cut off the Italians as they retreated before the 6th Australian Division.

The situation was soon reversed. Wavell's forces were depleted by the attempt to stem the German advance in Greece, and in February 1941 Hitler sent aid to his ally in North Africa. It consisted of General Erwin Rommel, the 5th Light Division and, in April, the 15th Panzer Division. Long before Wavell thought it possible, on 24 March, the Germans attacked, and by 11 April the British were very much back where they had started, while the port of Tobruk was isolated and surrounded behind enemy lines, defended by the 9th Australian Division under Major-General L.J. Morshead. Rommel was now a long way from his supply port of Tripoli, having ignored advice to be cautious by the Deputy Chief of Staff, Lieutenant-General Friedrich Paulus. Unable to go forward, Rommel concentrated on reducing the fortress of Tobruk and gaining the use of its harbour.

On 11 April, Good Friday, the Easter battles began with the armoured element of the 5th Light Division, the 5th Panzer Regiment, attacking west of the El Adem Road. The Australians were undeterred, and the 1st Royal Tank Regiment's cruiser tanks exchanged fire with the Panzers across the anti-tank ditch. That night intensive patrolling

and minelaying took place. On Easter Sunday, as the day cooled at 17.00 hours, the Germans broke into the perimeter through the Red Line. A half-dozen Australians including Corporal Jack Edmondson counter-attacked with grenades and fixed bayonets, an action that cost Edmondson his life and earned him the Victoria Cross. By 05.00 the next day 2nd Battalion, 5th Panzer had tanks inside the fortress and had advanced about half a mile (800 m). Morshead knew just where they were and deployed 1st and 3rd Royal Horse Artillery and 1st Royal Tanks to make ready for them once dawn had broken. As the Panzers pushed forward into the Pilastrino Escarpment they came under heavy, accurate fire both from the flank and from 1st RHA's guns firing over open sights. The German tanks pulled back, becoming mixed up with the next wave of Panzers. The British tanks then opened fire on the milling crowd. By 07.00 hours seventeen German tanks had been destroyed and the intrusion ejected. Supporting German infantry had been halted by Australian troops in posts flanking the breach in the Red Line and Rommel's men had suffered a bloody reverse.

The next German effort was made at the end of the month on the south-western corner of the enclave towards Hill 209. On the evening of 30 April the Red Line was breached again, and the Germans pushed towards Maccia Bianca, but were surprised at the tenacity with which the Australians, even when wounded and apparently leaderless, continued to resist from their scattered defence posts. Once again guns and tanks were readied to receive the next morning's attack. Seven Royal Tanks' Matildas were moved to Pilastrino in the path of the expected advance. As day broke, fog obscured the scene. Rommel was forced to delay his attack until 08.00 hours. When, finally, his tanks moved forward they brushed aside the infantry's anti-tank fire but then ran into a minefield that had hastily been laid. Seventeen Panzers were disabled. Further attacks on Red Line posts flanking the breach were tried, but suppressed in fierce hand-to-hand fighting.

25

Trenches and dug-outs made for the defence of Tobruk, 1941. (Taylor Library)

By the end of the day the Germans had gained a salient, but failed to make a breakthrough. In an attempt to cut the German position from the east the Matildas of 1st Royal Tanks moved along the Red Line westwards but were met both by enemy tanks and by 88 mm gunfire. To their dismay their previously invulnerable armour was insufficient to protect them; the British had encountered the Germans' versatile and deadly 88 mm gun.

The gallant defence of Tobruk brought pressure on Wavell to relieve the fortress. Operation Brevity under General Gott began on 15 May with an attempt to take Halfaya Pass, which succeeded, as did the attacks on Sollum and Fort Capuzzo, the keys to the two roads to the west. The left flank protection attempted by 2nd Royal Tanks was countered, and they were nearly cut off and had to withdraw, which led to the end of the operation. On 27 May the Germans regained the pass. The next effort was more ambitious. Operation Battleaxe followed the sending of a fast convoy to Alexandria from Britain to supply tanks and fighters. The tanks were a disappointment: 135 Matildas, each needing a two-day stay in the workshops, and 67 Crusaders, untried and untested. What was more, the operation's secrecy was blown; the repetition of the codeword 'Peter' had been given its correct significance by the Germans.

On 15 June the 11th Indian Brigade and its supporting Matildas ran into substantial anti-tank fire from the 88 mm guns and a newly laid minefield in Halfaya Pass, while the Crusader tanks of 7th Armoured Brigade which intended to sweep round the left flank broke down or fell to 88 mm guns at Hafid Ridge. The Tobruk garrison, known now as Tobforce, had been intended to break out. Their move was cancelled.

On 1 July Wavell was replaced by General Sir Claude Auchinleck who, in spite of pressure from London, took his time to prepare the next offensive, Crusader. In the meantime the Australians were relieved from the beleaguered fortress; having already suffered 3,194 casualties of the total 5,989 that would be sustained here, including the loss of 744 Australian lives, their government felt they had done enough. General Alan Cunningham was given command of the new Eighth Army, and the operation was launched on 18 November. At the same time Rommel had planned to make his next attack on Tobruk, this time from the south-east and along the Bardia Road. The British, New Zealand, Indian and South African troops followed the armour in a sweep around the southern end of the German line, and the men in Tobruk made a break-out to the south-east. Rain fell heavily, making aerial observation by either side impossible. Cunningham failed to keep his armour concentrated and Rommel took full advantage in preventing XXX Corps reaching the new salient out of Tobruk. Cunningham was dismayed and sought Auchinleck's permission to withdraw. It was not granted. Rommel then, on 24 November, mounted a thrust around the south of the British and attempted to reach Sollum and the coast, but found the 4th Indian Division unyielding. On 25 November Auchinleck replaced Cunningham with Major-General Neil Ritchie, but the battle had by now turned in his favour. The RAF had achieved air superiority and the resources of the Axis forces were seriously depleted. Rommel had to retreat. On the night of 26/27 November the New Zealanders linked with Tobforce, and despite a temporary incursion by the enemy, Tobruk was relieved. Crusader carried the British forward into Cyrenaica once more.

Axis Forces in North Africa, July 1941
Commander-in-Chief: General Ettore Bastico
Panzergruppe Afrika, General Erwin Rommel

Afrika Korps (DAK), General Crüwell
    15 Panzer, General Neumann-Silkow
    21 Panzer, General von Ravenstein
    90LT, General Sümmermann
    Recce Bns 3 and 33

Corpo d'Armata XXI, General Navarini
    Bologna, General Gloria
    Trento, General Stampioni
    Pavia, General Franceschini
    Brescia, General Gambon
    Savona, General di Giorgis
    Artillery Group Böttcher

Corpo di Manovra, General Gambarra
    Ariete, General Balotta
    Trieste, General Piazzoni
    Corps Artillery

Eighth Army, September 1941
General Alan Cunningham

XIII Corps, Major-General A. Godwin-Austen
    4th Indian Division, Major-General F.
    Messervy
    New Zealand 2nd Division, Major-General
    B. Freyberg, VC
    1st Army Tank Brigade, Brigadier H. Watkins

XXX Corps, Lieutenant-General C. Norrie
    7th Armoured Division, Major-General W. Gott
    South African 1st Division, Major-General
    G. Brink
    Oasis Force, Brigadier D. Reid

The exchange of the 9th (Australian) Division for 70th Division

Operation Treacle, 19–29 August.
Arrived: Polish 1st Carpathian Brigade and Cavalry Regiment
Departed: Australian 18th Brigade, 18th Indian Cavalry, 152nd Light Anti-Aircraft

Operation Supercharge, 19–27 September.
Arrived: British 16th Infantry Brigade, 32nd Army Tank Brigade, 4 Royal Tank Regiment
Departed: Australian 24th Brigade and 24th Field Park Company

Operation Cultivate, 12–25 October
Arrived: British 14th and 15th Infantry Brigades, a Czechoslovak Infantry Battalion, 62nd General Hospital
Departed: 9th Division HQ and Divisional troops, Australian 26th and 20th Brigades, Australian 4th Hospital

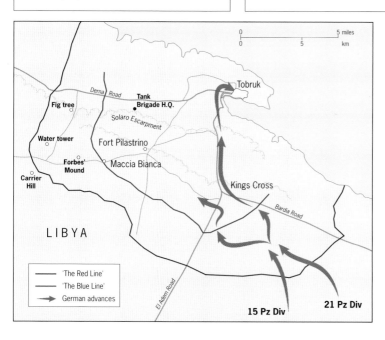

On 15 April 1941 officers of the *OKW* (*Oberkommando der Wehrmacht*), the German High Command, recommended to General Kurt Student, commander of XI Air Corps, that Malta should be subjected to an airborne invasion. He rejected the proposal, pointing out that Malta was too well fortified, and advocated Crete as the appropriate target. The island ran west to east, with accessible terrain on the northern side served by a single main road which could be cut and dominated. The island itself was important as a potential air base for the RAF to attack convoys in the Mediterranean and oilfields in Romania, as well as being the location of the Royal Navy base at Suda Bay. The idea was supported by the commander of the *Luftwaffe*, Göring, who saw a chance to restore the reputation of his service arm after the failure of the Battle of Britain. Hitler, in Führer Directive No. 28 of 25 April, authorized Operation Merkur (Mercury).

The forces that Student proposed to use would consist of paratroops, *Fallschirmjäger*, and mountain troops, *Gebirgsjäger*. The former would number 15,750 and the latter 7,000. Air transport would be provided by more than 500 Junkers Ju 52s and 80 gliders, supported by 280 bombers, 150 dive-bombers, 189 fighters and 40 reconnaissance planes from VIII Air Corps. The mountain troops would be transported by sea, and it was hoped that the air cover would protect them from the Royal Navy.

The Allied forces on Crete were composed mainly of those withdrawn from the failed attempt to stem the German advance in Greece itself. The 30,000 British and Commonwealth troops included the New Zealand 4th and 5th Brigades, the Australian 19th Brigade and the British 14th Brigade, fine soldiers but bereft of much of their equipment. Mortars lacked base plates and machine-guns their tripods, for example. The 11,000 Greek soldiers were no better off. There was virtually no transport. Armour consisted of sixteen light tanks of the 3rd Hussars, without radios or cooling equipment for their machine-guns, and six Matildas of 7th Royal Tank Regiment. Air cover ceased to exist when, on 19 May, the last five RAF fighters were withdrawn. In command of this array was Major-General Bernard Freyberg, VC, a New Zealander who had distinguished himself in the First World War. He had excellent information about German intentions because the Enigma codes used by the *Luftwaffe* had been easier to deal with than German army ciphers as a result of the inexperience of their signals personnel. Ultra thus provided the information that it was planned to drop paratroops at Máleme, Canea (Chanea), Retimo (Réthymno) and Heraklion (Irákleio) on 20 May. At Máleme and Canea the 21st, 22nd and 23rd New Zealand Battalions were deployed to meet them, at Retimo the Australians and some of the Greeks, while the balance were further east at Heraklion. As the German intentions became yet clearer as more

signal traffic was intercepted, Freyberg became aware that he could improve his dispositions, but dared not do so lest the Ultra intelligence was compromised.

A week of softening-up air raids preceded the invasion at 07.15 hours on 20 May. Glider-borne and parachuting troops, Group West, descended on Máleme airfield and in the Aiya Valley, west of Canea. They were slaughtered. The New Zealanders shot many before they even hit the ground. Of 600 men of 3rd Battalion, 1st Assault Regiment, attempting to take Máleme, 400 died that day. 1st Battalion, coming in by glider, ended the day with only 100 men alive and unwounded. Many paratroopers landing at a distance from their comrades fell victim to agricultural tools wielded by the inhabitants. 3rd Parachute Rifle Regiment took heavy casualties in the Aiya Valley, and 1st and 2nd were contained at Heraklion and Retimo. By the end of the day Student's men were in serious trouble and Freyberg had reason to rejoice. Freyberg's problem was that he had no way of knowing that.

The first of two fatal weaknesses of the British was now evident. Radio communication was almost completely lacking, so he was unable to obtain accurate information to assess, let alone give orders to counter, the disadvantages at which his subordinates were placing themselves. The British were close to the coast, but many of the Germans had come down further inland, with access to higher ground and also able to disrupt British troop movements that could lead to counter-attacks. The most serious error was made by the battalion commander in pulling 22nd New Zealand Battalion back to the east lest it be overrun the next morning. This opened the way for the Germans to occupy Hill 107, which overlooked Máleme airfield from the south, at dawn on 21 May.

With help from the *Luftwaffe*, the Germans held the New Zealanders off, and by afternoon Junkers transports were crash-landing at Máleme to deliver a battalion of 100th Mountain Regiment of the 5th Mountain Division. Wrecked aircraft were manhandled aside to allow the next plane to come in as the defenders' gunfire hailed down. The German hold was perilously fragile; all depended on the sea-borne troops' arrival.

The Royal Navy was most dangerously exposed. In a war in which mastery of the air was vital for the safety of fighting ships close to land, the RAF was absent, exhausted and deprived of aircraft in the battle for Greece. None the less Admiral Sir Andrew Cunningham, C-in-C of the Mediterranean Fleet put his ships at risk, and although two enemy convoys were prevented from reaching Crete, some 4,500 men of 5th Mountain Division landed together with artillery. The cost to the Royal Navy was high. On 21 May the cruiser *Juno* was sunk, and on 22 May the battleship *Warspite* and the cruiser *Naiad* were damaged, and the cruisers *Gloucester* and *Fiji* were sunk, as was the destroyer *Greyhound*. The next day Captain Lord Louis Mountbatten's destroyer *Kelly* and the destroyer *Kashmir* were lost. Before the end of the campaign two more ships – the cruiser *Calcutta* and the destroyer *Imperial* – would be sunk and another eight damaged. It was the costliest British naval battle of the war.

On 22 May an attempt by the New Zealanders to retake Máleme failed. Freyberg decided to pull them back before they were utterly destroyed. They fell back to Galatas, west of Canea, where they were attacked by the Germans on land and from the air. On 24 May Galatas fell, but the New Zealanders took it back and rolled the Germans west once more. The Germans came again. The line broke on 26 May, and Freyberg had to report to Wavell that the island could be held no longer. The Germans stuck to their original plan to secure the northern coast before anything else. The Royal Navy lifted some 4,000 troops from Heraklion before the Germans got that far east, and meanwhile the bulk of the defenders were making south over the

mountains to Sfakia (Sphakia) to wait under the cliffs for evacuation. Repeated and perilous voyages took 12,000 men off, but the last 5,000 had to be abandoned. Many scattered into the hills and were helped, at great risk to the helpers, to survive and even escape. The British and Commonwealth dead amounted to 4,200 soldiers and 2,000 sailors, while 11,835 were made prisoner. Some 10,000 Greeks had to surrender, about 1,000 having been killed.

The Germans had won an outstanding victory as a result of their courage and staying-power, but their losses were very great. German killed, wounded and missing totalled 6,698, two-thirds of them from 7th Air Division. Nearly 300 aircraft had been lost. Adolf Hitler remarked, 'Of course, you know that we shall never do another airborne operation. Crete proved that the days of parachute troops are over.' Events would show him to be only partly correct, for with proper support and as part of a well-structured combined operation, Allied paratroopers would contribute a great deal in Sicily, Normandy and on the Rhine.

Junkers Ju 52: the workhorse of the Luftwaffe's transport arm.

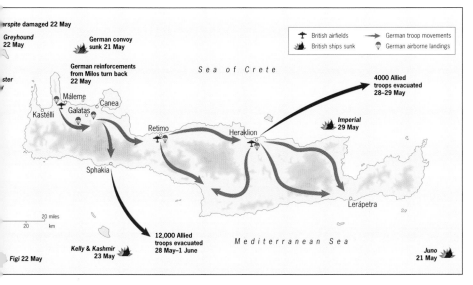

The success of Operation Crusader in November 1941 forced the Axis forces back to the southernmost point on the Gulf of Sirte, El Agheila. Here Rommel was significantly closer to his principal port of supply, Tripoli, and the British uncomfortably far from theirs. The Axis had lost 38,000 men as casualties, and some 300 tanks, while British losses were some 18,000 casualties. The scales appeared to be weighted in favour of Auchinleck and the British Eighth Army under Ritchie. A further attack was planned by the British for January.

In the previous September the Italians had succeeded in having the American Embassy in Rome broken into, and they acquired the cipher used by the military attaché in Cairo to report to Washington. This excellent source revealed to Rommel the extent to which Auchinleck was losing troops to the Far East, and in particular the extent to which the RAF was weakened. Encouraged by this and refreshed with reinforcements, he attacked first. On 21 January he drove for Agedabia, and by early February Cyrenaica was in his hands once more. Ritchie organized a defensive line from Gazala on the coast west of Tobruk to Bir Hacheim, more than fifty miles (80 km) to the south. The defences consisted of formidable minefields and a series of defensive boxes manned by XIII and XXX Corps, but even as a static defence system, the line had its faults.

First, it lacked depth; it was a strong set of beads on a string of minefields. Second, it had gaps not covered by the artillery within the boxes, notably in the south where some twenty miles lay between 150 Brigade in the Sidi Muftah box and Major-General J.P. Koenig's 1st Free French Brigade at Bir Hacheim. The armour was held back with 7th Armoured Division (the Desert Rats) in the south and 1st Armoured in the centre, neither properly integrated with the infantry in spite of recent attempted reforms. Auchinleck advocated locating the armour in the centre rear at a defensive position code-named Knightsbridge, but this was not done. The British were well supplied with tanks, 849 of them, of which 167 were American Grants with a 75 mm gun. The Gazala line was bisected by the

east–west Trigh Capuzzo highway; north of this Lieutenant-General William Gott commanded XIII Corps, while south of it Lieutenant-General Baron Willoughby Norrie commanded XXX Corps and the armour – a clumsy arrangement.

Rommel had some 90,000 men and 561 tanks, of which 333 were German and only 18 were armed with 75 mm guns. He was well supplied, as Malta had been subjected to such a bombardment that Field Marshal Kesselring had declared the place neutralized in April and convoys had been able to pass relatively freely from Naples to Tripoli. The Luftwaffe had about 260 serviceable aircraft available against the British Desert Air Force's 190 inferior fighters, so air supremacy was theirs. All in all, the opponents were fairly evenly balanced, which is, theoretically, not the situation favouring attack. Rommel's plans for Operation Theseus were circulated to a very small, secure group of his commanders on 1 May. He stated his objective as the destruction of the forces opposing him and the capture of that stubborn fortress, Tobruk. The scheme was to trick the British into the belief that the attack was concentrating on the northern half of the line and then to swing the Panzers around the southern flank. In the north Lieutenant-General Ludwig Crüwell's Gruppe Crüwell, (listed here from north to south) 15th Light Infantry Brigade, and the Italian Sabratha, Trento, Brescia and Pavia Divisions, were to attack the 1st South African Division and part of the 50th Division, while Rommel led (listed here from west to east) the 90th Light Division, 15 and 21 Panzer Divisions and the Italian Trieste and Ariete Divisions southwards. Crüwell struck in the early afternoon of 26 May, and Rommel started his move at 21.00 hours the same day, reaching a point south of Bir Hacheim in readiness to move at 06.00 on 27 May.

Crüwell's attack did its job but Rommel had miscalculated the strength of the armoured forces he faced. The 90th Light Division ran into opposition which it succeeded in overcoming, and by 10.00 it was at El Adem on the Trigh Capuzzo road, a mere fifteen miles (24 km) south of Tobruk, but there faced vigorous bombing attacks by the Desert Air Force, which drove it back before nightfall. On the other flank the Italians brushed the 3rd Indian Motorized Brigade aside with the help of 21 Panzer, but in the centre Rommel ran into fierce opposition from the 75 mm guns of the Grant tanks of 7th Armoured Division. In spite of their efforts being piecemeal and uncoordinated, the British armoured units prevented the German attack from developing. On 29 May a heavy counter-attack by 2nd and 22nd Armoured Brigades forced Rommel into a defensive posture south of Sidi Muftah and east of the box held by the British 150 Brigade. To his north and south were the British minefields and to his west the British armour. This should have spelled defeat.

The British armour, however, had suffered heavily in these exchanges. The Germans included

The Tocra Pass, near Benghazi, Libya, through which the British had driven the Italians in 1941 and which they were forced to yield to Rommel early in 1942. (Taylor Library)

the 88 mm gun in their mobile formations, having held the view from before the war that a Panzer unit should comprise armour, infantry and artillery, where the British still persisted in viewing each as a separate entity. Without artillery support to suppress the 88s, the British could not penetrate Rommel's front in the position now known as The Cauldron. Meanwhile, Rommel turned his attention on 150 Brigade to his rear, and by 1 June had reduced it, post by post, to the exhaustion of its ammunition and no choice but to surrender. With his supply lines to the west restored, Rommel could once again contemplate attack.

To his south lay the strongpoint of Bir Hacheim and the Free French, a threat that could not be allowed to persist. Operations to take the position began with a series of ferocious air raids, 1,300 of them between 2 and 9 June. On 6 June the French drove back an infantry attack, but from 8 June onwards the 90th Light and the Trieste Divisions, supported by 15 Panzer and the *Luftwaffe*, began to grind the position down. On the night of 10/11 June Koenig extracted 2,700 of his original force of 3,600, leaving 500 alive, mostly wounded, to become prisoners. The Free French had held until ordered to withdraw and won lasting honour in the process.

Ritchie attempted to destroy the Germans in The Cauldron on 5 June with an attack by 9th Indian Infantry Brigade and 22nd Armoured, but they failed to work together, lacking the training. That same afternoon the Germans launched their counter-attack with 21 Panzer and Ariete Divisions on the northern flank and 15 Panzer on the southern, and the next day over 3,000 prisoners, 96 guns and 37

anti-tank guns were in their hands. The British now held the area from Gazala to Tobruk, and south as far as the Trigh Capuzzo at Knightsbridge and east of that position, by no means a hopeless situation.

Ritchie now planned to have 2nd and 4th Armoured break out south-eastwards to hit 15 Panzer in the flank. On the morning of 12 June, as they were readying themselves to move, they themselves were hit by 21 Panzer and Ariete from the north and by 15 Panzer from the south. By the end of the day the British had lost some 200 cruiser and twenty medium tanks. The Gazala line could no longer be held. Auchinleck flew from Cairo to take over command, but it was too late. The South Africans retreated to Tobruk. Elements of the 50th (Northumbrian) Division broke out and succeeded in circling south to get back to Egypt. Auchinleck fell back to Alam Halfa, near Alamein, at which point the narrows between the sea and the Qattara Depression, where the land falls away steeply to about 430 feet (130 m) below sea level into an impassable basin, gave him a position he could hold.

Rommel dusted off his unused 1941 plan to attack Tobruk from the south-east, added *Luftwaffe* support by Stuka dive-bombers and smashed through the decayed defences. The fortress fell in days because the Germans cut clean through to the port itself, carving the fortress in two, and on 21 June the South African General D. Klopper surrendered. The Germans reported the acquisition of supplies for 30,000 men (the garrison they had captured) for three months and 10,000 cubic metres of fuel for their vehicles, quite apart from a port to supply further stores.

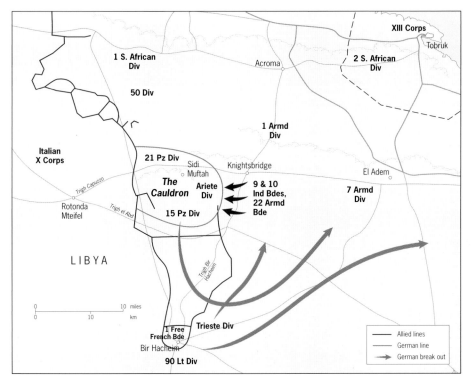

It was recognized that the eventual landing on the mainland of Europe would be an unprecedented undertaking in size and complexity, and soon after the return of much of the BEF from Dunkirk, planning was put in hand. When Lord Louis Mountbatten returned to Britain after the sinking of his flagship *Kelly* during the evacuation of Crete, he was promoted Vice-Admiral and became Adviser on Combined Operations. Pressure was being exerted for a European front both by the Americans and by Britain's new ally, the USSR, but the British were justifiably cautious; nothing like it had been tried since Gallipoli in 1915 and that was not an encouraging memory. Some small experience of landing on a hostile shore had already been gained in Norway and in France at St-Nazaire, but it was clear that a successful invasion would have to be resupplied, and in that case a port would be needed. Alderney, Le Havre and Cherbourg were considered and rejected. The location of Dieppe in relation to Newhaven commended it as the target for an exercise in illuminating the problems of such an operation.

The planning was conducted under the control of Lieutenant-General Bernard Montgomery, C-in-C South-Eastern Command, and Combined Operations Headquarters. Plans were made for a frontal assault without preliminary bombardment, as neither the Royal Navy nor RAF Bomber Command would undertake that task, for reasons of risk in the former case and of lack of accuracy in the latter. The principal force to be used was the 2nd Canadian Division under Major-General J.H. Roberts. The Canadians had landed briefly at Cherbourg in June 1940 but had been withdrawn when it became evident that France would collapse, and they had been fretting at the inaction of the last two years. The operation was scheduled for 7 July but then cancelled because of bad weather. Montgomery suggested it should be cancelled entirely, but he was then sent to command the Eighth Army in Egypt, and Mountbatten revived the plan under the name of Jubilee and fixed the date for 19 August.

The French coast near Dieppe is characterized by a succession of high chalk cliffs, into which narrow gullies are cut by streams, and beached-edged bays at Puys to the east and Pourville to the west. At Vasterival, further west, the lighthouse, the Phare d'Ailly, acted as a spotter platform for a battery of, it was thought, six 150 mm guns, and another battery, of four similar guns, was at Berneval-sur-Mer to the east. Aerial photography revealed many, but by no means all, aspects of the German defences, and in particular the cliff-based gun emplacements overlooking the shingle beach at Dieppe itself went undetected.

The landing force of 4,963 Canadians, 1,075 British (including 3 and 4 Commando), 51 US Rangers and fifteen French Marines of 10 Commando was transported and supported by a naval force of 237 warships and landing craft, including eight destroyers. The air support, 74

squadrons strong, under Air Vice-Marshal Leigh-Mallory, included 66 fighter squadrons. The raiding fleet sailed on the evening of 18 August, and at about 03.45 hours on 19 August had the misfortune to encounter a small German convoy sailing west. In the encounter, fortunately given no significance ashore, the vessels carrying 3 Commando were damaged and scattered.

The action on the western flank was successful, if bloody. Lieutenant-Colonel the Lord Lovat put a diversionary force ashore at Orange I at 04.53 hours and took his men in a sweep inland from Orange II to put the battery out of action, a fight in which Captain Patrick Porteous won his Victoria Cross. By 07.30 4 Commando had embarked once more. The South Saskatchewans landed on Green at 04.50, but instead of straddling the little River Scie, they all came ashore to the west of it. Having to cross the river cost time (which the Germans used to recover their composure), although, led by Lieutenant-Colonel C.C.I. Merritt they got through Pourville. But even when the Camerons joined them at 05.30, they could not take the hills. The force withdrew with some 350 casualties and Merritt was awarded the Victoria Cross. On the other flank, to the east, the remnants of 3 Commando came ashore at about 04.50. At Yellow I they engaged beach defences but got no further. At Yellow II Major Peter Young, with the defenders distracted by the action on his left, got behind the battery and so harassed it with sniper fire that it actually tried to fire back with one of its huge guns, traversed full around to point inland. As German reinforcements arrived, these men also were taken off by the Royal Navy.

The frontal attack on Dieppe began at 05.20 hours. Between the harbour to the east and the castle-topped cliff to the west is a broad, flat beach in front of a sea wall, and between that and the town itself fronting the Boulevard de Verdun, the promenade, a wide and pleasant space for strolling and taking the air. On 19 August this formed Red and White Beaches. The RAF laid a smoke-screen, and four destroyers put down a barrage before eight squadrons of Hurricanes added their rocket fire to the attack. By the time the RHLI and the Essex Scottish had got as far as the sea wall they had taken heavy casualties. The tanks were delayed and had to attempt a landing without covering fire. Of the first wave of nine vehicles, four reached the promenade and only eleven of the next twenty made it that far. The streets leading into the town had been blocked with barricades and the tanks could get no further. A platoon of the RHLI led by Denis Whitaker succeeded in reaching the casino, and Whitaker himself got into the town for a short while, but to no good purpose. The Essex Scottish reported a few men 'in the buildings', which was interpreted at General Roberts's HQ on HMS *Calpe* as meaning into a house on the Boulevard de Verdun – encouraging news. The Fusiliers de Mont-Royal were therefore sent to support the Essex

Scottish. They approached the beach at about 07.00 and came under heavy fire. Small groups of them were spread all along Red and White Beaches and some reached the casino, others the edge of town. Again a misleadingly optimistic report reached Roberts, and more reinforcements were sent – the Royal Marine A Commando. To some extent they were fortunate. As his landing craft got nearer the beach, the commanding officer, Lieutenant-Colonel J. Picton Phillips, saw that the leading craft were being shot to ribbons and realized that he was leading his men into an impossible situation. Pulling on white signal gauntlets, he jumped up onto the foredeck. He waved the following vessels to go back and as he did so was shot in the head.

The landing at Blue Beach was the least successful of all. The Royal Regiment of Canada, with three platoons of the Black Watch of Canada, had to land on a narrow beach overlooked by cliffs. They planned to use the dark and surprise, but they arrived at 05.10 instead of 04.50, just late enough for dawn to reveal them to the defenders. At 08.30 the 97 unwounded survivors surrendered. Their casualties amounted to 227 killed and 327 wounded.

By 09.00 it was clear that the attack had failed entirely. Roberts had to liaise with the RAF to arrange cover for a withdrawal and it was not until 11.00 hours that landing craft edged in towards the beaches in front of Dieppe. An hour later the attempt was abandoned, with only some 400 men retrieved.

More than 900 Canadian soldiers lost their lives at Dieppe. The total casualties, including wounded and prisoners, amounted to 3,367 Canadians and 275 British. The Royal Navy lost a destroyer and 33 landing craft and suffered 550 casualties. In the air the RAF lost 106 aircraft to the *Luftwaffe*'s 48. On land the German casualties totalled 591.

As an experiment in making a landing, Dieppe was extremely expensive. It did demonstrate that taking a port was very difficult and that if an alternative method of securing supply could be found it would be vastly preferable. Numerous other shortcomings gave food for thought. That it was a necessary experiment remains open to question.

Landing Beaches and Landing Units, West to East

Orange I:	Ste-Marguerite	4 Commando
Orange II:	Vesterival-sur-Mer	4 Commando
Green:	Pourville	South Saskatchewan Regiment
		Queen's Own Cameron Highlanders of Canada
White:	Dieppe, west	Royal Hamilton Light Infantry
		14th Canadian Army Tank Regiment (Calgary Regt)
		Royal Marine A Commando
Red:	Dieppe, east	Essex Scottish Regiment
		Les Fusiliers de Mont-Royal
Blue:	Puys	Royal Regiment of Canada
Yellow II:	Bernevàl	3 Commando
Yellow I:	Berneval	3 Commando

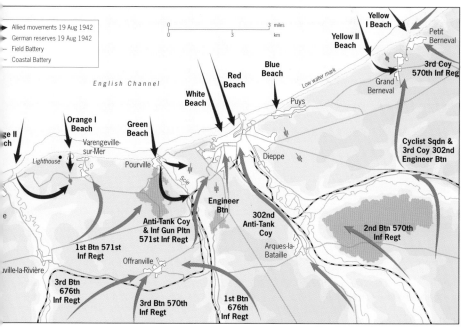

Shells burst close to a South African radio car being used by a British officer to communicate with the CO. (Taylor Library)

After the serious defeat on the Gazala Line in May and the fall of Tobruk in June, the British retreated towards Egypt. German elation at Rommel's victories was immense. Hitler promoted him to the rank of Field Marshal on 22 June and pressed Mussolini to support the advance into Egypt. In Britain Winston Churchill was obliged to fight off a motion of censure in Parliament. Rommel was successful once more at Mersa Matruh, inside the Egyptian border, on 27 June. Here the New Zealand Division was surrounded and broke out at the point of the bayonet. XX Corps was also forced to break out and retreat. Auchinleck fell back to a defensive line between the coastal railway halt of El Alamein and the Qattara Depression. The fighting had reduced the Axis strength, in spite of stores acquired at Tobruk, to a level which included only fifty-five German and thirty Italian tanks. The troops were near to exhaustion, but Rommel refused them rest.

The British defensive lines at El Alamein had been planned by Lieutenant-General Eric Dorman-Smith, and it was against these lines that Rommel failed. The attack of 2 July was turned back by much improved use of the artillery and the co-ordination of the gunnery with infantry attacks demonstrated by the New Zealand Division. Axis endurance was worn down in the fighting over the Ruweisat Ridge, and finally, the 9th Australian Division returned to the front and threw the Italians off Tell el Eisa, west of El Alamein. These counter-attacks on Italian units forced Rommel to waste fuel and men in coming to their support. By this date, 11 July, both sides were utterly worn out.

In August Churchill flew to Cairo and replaced Auchinleck with General Harold Alexander, and sent for Lieutenant-General William Gott, whom he wished to appoint as commander of the Eighth Army. On 7 August the aircraft in which Gott was flying to the meeting was shot down and the general was killed. In his place Lieutenant-General Bernard Montgomery was chosen. On both sides reinforcement and resupply built the armies up once more. Rommel, however, was unwell, and on 21 August he suggested Colonel-General Heinz Guderian should be sent to relieve him; but this, because Guderian was at odds with Hitler, was denied. However, by the end of the month Rommel had 203 tanks with which to mount his attack on the last line of British defence in Egypt. Montgomery, too, had been able to build up his force. The Americans had made provision of tanks to North Africa a priority and substantial numbers of the 6-pounder anti-tank gun had arrived. Rommel seemed to be unable to come up with fresh ideas and, predictably, planned another right hook. Ultra intelligence confirmed that this plan, anticipated by Montgomery, was real. Moreover, the desperate shortage of fuel that the Axis was attempting to make good was, like the means of supply, revealed by Ultra, and four tankers of the six sent were sunk by the British.

The attack began on the night of 30 August, at 23.00 hours. Diversionary attacks in the north were intended to distract from the main armoured thrust south of the New Zealanders' position to the south of Ruweisat Ridge and north of the Qattara Depression. From north to south, the 90th Light Division, the Italian Motorized Corps with the Ariete and Littorio Divisions and 15 and 21 Panzers rumbled forward. They were soon caught in minefields much more substantial than they had anticipated and came under heavy fire. The Afrika Korps commander General Walther Nehring was severely wounded, and Major-General Georg von Bismarck, commander of 21 Panzer, was killed. Parachute flares illuminated the scene and British aircraft bombed and strafed the Axis armour. The advance stalled.

Rommel spent the morning assessing the situation. He then changed his objective just as Montgomery had anticipated. Instead of seeking to pass east of the Alam Halfa Ridge, the way being barred by the British 7th Armoured Division, he would attack the ridge itself. Under the cover of a sand-storm the Axis armour pushed forward and turned towards the ridge, only to be revealed to the waiting artillery as the dust cleared at about 16.30 hours. There the tanks remained pinned down by shellfire until dusk and by British bombers thereafter. On the morning of 1 September Rommel himself went forward to see for himself. During the morning six further air raids took place, and by the middle of the day he had no choice but to order a retreat. He lost 536 men killed and 38 tanks, and more importantly, he lost his reputation of invincibility. Montgomery gained a reputation for clinical efficiency in destroying the enemy and inspiring confidence in his troops, as well as demonstrating his skill in organizing co-operation with the RAF.

On 19 September General Georg Stumme arrived to relieve Rommel and received detailed orders for the fortification of the line in front of El Alamein.

Extensive minefields made up of anti-tank mines in box formations with anti-personnel mines and booby-traps within them were laid. The Germans put down 248,849 anti-tank mines and 14,509 anti-personnel mines which, together with British minefields now under their control, took the total to close on half a million mines. In forward positions were infantry outposts, then the main infantry positions, behind which were the artillery and the armour as a mobile reserve. Rommel expected an attack before December and went on leave on 23 September.

A sand-storm blocks out the sun. (Taylor Library)

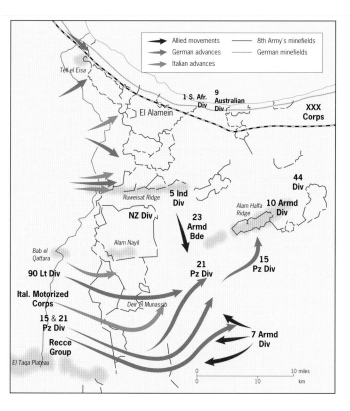

The Battle of El Alamein

With the Axis forces so short of supplies that attack could not be contemplated, it now fell to the British to take the initiative. They faced, as had Rommel at Alam Halfa, the problem of breaking a continuous front from the sea to the Qattara Depression secured with a complex of minefields.

Montgomery's plan was to fight the battle in three distinct phases. While Lieutenant-General Brian Horrocks's XIII Corps mounted a diversionary attack in the south, Operation Lightfoot would consist of an attack in the north by Lieutenant-General Sir Oliver Leese's XXX Corps after a massive artillery bombardment. While the Axis infantry was undergoing reduction, the Royal Engineers would detect and lift mines to create gaps for the armour to pass through. When the initial crowbar had made the first breach, it would be wiggled about, in Montgomery's metaphor, to crumble the Axis defence and widen the hole for the tanks to rush through in due course. In other words, when a notional line codenamed Oxalic had been reached, touching Kidney Ridge on the far side of the minefields, the armour of X Corps would pass through. The impression of a massive British presence in the south was created by the illusionist skills of the Royal Engineers' Camouflage Corps under Jasper Maskelyne. On the German side, Rommel's temporary replacement, General Stumme, could not know where the blow would fall, and had to cover the whole 40-mile (65 km) front. The Italian armour in the north, the Littorio Division, was stiffened by combining it with 15

Panzer, and in the south the Ariete was with 21 Panzer. The 90th Light Division was held in reserve in the north. Fuel was a real problem, as there was enough to move the armour from, for example, the south to the north, but if that proved to be an error, not enough to send it back.

Montgomery wrote, just before the action commenced: '... let no man surrender so long as he is unwounded and can fight. Let us pray that "the Lord mighty in battle" will give us the victory.' The battle began at 21.40 hours on 23 October with the biggest artillery bombardment since 1918, and the infantrymen of the 9th Australian, the 51st (Highland), 2nd New Zealand and 1st South African Divisions made swift progress for as long as surprise and shock lasted. Then the fighting became progressively harder. In the dark, clouds of dust further obscured the scene. The mine-clearing of the previous ten days had dealt with only part of the obstacle, and on the left the South Africans were soon stopped. In the centre the New Zealanders did well, and the Highlanders also did so on their left, but failed to attain their objectives on their right, although they made fair progress. On the extreme right the Oxalic Line was reached by the Australians. The mine clearance work went much more slowly than expected. The new detectors were so sensitive that they were activated by trivial objects, and the Scorpion flail tanks raised so much dust that they put themselves out of action. The sappers were reduced to probing with the bayonet. Thus, on the morning of 24 October, four gaps had

A British gun crew in action in the desert sand and dust. (Taylor Library)

A Grant tank pushes west. The Allied pursuit of the retreating Axis forces was hampered by heavy rainfall in Libya. (Taylor Library)

been made up to the Oxalic Line at Miteirya Ridge and another to the right of it, but not all the way through. At Montgomery's insistence, Major-General A.H. Gatehouse ordered his 10th Armoured Division to advance, but they ran into heavy anti-tank fire and by the end of the day no further progress had been made, in spite of serious losses. The Axis command was in confusion because General Stumme had gone forward that morning to see what was happening and fell from his command vehicle, suffering from a heart attack, as an artillery barrage engulfed his party. General Wilhelm Ritter von Thoma took command and Rommel was summoned from his holiday.

On 25 October the planned attack by the British in the south was made by the 50th (Northumbrian) and 7th Armoured Divisions, who encountered spirited resistance from the Folgore Parachute Brigade. No progress was made, but enough uncertainty spread to prevent any movement of Axis troops to the north. Meanwhile Montgomery pulled out the mauled armour and suspended attacks on the Oxalic Line by the New Zealanders for the day, directing the Australians to push northward next. Rommel arrived late that evening.

While the Australians, supported by 1st Armoured Divsion, began their drive towards the coast that night, a small force of the 2nd Battalion The Rifle Brigade and 239th Battery Royal Artillery penetrated the German lines at a point code-named Snipe, on Kidney Ridge, and did significant damage with their anti-tank guns during a full day of attempts to oust them. A troop under Second Lieutenant Jack Toms destroyed three enemy tanks at close range when down to their last gun, and accounted for twenty-three tanks in all that day. Such actions, coupled with continuous air raids and artillery strikes, wore down Rommel's resources.

The crumbling process was in hand. On the night of 30/31 October the Australians mounted a fresh attack towards Thompson's Post, a strongpoint near the coastal railway. They made little progress and took heavy casualties, but drew the Axis defence further north again.

Montgomery now planned a renewal, with modifications, of his Lightfoot opening. The new operation, Supercharge, was to drive for Tell el Aqqaquir, west of the northern flank of Kidney Ridge, to open the way for the armour to pour through. Major-General Bernard Freyberg was given the command of two brigades, and the operation was scheduled for 1 November, but had to be delayed for twenty-four hours because of the complexity of its planning. Early on 2 November another massive barrage fell on the Axis lines and the infantry made excellent progress, but 9th Armoured Brigade, tasked with the destruction of the German anti-tank guns, was half an hour late, and dawn broke with the job unfinished. The brigade was shot to shreds, losing seventy-five of its ninety-four tanks. 1st Armoured, also late, made use of the gap and took up defensive positions. The British artillery was made ready, so that, when Rommel threw in his armour as expected in a typical counter-attack, they were waiting for him. Throughout the day the tank battle raged at El Aqqaquir, and 117 Axis tanks were destroyed. By evening von Thoma reported that there remained thirty-five serviceable tanks. Rommel had no option but to withdraw, and signalled Berlin accordingly. As his decision to pull back to Fuka, sixty miles (100 km) to the west, was being put into action, a signal came ordering him to stand firm. Rommel attempted to implement it, but it was hopeless.

While the mobile troops had been hurled at the British bridgehead at El Aqqaquir, the line north and 37

Miles of barbed wire strung across the desert. (Taylor Library)

officers and over 2,000 men of the Italian army were captured.

At the same time as the Indians had attacked, the 51st (Highland) Division smashed forward towards El Aqqaqir. In the morning of 4 November they found the place abandoned. Everywhere the Axis line was collapsing, and at last Rommel was given permission to retreat. He had lost over 35,000 men as prisoners and his army was broken. It had cost the Allies 13,560 casualties and 200 tanks destroyed, with 300 for the time being unserviceable. The battle had not developed as Montgomery had planned, but the result was the one desired, and it had lasted, as predicted, twelve days.

Comparative strengths

	Axis	Allied
Men	104,000	195,000
Infantry battalions	71	85
Medium tanks	496	1,029
Anti-tank guns	800	1,451
Field and medium artillery	500	908
Aircraft	500	530

south was still held by the Axis. The 5th Indian Brigade was given the task of breaking through to allow British armour to pass, and on the evening of 3 November made a twelve-mile approach march in order to attempt the penetration of the line at Kidney Ridge in the dark. At 02.30 hours on 4 November a solid barrage was laid down which was to move forward at 100 yards (90 m) per three minutes. And so it did, the Essex, Rajputana Rifles and the Baluchis advancing behind it. At 05.00 it stood still for half an hour and then moved on again. At dawn it ceased, and through came the tanks, after which the 4th Indian Division moved south to trap as many of the enemy as they could. One column, consisting of a company of the 2nd Gurkhas, six armoured carriers and a machine-gun platoon of the Rajputana Rifles, ran into the Brescia Division moving west. The carriers moved to stop them, the anti-tank guns drove off four German tanks lending support and 100

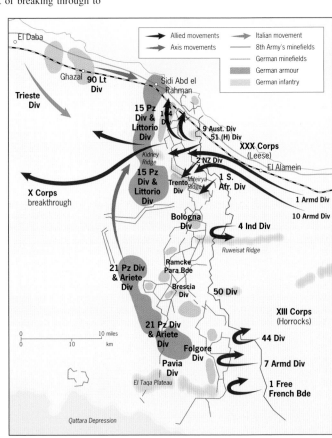

38

Immediately after Montgomery's victory at El Alamein, American troops landed in north-west Africa. Operation Torch was the first undertaken by the United States in the Western Theatre and was intended to roll up the Axis from the west as well as to bring more of the French into the Allied camp. In command was Lieutenant-General Dwight D. Eisenhower, and his deputy was Major-General Mark Clark. The commanders were not all Americans, however, and he had Air Marshal William Welsh as Eastern Air Commander with No. 333 Group, RAF, Lieutenant-General Kenneth Anderson who was to take over Eastern Task Force once landing was complete, and Admiral Cunningham of the Royal Navy reporting to him. Eisenhower's ability to work with officers of other nations and to contrive that his subordinates worked together more often than not was an outstanding and unusual talent that outstripped his lack of strategic vision in attaining war objectives.

The landings on 8 November 1942 were, it was hoped, to be largely unopposed. From the United States, Western Task Force (2nd Armored, 3rd and 9th Divisions) under Major-General George S. Patton landed at Casablanca; sailing from Britain, Central Task Force (US 1st Armored and part of 82nd Airborne Divisions) under Major-General Lloyd Fredendall went to Oran, and Eastern Task Force (British 78th and US 34th Divisions) under Major-General Charles Ryder landed at Algiers. The force totalled 65,000 men. In the event the reaction to the landings was more hostile than anticipated. Attempts to land troops from British warships at Algiers and Oran ran into heavy fire and an intended air drop at Oran was scattered by adverse weather. Those aircraft that did get through dropped their men off target. The heaviest fighting was at Casablanca, where the French battleship *Jean Bart* acted as a static gun battery, engaging the American battleship *Massachusetts* until battered into submission. The French flotilla sallied forth and, all seven ships and three submarines, was destroyed by the Americans. The Americans sustained 1,400 dead and the French 700 killed in the landings. The decision of Admiral François Darlan, Commander-in-Chief of the Vichy forces and by chance in Algiers, to surrender brought a general cease-fire on 10 November, but the Vichy Government repudiated the capitulation, the Germans occupied Vichy France and the Italians Corsica. Meanwhile Admiral Jean-Pierre Estéva, Resident-General of Tunisia for Vichy France, lent every co-operation to the Germans in rushing reinforcements to Tunis to prevent the retreating Rommel from becoming isolated. Darlan was assassinated in Algiers on 24 December, but by then the French forces there had either ceased to oppose or actually joined the Allies, and the French fleet at Toulon kept faith with Darlan by scuttling itself.

The campaign became a race for Tunis. North Africa from Morocco to Tunis consists of a narrow

Men of the Royal West Kents man a 25-pounder field gun in support of French troops in the Eastern Dorsales in January 1943. *(Taylor Library)*

coastal plain with the barrier of the Atlas Mountains inland. The mountain range ends before Tunis in the north-to-south hills of the Western Dorsales, and another, lesser, line of hills, the Eastern Dorsales, lies between them and the coast. At Tunis the coast turns south and then east at Mareth, to the west of which an area of lake and marsh runs south of the mountains. The terrain channels and limits movement severely, and in the gap between the lakes and the coast in the south the French had built, in the 1930s, the defensive Mareth Line for protection against a possible Italian invasion from the east.

General Jürgen von Arnim arrived in December when some 17,000 additional Axis troops had already been sent to Tunisia. He took command of the Fifth Panzer Army, of which 10 Panzer, Hermann Göring Panzer Parachute and 334th Divisions were the main units. The Allies were also opposed by German aircraft. The drive along the northern coast to Tunis by what had been Eastern Task Force, now transformed into the First British Army under Anderson, was stopped by 10 Panzer at Tébourba and by stout resistance at Longstop Hill, some twenty-five miles (40 km) west of the objective. The American intention to use 2nd Corps under Fredendall, 1st Armored and part of the recent arrival, the 1st Division, to strike in the south and isolate the Tunisian garrison was frustrated by a German attack on French troops in the Eastern Dorsales, close to their junction with the Western Dorsales at Pont du Fahs, some forty miles (65 km) south-west of Tunis. By 24 January the Germans were in control of the whole range of the Eastern Dorsales. Fredendall was put in command of all

Allied troops to combat the crisis and a withdrawal to the Western Dorsales was begun.

The information from Ultra intelligence was not correctly interpreted, and the Allies believed that the Germans intended to attack the northern end of their line. The important pass through the Western Dorsales at Kasserine was therefore defended by a small force comprising the US 26th Infantry Division, part of the 19th US Combat Engineer Regiment, 33rd US Field Artillery and 805th Tank Destroyer battalions and the French 67th African Artillery when Rommel's Panzer Army, with elements of 10 Panzer, attacked on 19 February 1943. By 21 February the Panzers were through the pass, having made use of the new *Nebelwerfer* rocket-firing weapons. Rommel's troops were headed for Tébessa, while 10 Panzer made for Thala, with El Kef yet further north beyond that town. East again, pushing towards Sbiba, was 21 Panzer. Fortunately Rommel was then ordered to join the drive for El Kef instead of following up his dangerous left hook, and the British 6th Armoured Division pushed the 26th Armoured Brigade south from El Kef towards Thala and the 1st Guards Brigade towards Sbiba. Rommel turned away, disheartened by what he saw as a mistake by the Italian High Command and also by the denial of a loan of the new Tiger tanks by 10 Panzer, back to the Mareth Line to face the advancing Montgomery and his Eighth Army. In March Patton replaced Fredendall in command of 2nd Corps.

On 23 February Rommel was made C-in-C Army Group Africa and began to plan Montgomery's defeat. His intention to use all three Panzer divisions was revealed by Ultra on 28 February, and his attack at Medenine was defeated on 6 March. Rommel was recalled to Germany. Command passed to the Italian General Giovanni Messe. The Allies also reorganized, creating Eighteenth Army Group, comprising both the First and Eighth Armies, under General Alexander.

Montgomery sent XXX Corps to carry out a frontal assault on the Mareth Line, between the sea and the Matmata

Hills, on 19 March. The attempt was held by Rommel's former troops, now called the First Italian Army. However, a New Zealand Corps under Freyberg had been sent to probe westwards, and discovered, with Long Range Desert Group intelligence, that the line could be outflanked. Montgomery reinforced the manoeuvre with artillery and the air force, and on 27 March Freyberg broke trough the Tebaga Gap. The defenders were driven back to the Eastern Dorsales.

The pressure on the Axis forces was inexorable. In spite of attempts to resupply and reinforce them, they were running out of fuel, ammunition and equipment. They were pressed back until they held an enclave around Tunis. A final offensive, code-named Vulcan began on 22 April. In the extreme north Lieutenant-General Omar Bradley, now in command of 2nd Corps, made for Bizerte, in the centre the First Army went for Tunis, on their right the 19th French Corps for Pont du Fahs and, on the eastern coast, Montgomery's Eighth Army was up against the defences of Enfidaville. The latter failed, but Montgomery advised reinforcing the thrust in the centre in Operation Strike, which succeeded. The Axis forces collapsed, surrendering 238,000 prisoners. The campaign had cost the Allies 76,000 killed, wounded and missing.

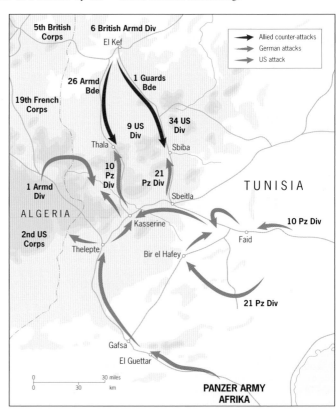

H-Hour on D-Day, 10 July. British troops land in Sicily. (Taylor Library)

The decision to invade Sicily was taken at the conference, codenamed Symbol, held in Casablanca in January 1943 at which British Prime Minister Winston Churchill and US President Franklin D. Roosevelt discussed strategy. Marshal Iosif Stalin was invited to come from the USSR, but the battle of Stalingrad was at a critical stage and he did not attend. The Americans were still in favour, as they had been from the outbreak of the war, of a second front in north-western Europe. It had been impractical then, and now Churchill persuaded them that an Italian campaign would be a useful prelude to the eventual aim, that Europe would be more vulnerable attacked by way of the 'soft underbelly'. Then, and in retrospect, the argument was questionable, although it has to be recognized that the Allies could not have invaded France in this year. The question of what the next move would be after the victory in North Africa also exercised the Axis, and they were assisted in their speculation by Operation Mincemeat. This involved a corpse which was apparently that of a military messenger. The body of the fictitious Major Martin, Royal Marines, was put over the side of a submarine off Huelva,

Spain, on 30 April, an attaché case chained to his wrist. In the case were documents suggesting that the preparations to invade Sicily were cover for the real plan, an invasion of Greece. Ultra intelligence received on 14 May showed that the ruse had worked, and a signal was sent to Churchill saying, 'Mincemeat swallowed whole'.

The invasion of Sicily was the largest combined operation undertaken so far in the war. The Allies landed 180,000 troops and employed 2,590 ships in Operation Husky. Major-General Harold Alexander's 15th Army Group consisted of, on the west, Patton's Seventh US Army, and on the east, Montgomery's British Eighth Army. The plan was for the American 2nd Corps, under Bradley, to land on the shore of the Gulf of Gela to the east of the town of Gela (from west to east, 1st Division and Rangers, 45th Division) while the 3rd and 2nd Armored Divisions were to land near Licata, further west. The British XXX Corps (1st Canadian and 51st (Highland) Divisions, 231st Brigade and Commandos) were to land astride the southernmost tip of the island, Cape Passero, while XIII Corps (5th and 50th Divisions and Commandos) were to

41

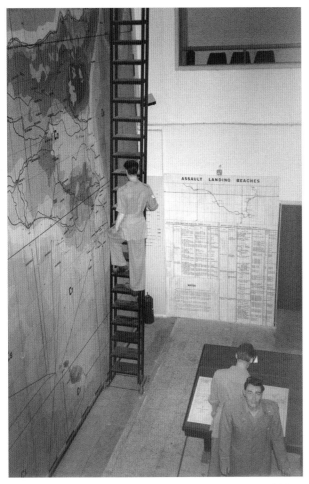

ASSAULT LANDING BEACHES

NOTES

The Combined Operations room, Lascaris War Rooms, Valletta, Malta. The preparations for Operation Husky are displayed. (Nigel Cave)

for the defence, both from General Hans Hube's 14th Panzer Corps, the Hermann Göring Panzer Division and 15th Panzer Grenadier. There were ten Italian divisions and the island was under the command of General Alfredo Guzzoni. During the course of the campaign two further German units, 1st Parachute and 29th Panzer Grenadier Divisions, would arrive as reinforcements. At the outset the Hermann Göring were in the Piana de Catania and the 15th Panzer Grenadiers in two parts, one overlooking Licata and the other in the north-west, west of Corleone.

The start of Husky came as a surprise to the Axis forces because the weather was so bad that an attack seemed impossible. The landings were intended to be preceded by airborne troops, but weather and poor execution of the task by those who carried them inflicted heavy casualties on the US 82nd and British 1st Airborne Divisions. On D-Day the American-crewed Dakotas released the gliders of British 1st Air Landing Brigade too early and they never made it to land. The next day an attempt to insert 2,000 American parachutists into the beachhead resulted in the Allied fleet opening fire on the Dakotas carrying the 504th Regiment with considerable loss of life. The seaborne landings went much more satisfactorily. The British came ashore against trivial resistance and captured Syracuse on the same day. The Americans were more exposed to the rough seas, but also landed with comparatively little trouble. On the next day 1st and 4th Rangers at Gela were counter-attacked by the Italian Gruppo Mobile E, equipped with thirty-two French ten-ton tanks. They managed to knock out three tanks in the streets of the town and the remainder withdrew. General Patton came ashore that day to see what the delay was in pushing inland, and discovered that the rough sea was holding up disembarkation of the tanks and guns. The Germans now joined the fray with Tiger tanks of the Hermann Göring Panzer Division. These formidable AFVs were armed with 88 mm guns, and there were seventeen of them in Sicily. The Rangers found some Italian 77 mm anti-tank guns and engaged the Tigers. The Navy joined in. Amphibious vehicles, DUKWs, brought some of the divisional artillery ashore. By noon the attack had been fought off. In the first three days of the

come ashore further north in the Gulf of Noto, south of Syracuse.

The terrain of Sicily is marked by a substantial range of mountains along the northern coast rising to the volcanic Mount Etna, which overlooks the Ionian Sea on the east of the island. South of Etna is a great bowl of a valley, the Piana de Catania, through which numerous rivers from the surrounding mountains drain into the Gulf of Catania. The south-western side of the island is more gentle country facing the north-west–south-east line of the high hills.

The Italians had sustained considerable losses overseas, not only in North Africa but also at Stalingrad, and the troops remaining to them were not of the first quality, courageous though they might be. There were two German units available operation ten of the Tigers were put out of service and destroyed to prevent their capture. Only one of them survived to be sent back to Italy.

Alexander now ordered Patton to cover Montgomery's western flank while the British advanced to Messina at the extreme north-eastern tip of Sicily. The chance to let Bradley hurry north and cut the island in two was missed, and the resistance of the Hermann Göring Panzer slowed Montgomery. On the night of 13 July an operation was mounted to take two bridges on the line of advance. Ten miles (16 km) ahead was the Ponte dei Malati, which 3 Commando was to take after landing at Agnone, and a further ten miles on was the Primasole bridge, the objective of the paratroopers. The Commandos landed under fire and pushed on to their bridge. They took the north end and removed as many demolition charges as they could discover, but found themselves on the route being used to reinforce the Germans facing the 50th Division to the south, and held as long as they could. By dawn it was clear their comrades would not be arriving soon. They dispersed and lay up during the day, and when the 50th arrived in the late afternoon the bridge was still intact. It had cost 3 Commando 153 casualties. At Primasole bridge the 1st Parachute Brigade had suffered even greater losses, but had held the bridge for two days with a force of some 250 men before being swamped.

Patton protested against Alexander's continuing instruction for the protection of Montgomery's flank, and was permitted to send his Provisional Corps under Lieutenant-General Geoffrey Keyes to take Palermo, an operation that netted a large number of ineffectual Italians but achieved little else. German reinforcements slowed the advance. Montgomery failed to push past the solid resistance on the coast and by 17 July General Hube had set up the first of three robust lines of defence, this one from south of Catania in the east to San Stefano in the north. Except for the narrow coastal plains, this was all mountain country, easy to defend and difficult to attack. On 22 July the 1st Canadian Division took Leonforte in the centre, and Bradley's 2nd Corps, to their left, at last reached the coast. The pick of the Germans and Italians were, however, all to the north-east of the line. By early August the US 1st Division was gaining Troina in a five-day battle, while the British beset Adrano. When they fell the Germans began their evacuation of the island in an operation that took some 40,000 German and 62,000 Italian soldiers to the mainland, complete with their weapons and equipment. When, in an irrelevant show of one-upmanship, the American 3rd Division beat the British into Messina on 17 August, the enemy had escaped. Sicily was no longer available to the Axis as a base for aircraft to threaten shipping in the Mediterranean, but an opportunity to inflict real damage on the principal adversary, the Germans, had been wasted.

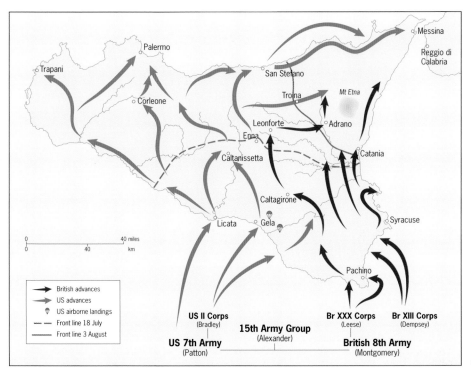

The fascist leader of Italy, Benito Mussolini, was displaced on 24 July, and secret negotiations began for a surrender to the Allies. The danger was that Hitler would order his troops into Italy to replace the Italian contribution to the war, and it was in the hope that the armistice could remain secret that the Italians agreed the terms; in effect they amounted to unconditional surrender. The secrecy was needed to prepare for the inevitable German response, but the armistice was made public just as the Salerno landings began, and the Germans put Operation Alarich into force, bringing 1st SS Panzer from Russia and putting Rommel in charge of the subjugation of north and central Italy, while Field Marshal Kesselring used the troops who had escaped from Sicily to counter the new invasion.

On 3 September a grumpy Montgomery landed his Eighth Army at Reggio di Calabria, on the toe of Italy just across the Straits of Messina from Sicily, and began to advance on what he saw as a backwater of this theatre of war. On 9 September the British 1st Airborne Division took Taranto, the naval base inside the heel of Italy. The Germans paid small attention to these two diversions, fully expecting a landing in the Gulf of Salerno, where welcoming beaches offered easy access. These beaches were, however, overlooked on all sides by hills primed for the defence of the area. On 9 September Operation Avalanche sailed into the bay. The attacking force, under Lieutenant-General Mark Clark, was the US Fifth Army, comprising the British X Corps under Lieutenant-General Richard McCreery and US VI Corps commanded by Major-

General Ernest Dawley. X Corps landed astride Salerno on the north and east side of the gulf with, from left to right, 1st, 3rd and 9th US Rangers at Maiori, 2 Commando and 41 Royal Marine Commando at Vietri and the 46th and 56th Divisions south of Salerno. On their right the 36th Division landed at Paestum with 45th Division as a floating reserve. The opposition from Lieutenant-General Hans Hube's 14th Panzer Corps was, for the time being, light. The commander of the German Tenth Army in southern Italy was General Heinrich von Vietinghoff, who immediately moved 76th Panzer Corps back from Calabria and the fight with Montgomery's army and more men from Rome. The Allies scarcely moved beyond the beaches as the German defence gained coherence.

On 12 September the Panzers attacked the British in the village of Battipaglia, and Panzer Grenadiers joined the fray the next day. The danger of the beachhead being cut in two was very real. The warships in the gulf unleashed a massive barrage in reply. At Altavilla and Persano just to the south the Americans were pushed back, and the artillerymen of the 45th Division hung on stubbornly to halt the Panzers in spite of having been abandoned by their infantry. On 13 and 14 September the US 82nd Airborne were dropped in to stiffen the resistance of the American beachhead. The entire air strength of the Allies in the Mediterranean was brought into action and two British battleships joined the naval artillery bombardment. In the hills to the north the Rangers and Commandos were conducting mountain warfare, while on the beaches a siege was

In the wake of the retreating Germans and the wreckage they abandoned, British forces move from Vietri towards Cava on 23 September. (Taylor Library)

in progress. Reinforcements were shipped from Libya to shore up the Allied force. By 15 September it was becoming clear to General von Vietinghoff that the Allies were going to hold, but by then a precious week had been gained in the preparation of defensive positions further north on the Italian peninsula.

On 16 September the first units of the British Eighth Army made contact with the Americans from Paestum. On 18 September the Germans began a fighting retreat to the north, blowing bridges behind them as they went. Inland the 1st Canadian Division advanced through Potenza towards the airfields at Foggia, which they took on 27 September, and the next day they were on the Adriatic seashore. On 1 October British troops entered Naples. There they found the results of the abortive rising of 27 September, when, in the belief that the Allies were just about to arrive, the citizens rose up against the Germans. They were shot down without mercy.

The Italian campaign now entered what was to be a long, difficult fight. The terrain is characterized by the range of mountains that runs down the centre of the peninsula, the Apennines. Not only are they high, but they are cut, east and west, with steep river valleys which reach out to the narrow coastal plains. Advance by an army on a broad front is impossible, and the steepness of the hillsides makes aerial bombardment inaccurate and wasteful. It is country well suited to defence. Kesselring had fixed on a line to hold, known as the Gustav Line, along the rivers Garigliano and Sangro, though Cassino. Here he could leave the mountainous centre virtually undefended and concentrate his forces between the mountains and the sea, east and west. On the west, facing the US Fifth Army, were 3 and 15 Panzer Grenadiers, with the Hermann Göring Division in reserve, while on the Sangro to the east, facing British Eighth Army's XIII and V Corps, were 16 and 26 Panzer, 29 Panzer Grenadier and 1st Parachute Divisions. A long, hard, cold winter was in prospect.

Landing Forces

US Fifth Army, Lieutenant-General Mark Clark
US VI Corps, Major-General Ernest J. Dawley
   36th (Texas) Division, Major-General Fred L. Walker,
   36th Cavalry Recce Regt,
   132 Field Artillery Bn,
   158 Field Artillery Bn,
   189 Field Artillery Bn,
   323 Glider Regt,
   191 Medium Tank Bn,
   141 Regimental Combat Team,
   142 RCT, 143 RCT, 157 RCT
82nd Airborne Division, Major-General Matthew B. Ridgeway
   504th Parachute Regiment, Lieutenant-Colonel Reuben H. Tucker;
   505th, Colonel James M. Gavin;
509th, Lieutenant-Colonel Doyle Yardley.
45th Division, in reserve.
British XX Corps, Lieutenant-General Sir Richard McCreery
46th Division, Major-General John Hawkesworth,
   16th Durham Light Infantry,
   1/4 Hampshires, 1/5 Hampshires,
   2nd Hampshires, 2/4 King's Own Yorkshire Light Infantry,
   2/5 Leicesters, 6th Lincolns,
   5th Sherwood Foresters,
   6th Yorks and Lancs,
   46th Recce Regt,
   2nd Bn Royal Northumberland Fusiliers, Royal Artillery,
   Royal Engineers Commandos,
138 Brigade, Brigadier Robert Laycock
US Rangers, Lieutenant-Colonel William Darby
56th Division, Major-General Douglas Graham
   6th Oxfordshire & Buckinghamshire Light Infantry, 2/5th Queen's,
   2/6th Queen's, 2/7th Queen's,
   44th Recce Regt, Cheshire Regt,
   8th Royal Fusiliers, 9th Royal Fusiliers, The Grenadier Guards,
   The Royal Scots Greys,
   3rd Coldstream Guards.

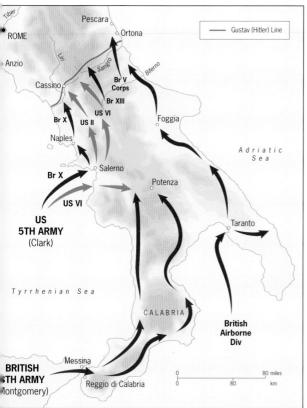

The Four Battles of Monte Cassino

The ruins of the Abbey finally taken by Polish troops. (Taylor Library)

As winter approached, the Germans withdrew to a defensive line, known as the Gustav Line, based on the river system flowing into the sea to the west as the Garigliano. On the eastern side of the Apennines the defence was organized on the River Sangro. The British Eighth Army crossed the Sangro in late November after heavy rains had imposed a cessation of hostilities for a week. The 1st Canadian Division then pushed up the coast to the Bernhardt Line on the River Moro, south of Ortona. It was defended by 90th Light Panzer Grenadiers and 1st Parachute Division, who held out for nearly a month. The town of Ortona itself was taken only after bitter street fighting, and fell to the Canadians on 27 December. There they were to stay until the following May, awaiting tangible progress on the western flank.

North-west of the wide coastal plains on which Naples stands in the south, the River Garigliano comes down at right angles to the sea from between the high hills inland. Some fifteen miles from the sea, at Sant' Ambroglio, the river is fed by two other streams – the Liri, which runs parallel to the sea and is separated from it by the Aurunici mountains, and the Rapido, which runs further inland past the town and monastery of Cassino. All these rivers run in valleys between substantial hills and mountains, so the approach of the Allies from the south was itself a mountain-to-mountain fight interspersed with river crossings with blown bridges and enemy resistance that lasted until the end of the year.

The Liri valley led towards Rome, and in January 1944 Lieutenant-General Mark Clark's Fifth Army was intended to use that route. General Alphonse Juin's French Expeditionary Force, consisting mainly of Algerian and Moroccan troops, pushed the German 5th Mountain Division back across the Rapido on the right of the line, while the British 5th and 56th Divisons crossed the Garigliano near to the sea. However, the Germans opened sluices on the Liri to rush the Garigliano into flood south of its junction with the Rapido, and the British 46th Division failed to cross the torrent. In the centre the US 36th Division was given the task of making an approach to the Rapido from the east across an open plain and then crossing the river. This was attempted on 20 January. It was a disaster. Three days' fighting left 1,000 Americans dead out of a force of 6,000, and no progress made. The minefields, the river and 15 Panzer Grenadiers had done great damage. The attack on the Gustav Line stalled. The situation was not without hope, for a move was afoot to outflank the Gustav Line by making a landing at Anzio, further north, but that, too, was to stagger to a standstill.

The town of Cassino is in the valley, on the Rapido River, while the monastery stands high above on the end of a ridge that stretches away to the north-west. It was understood by all that possession of that ridge was the key to the security of the German front. On 24 January a long fight for the ridge began. The French 2nd Moroccan Division drove towards Atina, north of Cassino, while the 3rd Algerian Division attacked the Colle Belvedere, halfway between the two towns. To their left the US 34th Division battled for points of vantage along the ridge adjacent to the monastery, but failed to take and hold summits close to the objective.

On 15 February a second major attack was undertaken after the monastery had been bombed. Lieutenant-General Freyberg, commanding the New Zealand II Corps, went over Mark Clark's head to Alexander to demand this, and every man at the front, oppressed by the baleful, all-seeing presence of the monastery, would have supported him if asked. The Germans themselves had no soldiers in the buildings, nor were they using it as an observation post as they felt it was too obvious a location, and it would certainly be destroyed as a matter of necessity by an attacker. The commander of the unit there, Lieutenant-General Fridolin von Senger und Etterlin of XIV Panzer Corps, expressed just such a view. Clark, in addition to a distaste for the destruction of an historic building, thought the result would be an enhanced defensive position, and doubted reports of the presence of enemy troops there. None the less the bombing was approved and took place at 09.30 on 15 February. The New Zealanders attacked with a view to capturing the station in Cassino, and the 4th Indian Divsion pushed along Snakeshead Ridge towards the monastery. By 18 February both formations, severely mauled, were back on their start lines.

The third battle began, after a prolonged period of foul weather, on 15 March. This time the Indians and New Zealanders attacked from the north-east, the Indians on the right towards the monastery and the New Zealanders towards to town. The renewed shelling and bombing reduced the whole area to rubble, and the defenders exploited this wasteland with skill. The ruins prevented the use of armoured vehicles and all movement was on foot. By 23 March the Allied troops were exhausted and Freyberg had to ask Clark for permission to disengage. The line now ran from the end of Snakeshead Ridge (Point 593) to Castle Hill, which the New Zealanders had taken, and along the flank of the ruined town to the railway station – a small gain at great cost. The remnants of the gallant Indian Division were withdrawn from the line for a deserved rest.

The battles here and at Anzio now became stalled, and the final advance at Cassino took place as part of Alexander's spring offensive, Operation Diadem, which began on 11 May 1944 at 23.00 hours. General Juin had advised at the very start of the campaign against the Gustav Line that pinprick efforts against limited targets would not solve the problem, and now an attack on a much broader front was made, from Cassino in the north to the southern seashore. It was in the southern part of the line that the major breakthrough took place. The French Expeditionary Corps penetrated the German defences in the Aurunici Mountains south of the Liri valley. The Third Algerian Division forced its way up the Ausente River valley to take Ausonia by 14 May, and the 2nd Moroccans took Monte Faito on the 12th and Monte Maio on 13 May. It was clear that the Gustav Line was fatally compromised and that the Germans would have to fall back to the Führer-Senger Line and abandon Monte Cassino. This outcome was not known to the attackers when, on 11 May, the final assault on Monastery Hill was mounted. While the British 4th Division attacked along the low ground south and east of the hill, II Polish Corps, under Lieutenant-General Wladyslaw Anders, came from the north. During the early hours of 12 May they gained, at a cost, highpoints on the infamous ridge. When day dawned the Germans started methodically to pick them off. By afternoon Anders was forced to recognize that the attack had failed, and it was small comfort to know that the German 1st Parachute Divison had been unable to bring sufficient fire to bear on the British south of the hills to slow their progress. On 16 May, at 18.00 hours, he tried again. It took more than two days of relentless attritional fighting before, at 10.20 hours on 18 May, the 12th Podolski Lancers raised the Polish flag over the ruins of the monastery.

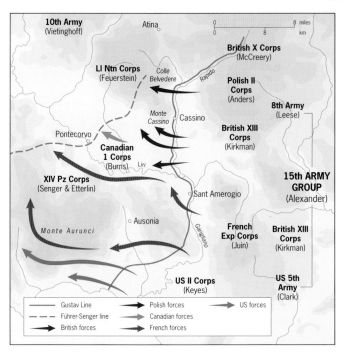

The Anzio Beachhead

A number of plans had been laid but abandoned unhatched for a landing near the holiday resort of Anzio-Nettuno, thirty miles (50 km) south of Rome. A mere twenty miles (32 km) inland were the Alban Hills commanding the main routes to the south-east and the Gustav Line. On 7 and 8 January Churchill held a conference at Marrakesh at which the operation, codenamed Shingle, was revived. It had to be undertaken quickly because the LCTs (Landing Craft Tanks), the large vessels needed to carry bulk supplies and armour, were due to be moved to Britain for refurbishment and use in the invasion of France. They could be kept in the Mediterranean up to late January and no longer. Thus the plan of landing a force of two divisions at Anzio to hurry inland and seize the Alban Hills was proposed from on high. Detailed planning now had to be done, and Lieutenant-General Mark Clark issued orders for a beachhead to be established at Anzio and an advance to be made on, not to, the Alban Hills – a crucial modification of the concept made because Clark thought the force too small.

The operation was undertaken by a mixed force, the US VI Corps, under the command of Major-General John Lucas. They amounted to some 40,000 men and 5,200 vehicles and were transported to the landing beaches in 289 vessels. They anchored off Anzio just after midnight on 22 January and, unobserved, began preparing for landing. At 02.00 hours the night was lit with rocket fire as the beaches came under bombardment and naval gunfire followed. The troops made for the shore. On the left the British 1st Division landed on the beaches north of Anzio and were soon two miles inland, virtually unopposed. In the centre the US Rangers and Parachute Infantry swarmed through Anzio itself, and engineers followed up and cleared the port installations for Allied use. On the right the 3rd Division were three miles inland by noon, again almost unopposed. By the end of the day 36,000 men, 3,200 vehicles and almost all supplies had been landed. Casualties so far were thirteen killed, ninety-seven wounded and forty-four missing. A German counter-attack was sure to come, and Kesselring had, indeed, devised a plan called Case Richard which would pull in troops from Northern Europe. Mark Clark had instructed Lucas to prepare for counter-attack and softened the definition of the operation's objectives by making vague references to the Alban Hills. A massive attack on the Gustav Line was in progress, and Kesselring's opportunity to use either his reserves or Gustav Line troops to quell this incursion at Anzio was evidently severely limited. In addition, Ultra intelligence was giving a clear picture of what the Germans were doing to deal with the situation, and it was taking them time. Lucas, with Clark's full approval, stayed put and dug in. Alexander sent Lucas his congratulations. By 24 January the beachhead was seven miles (11 km) deep and sixteen miles (26 km) wide. No one seemed to be in any hurry, except the Germans.

General Eberhard von Mackensen was placed at

Naval escorts lay a smoke screen for the landings at Anzio. (Taylor Library)

October 1944: heavy rains slow the advance on Bologna. (Taylor Library)

he struck at the British in the salient near Campoleone with a pincer movement that cut them off from the beachhead, and 3 and 24 Guards Brigades were isolated at 'the Factory'. It now remained to eliminate this Allied fragment. The fight went on all day and the British refused to yield. Eventually they regained contact with their comrades, but at the cost of 1,400 killed, wounded or missing. The Germans had been hurt as well: some 500 killed, 300 made prisoner and tanks and equipment lost. The vulnerability of the British salient was evident to Lucas, and a well-conducted withdrawal was achieved by night. Further attacks on 7 and 9 February resulted in the fall of the Factory to the Germans and much fighting on the railway at Carroceto. The British 1st Division was then relieved by 179th and 180th Infantry of the US 45th Division, who counter-attacked but made small gains.

The major effort by the Germans came on 16 February. Attacks came in from all sides, but the main thrust, known to the Allies through Ultra, was down the Albano–Anzio road, past the Factory. The ground was soft and armour had to keep to the roads, which slowed German progress, but progress they did. The Allied air forces bombed the attackers and the naval guns plastered the area with shellfire. The Infanterie-Lehr-Regiment, Hitler's favourites,

the head of an improvised Fourteenth Army to oppose Lucas. The German intention in such situations was to create a *Kessel*, a cauldron, in which to cook the enemy's goose. To do so von Mackensen assembled 90,000 men. From forces already in Italy came the Hermann Göring Parachute Panzer, the 16th SS Panzer Grenadier, the 35th, 26th and 29th Panzer Grenadier Divisions. Artillery designed to smash the Maginot Line was brought – two 240 mm railway guns. Added to these were 210 mm railway guns and 170 mm artillery, all able to outrange the weapons the Allies had ashore. Clark had news of this through Ultra.

Now, on 28 January, it dawned on Clark that it was about time Lucas attempted to push forward and he visited his subordinate to say so. Lucas planned to have the British push towards Campoleone, north, and the 3rd Division towards Cisterna, north-east. The attacks began in the early hours of 30 January. The British 1st Division made progress but the supporting US 1st Armored ran into mines and mud and could not give the planned support. The next day the British got as far as the railway embankment south of Campoleone but could not get further, nor could the American armour advance any further: the German force was stronger than anticipated. The efforts of the 3rd Division were to be spearheaded by the Rangers, but they were caught in an ambush and two battalions were wiped out, losing sixty per cent killed or wounded and the rest taken prisoner, while 4th Battalion suffered fifty per cent casualties. The 3rd's infantry ran into a solid wall of Germans before they reached the railway. Here they were held. The landing force was well contained and at the mercy of German guns, but it had been a close thing for the Germans, and they had been forced to commit their entire force to containing the Allies and had taken heavy casualties in the process.

The plan that had previously been devised by von Mackensen was to cut the beachhead in two and reduce the remaining halves in turn. On 3 February

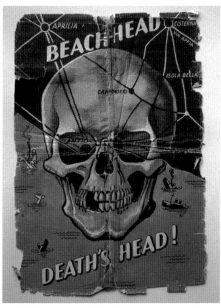
A German propaganda leaflet that tried to persuade the Allies that their fight at Anzio was doomed. (Tom Roe Collection)

A bulldozer being brought into use to move a 5.5-inch gun in the Apennines in the rain of late 1944. (Taylor Library)

Initial Landing Forces
US VI Corps, Major-General John Lucas
US 3rd Infantry Division, Major-General Lucian Truscott
  7th,15th, 30th Infantry Regiments
  9th, 10th, 39th, 41st Field Artillery Battalions
US Ranger Force, Colonel William O. Darby
  1st, 3rd, 4th Ranger Battalions
  509th Parachute Infantry Battalion
British 1st Infantry Division, Major-General W. Penney
2 Infantry Brigade: 1st Loyal Regiment, 2nd North Staffordshire, 6th Gordon Highlanders
3 Infantry Brigade: 1st Duke of Wellington's, 2nd Sherwood Foresters, 1st King's Shropshire Light Infantry
18 Infantry Brigade (from 24 February): 1st Buffs, 14th Sherwood Foresters, 9th King's Own Yorkshire Light Infantry
24 Guards Brigade (until 24 March): 5th Grenadier Guards, 1st Scots Guards, 1st Irish Guards.
2/7th Middlesex
9 and 43 (RM) Commando
2nd, 19th, 67th Field Regiments, Royal Artillery

broke. The pressure was maintained on the Allies through the night, and was followed by a tank attack the next morning. By noon a deep wedge had been driven into the 45th Division. Lucas called in every reinforcement he had in the beachhead and all the fire-power he could summon from outside and the battle raged all day, but the American line held. The critical day was 18 February. The shattered 179th Infantry was close to collapse but managed to hold. On 19 February Lucas was actually able to mount some limited counter-attacks, and by the next day the Germans had to admit that they had failed. They had suffered 5,389 casualties, most to artillery fire. The Allied losses came to 3,496. The beachhead settled into an uneasy, static stand-off. General Lucas was relieved of his command on 22 February and Truscott took over from him.

When Operation Diadem began on 11 May, a breakout from the beachhead became possible, and on 23 May Truscott advanced. The opportunity to take the Alban Hills at last, to carry on to Valmontone on Route 6 and capture the retreating Germans pouring back from the Gustav Line was there, but General Mark Clark had other ideas. The glamour of entering Rome was not resisted, and on 26 May he directed Truscott to wheel left and go for the capital city. At 11.00 hours on 27 May the US 3rd Division alone was near Valmonte to oppose the German retreat, and Hermann Göring Division was in place to stop them. That was enough to keep the Germans' exit open.

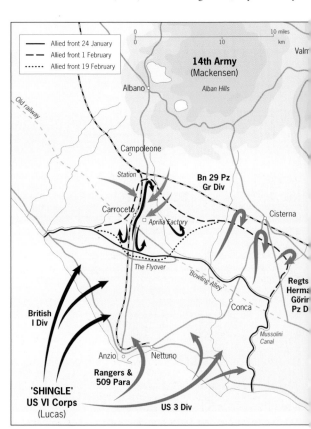

50

The Battle of the Flying Bombs

The development of self-propelled, pilotless devices for delivering explosive weapons was in hand in Germany in the early years of the war. When they came into use in 1944 the Allied bombing campaign on Germany had inflicted considerable damage, and the name given to these flying bombs, *Vergeltungswaffen*, retaliation weapon, appeared appropriate.

Three types of weapon were created, of which two were used. The V1 flying bomb was a cruise missile, the V2 a ballistic missile and the V3 was a long-range gun. The V1 was a pilotless aircraft with a wingspan of 5.3 metres (17 ft 4.5 in) and a length overall of 8.32 metres (27 ft 3.5 in), capable of carrying a warhead of 850 kg (1,875 lb) of high explosive. It was powered by a pulse-jet engine, an air-breathing type of ramjet which produced a top speed of over 400 mph (670 kph) and gave a range of about 125 miles (200 km). The missile was launched either from a ramp using a catapult or from a flying aircraft. Of the two methods the former gave the best results in terms of target attainment. The first example was test-launched, soon after the first V2, in December 1942 at Peenemünde, a remote location on the shore of the Baltic Sea some sixty-five miles (105 km) east of Rostok. The technical director of the project was Wernher von Braun.

The V2 was a rocket-powered device intended for use by the Army. It ran on a 3/1 water/alcohol mixture and liquid oxygen, and had a subsidiary power system for working the pumps which used hydrogen peroxide and calcium permanganate. It

was 14.04 metres (46 ft 1¼ in) long and the fins had a span of 3.56 metres (11 ft 8¼ in). The warhead weighed 975 kg (2,150 lb). It had a maximum speed of 3,600 mph (5,750 kph) on impact with its target, and reached an altitude of 60 miles (96 km) in attaining its maximum range of 200 miles (320 km).

The V1 flying bomb was known to the British as the Doodle-Bug. The first was launched against London on 13 June 1944, soon after the D-Day landings in Normandy, and 2,452 had been sent by the end of the month. Their characteristic, pulsing engine-noise soon became familiar to the English. They would cease their activity and stay still and silent when they heard one, waiting for the engine to stop, the event preceding its descent. If it ceased its noise immediately overhead, the news for the listener was good, for the bomb would glide and fall elsewhere. Fighters were deployed to shoot them down but had to be fast enough to do so. The Spitfire IX, which came into service in 1942, was in theory capable of 416 mph (669 kph), and the Tempest, of 1944, of 435 mph (700 kph), while the first operational jet fighter in the RAF, the Meteor, had a top speed of 490 mph (788 kph), but they were few in number. The first squadron to have Meteors was No. 616, and in July 1944 it had seven aircraft at Manston, Kent. On 4 August, near Tonbridge, Flying Officer Dean, his 20 mm cannon jammed, tipped a V1 over with his wing-tip and became the first jet pilot to down a flying bomb. Later that day FO Roger shot one down near Tenterden, Kent. Conventional fighters had shot down about a hundred V1s over Kent in the first

A V1 'Doodle-Bug' that crash-landed in southern England without exploding. (Taylor Library)

week of the attacks. The other important weapon against the V1 was the anti-aircraft gun. In July anti-aircraft guns were massed on the Kent coast between Dungeness and Dover and claimed some 1,000 enemy bombs destroyed by the end of August. The first campaign ceased in September as the Allies advanced in France and overran launch sites. The attack by V1s launched from Heinkel 111s had already begun, and was built up during the autumn. Of the fifty per cent of launches that functioned properly a low rate of accuracy was achieved, and the shortage of aircraft fuel brought the campaign to an end in January 1945. The V1 was used against Belgian cities in 1945, and a brief renewed attack on London was made from the Netherlands in March that year. Some 10,000 V1s were launched against Britain, of which 7,488 made it across the sea. Of these, 3,957 were shot down. London suffered hits from 2,419 flying bombs, Southampton and Portsmouth received about thirty and Manchester one. The British dead totalled 6,184 and the injured 17,981.

The V2 rocket was first flown in October 1942, but was much more difficult to perfect than the V1. It went into production in May 1944 in an underground factory at Nordhausen in the Harz Mountains, 150 miles (240 km) south-west of Berlin. The labour was supplied by a concentration camp codenamed Dora, Mittelbau KL, to which some 60,000 people were sent, of whom about fifty per cent died. Another V2 assembly factory was built at Eperlecques, north of St-Omer, and yet another just west of St-Omer, which also used forced labour. The first missile launched against England hit Chiswick, London, on 8 September 1944, and by 27 March 1945 1,054 rockets had been fired successfully, half of them on London. Some 2,700 Londoners died. Antwerp, Belgium, was also a target, receiving about 900 V2s by the end of 1944. Defence was impossible and locating launch sites very difficult, as the highly mobile weapon could be launched from a small concrete base used only temporarily. The cessation of this form of attack depended on the advance of the Allied armies to deny the Germans launch sites within range.

The V3 was a long-range, smooth-bore gun which was intended to fire fin-stabilized shells, the largest of which was 3 metres (9 ft 10 in) long with a calibre of 11 cm (4¼ in) and with a 10 kg (22 lb) high-explosive warhead. The shells were to be fired by a series of explosive charges in side chambers along the length of the 150 metre (492 ft) barrel. The bore was 15cm (5‰ in) and the shell had sabots, disposable cuffs, around it to achieve a seal, which were to fall away after it emerged. The construction of two sites at Mimoyecques, near Calais, began in late 1943. Each site was intended to have twenty-five barrels capable of giving a rate of fire of five shells a minute to hit London. One site was damaged by an air raid and the other had only achieved a range of about sixty miles (96 km) by July 1944. The barrels were inclined to split. The RAF bombed the site once more that month, and it soon fell to the advancing Allies. The concept was not abandoned, however, and a modifed version of the gun was brought into action in December. It had one barrel 60 metres (197 ft) long, and a shorter range, about forty miles (65 km). With this gun the Germans fired on Antwerp, and another such weapon was used against the Americans in Luxemburg, but with no significant results.

Wernher von Braun and about a hundred of his colleagues at Peenemünde managed to escape from the invading Soviet forces in March 1945 and go to the USA. They became part of the American space programme personnel.

The V3 supergun, intended to fire a missile from northern France to London. (Taylor Library)

Bocage country near Méautis, south-west of Carentan. The banks flanking this cart track are considerably higher than a grown man. (Author)

The return to the mainland of Europe had been advocated by the Americans and Russians for more than two years before Operation Overlord actually took place. The resources required were immense and the intelligence needed was complex and extensive. Detailed planning began as a result of the Casablanca Conference of January 1943, and General Frederick Morgan was ordered to build an organization, codenamed COSSAC, to make the necessary plans. The proposal to invade the French coast in the Baie de la Seine between Le Havre and Cherbourg was approved at Quebec in August.

The experience of the Dieppe raid made it clear that a direct assault on a major port was doomed, but resupply of a landed force was vital. It was hoped that Cherbourg could be taken quickly, but temporary arrangements were possible with the building of Mulberries – harbours formed with blockships and floating caissons. Fuel was to be supplied by an undersea pipeline codenamed Pluto, Pipe Line Under The Ocean. The Germans were in the process of constructing the Atlantic Wall, a line of fortifications from the Netherlands to Spain intended to be the frontier of Hitler's Fortress Europe, but the section in Normandy was incomplete. Deception schemes such as Fortitude South, the pretence that Lieutenant-General George Patton's Third Army would be landed in the Pas de Calais, were mounted to keep troops and defence construction concentrated in the wrong place.

The structure of the German armed forces was not conducive to co-operation either between arms of service or within the Army itself. Field Marshal von Rundstedt was of the opinion that the Allies would, no matter what, get through the Atlantic Wall, and so he favoured having a strong mobile force ready to round them up when they did. His theoretical subordinate, Field Marshal Rommel, on the other hand, declared that the battle would have to be won on the beaches, and as Rommel had a direct line of communication to Hitler, who agreed with him, the plan put into action was for beach defence. Elaborate arrangements had already been started and to these were added more 'hedgehogs', girders welded into six-pointed structures like jacks, and 'Rommel's Asparagus', poles planted to prevent aircraft landing on open fields. The rivers had also been released to form flood hazards, notably in the marshy area around Carentan at the base of the Cotentin Peninsula to the west and in the valley of the River Dives, east of Caen, and the River Orne which flows through it.

The countryside facing the Baie de la Seine is varied. Sandy beaches alternate with steep cliffs and marshy river mouths along the shoreline, and inland the land rises at first to open hills, but these are cut by steep river valleys. South of Caen the landscape opens out into a broad plain rising gently towards Falaise, to the east of which the valley of the Dives separates it from more high country. To add to the natural obstacles, hundreds of years of agricultural use had changed the landscape. Particularly where the land is wet, ditches had been dug alongside access tracks and around fields for generations past and the spoil dumped alongside. These soil banks had then been planted with hedges and trees, binding the soil with their roots to form boundary walls to the fields up to ten feet (3 m) high. This kind of country is known as the *Bocage* and it was to become notorious as a land ideal for defence.

The plan for the landings was to secure the western and eastern flanks with paratroops before the amphibious operation Neptune put soldiers ashore on four main beach areas. These would be joined together into a continuous beachhead some forty miles (65 km) wide and ten miles (16 km) deep. The British and Commonwealth forces on the east would absorb the energy of the German counter-attack south of Caen before pushing forward, while the Americans would move at once to take Cherbourg, the key port of supply. A breakout by the Americans from the Cotentin Peninsula would then clear Brittany and give the Allies more vital seaports, as well as turning east to render the German defence untenable. But few plans work out in real life.

By early June the Allied forces had made ready in England. There were twenty American divisions, fourteen British, three Canadian and one each from Poland and France. There were nearly 8,000 aircraft. Under Admiral Sir Bertram H. Ramsay 4,000 landing craft and vessels and nearly 300 fighting ships were prepared to carry, defend and support the land forces. Now what was required was suitable weather, for midsummer in Europe is not always quiet and sunny. The landings were scheduled for the morning of 5 June, but a storm forced cancellation, and a window of comparative calm that was forecast prompted Eisenhower to order D-Day for 6 June.

Omaha Beach seen from a German bunker that is well protected from naval shellfire but covers the landing beaches efficiently. (Author)

The US First Army: Utah and Omaha Beaches

Inland of the intended landing beaches on the south-eastern flank of the Cotentin Peninsula wide salt marshes lie, and through them thread a few raised roads to the ridge inland. To the west and south of the ridge were flooded river valleys and marshes. This ridge, the villages of Ste-Mère-Eglise and Ste-Marie-du-Mont and the causeways over the marshes from the beach were the objective of the American 82nd and 101st Airborne Divisions. At 01.30 hours on 6 June the 101st went in, to be followed by the 82nd an hour later. The aircraft approached from the west, across the line of the ridge, and with enemy gunfire coming up at them and the sea ahead, the drop was scattered. Many men, laden with supplies, weapons and equipment, drowned in the floods. Others found themselves lost and alone. Some dropped right into their target towns; John Steele of 505 Parachute Infantry got hooked up on the church tower in Ste-Mère-Eglise and had to feign death to survive. Their natural confusion was more than matched by the bafflement of the defenders, who were taken entirely by surprise. The Americans formed themselves into workable units, secured their objectives and waited for the men from the sea.

The Cotentin Peninsula sheltered the sea approaches to Utah Beach from the westerly gales that had delayed the invasion, but the wind had pushed the waters of the English Channel to create a higher tide than normal and a north-to-south current along the shore. As the covering bombardment from the Navy crashed on German defences, Brigadier-General Theodore Roosevelt Jr saw that his 4th Division was being swept south, that they were going to miss Uncle Beach entirely and that all would be compressed onto the Victor section of Utah Beach. A veteran of the previous war, he realized that it was best to keep moving in battle if there was no cover, and pressed on. By chance the defences here were light, and they came ashore and moved up to the ridge to meet the airborne troops without much resistance. By nightfall 23,250 men had come ashore with the loss of 210 killed.

Further east the sea was considerably rougher and the defending troops of a different calibre. The Allies' intelligence had shown that the German 352nd Infantry Division was at the southern end of the Cotentin, south of St Lô, and that this coast was defended by 716th Coastal Defence Division, a unit not noted for its martial prowess. In fact the crack 352nd was here on exercise. The landings were made by 116th Infantry of 29th Division and 16th Infantry of 1st Division together with the US 5th Rangers. The American approach and attack had been prepared meticulously, and was immediately put out of gear by the adverse conditions. The landing run began, as planned, twelve miles (19 km) off shore instead of being brought closer in, and the amphibious tanks, D-D Shermans, were launched 6,000 yards (5,500 m) off the beach. Of the thirty-two that started, twenty-seven sank. The height of the tide covered the mine-topped posts, and tanks and landing craft ran foul of them. The amphibious trucks, DUKWs, carrying the support artillery and ammunition had been overloaded for the conditions and capsized. Without supporting armour or artillery on the beach, the infantry were exposed to heavy fire from secure gun emplacements built into the western cliffs, from which the Germans could fire down the length of the shore. The losses were terrible. Men and landing craft poured into the cauldron of fire and became casualties or got pinned down in turn, huddled under the sea wall. By noon

The Rangers' memorial crowns one of the bunkers they took on Pointe du Hoc. (Author)

DUKWs of the 51st (Highland) Division leaving Sword Beach. *(Taylor Library)*

East of the River Orne the hills rise to Merville before dropping away to the broad Dives valley. The Orne is supplemented with a canal for seagoing vessels and is crossed near Bénouville with a lift-bridge. The eastern flank of the landing grounds had to be secured and men of the British 6th Airborne were sent to do it. At 00.16 hours on 6 June three gliders landed next to the lift-bridge and men of the Oxfordshire and Buckinghamshire Light Infantry took it. The battery at Merville was dealt with by 9th Parachute Battalion, although they found only old Czech guns in place. The bridges over the Dives at Troarn were blown to secure the flank, and the Airborne awaited the arrival of men from Sword Beach.

they were still there and Bradley considered evacuating them. The Rangers managed to penetrate the defences and gained the road east of Vierville. Others managed to scramble up the cliffs and, one by one, knock out the gun emplacements. By the end of the day the Germans were low on ammunition, and their reserves had been sent on a hunt for non-existent parachute troops inland, fooled by a drop of dummies. The American pressure began to tell and two of the exits from the beach were secured. When night fell there were 34,000 men ashore at a cost of over 2,000 casualties, more than half of them fatal.

To the west 2nd Rangers had been given the task of neutralizing an emplacement of heavy guns on the Pointe du Hoc. Under the command of Lieutenant-Colonel James E. Rudder, most of the boats eventually made it to the beach below the cliffs, but the DUKWs with extending ladders proved useless, as shellfire had pitted the beach so much that they could not get near. Grapnels shot up were pulled back by wet ropes, and the Germans above started rolling grenades down upon them. Some grapnels held. A few men hauled themselves up, and more followed, enough to mount an attack across the moonscape created by shells from USS *Texas*. The gun emplacements were empty. The guns, ready for installation, were found inland, but not the men from Omaha Beach whom the Rangers were to meet. They had to hold this place for two days before they met their comrades coming from the east, and by that time they had suffered sixty per cent casualties.

It had been intended that, by the end of the first day, the Americans would control all the land in from Utah Beach as far as the valley of the Merderet River, but in fact they still held only pockets of that area and had yet to consolidate. East of the Douve estuary the whole coast should have been taken, but they actually held only the Pointe du Hoc and a small beachhead at Omaha. But they were ashore, they had not been defeated on the beaches.

The landings at Sword were hampered by the extra-high tide, but met modest resistance and suffered more from the traffic jam caused by the cramped area available for getting ashore and organized. By 11.00 hours 185th Brigade was in formation and starting to move inland, despite the absence of their supporting armour, still stuck in traffic. Lord Lovat's 6th Commando extracted itself and dashed off to support the 6th Airborne. At Juno the Canadian 3rd Infantry met a more determined defence from the German 716th Infantry, but by noon they were four miles (6 km) inland. Both were vulnerable. The fort overlooking Ouistreham from the hill above, named Hillman, offered serious resistance, and the Suffolk Regiment's naval liaison officer had been killed, preventing them from calling for covering fire from the sea. The fort held until evening, slowing the exploitation of the beachhead and allowing a gap to open between them and the Canadians. Into this space 21 Panzer penetrated as far as Luc-sur-Mer, and over the next four days 46th Royal Marine Commando, the Canadian Regiment de la Chaudière and Sherman tanks reduced this salient.

On Gold Beach the effect of the storm was so great that it was decided to run the landing craft carrying the D-Ds all the way in to the shore. Here the specially equipped tanks known as Hobart's Funnies did good service in bridging ditches and destroying pillboxes. By the end of the day, when a continuous beachhead should have been established, there was still a gap between Sword and Juno and the intention of reaching Caen had not been realized. The Allies were firmly established, however, and the slowness of the German response permitted them to consolidate their hold over the next seven days.

Altogether 75,215 Commonwealth troops and 57,500 US troops were landed on D-Day. There were about 4,300 British and Canadian casualties, and 6,000 American.

The first task of the Americans was to take Cherbourg, but fighting through the *bocage* was tougher than anyone had anticipated. The western coast of the Cotentin Peninsula was reached on 18 June, but although the German command in Cherbourg surrendered on 26 June, full control of the port was not attained until 1 July. By then demolition crews had reduced the harbour to wreckage, and it would be September before Cherbourg became fully operational once more. The need for Mulberry harbours was thus absolute. At Arromanches the so-called Gooseberries, concrete-filled block ships, were sunk and the caissons and piers towed into place, the product of a huge cross-Channel effort that began on 9 June. By 18 June the great curve of the artificial harbour was in place and on 19 June another storm blew up. The Mulberry under construction at Omaha Beach was destroyed and abandoned, but at Arromanches the harbour held out. In the meantime supplies had been delivered by running large landing craft up on the beaches to unload. They were then able to float off on the incoming tide.

On the Caen front the British mounted actions to the west of the town, culminating in Operation Epsom on 25 June, but little ground was gained. By 10 July the battered city of Caen fell to the British and Canadians, but an effort to grasp the open country to the south in Operation Goodwood on 18 July failed to break through. On that day the Americans at last managed to enter St-Lô. Goodwood had, however, made its contribution by the time the heavy rain of 20 July stopped it. The last of the German armoured units in the north of France, 116 Panzer, was ordered to the Caen sector. German Army Group B had lost over 90,000 men and 200 tanks. Panzer Lehr, west of St Lô, was down to 40 tanks and 2,200 men. Eisenhower, putting aside all suggestions that he should replace his subordinate, encouraged Montgomery to throw caution to the winds.

The Mulberry harbour at Arromanches. (Taylor Library)

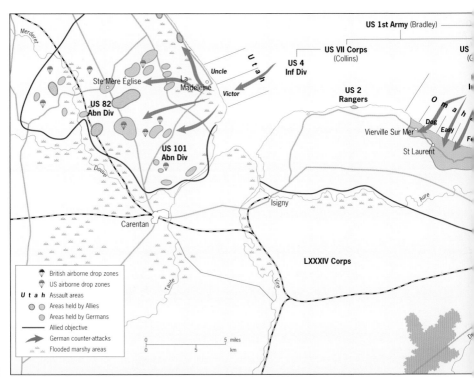

Allied Commanders

Supreme Headquarters Allied Expeditionary Force (SHAEF)
Supreme Commander: General Dwight D. Eisenhower
Deputy Supreme Commander: Air Chief Marshal Sir Arthur Tedder
Chief of Staff: Major-General Walter Bedell Smith

21st Army Group, General Sir Bernard L. Montgomery
Second British Army, Lieutenant-General Sir Miles Dempsey
First Canadian Army (from 23 July), Lieutenant-General H.D.G. Crerar

12th Army Group (from 1 August), Lieutenant-General Omar N. Bradley
First US Army, Bradley (to 1 August), Lieutenant-General Courtney H. Hodges
Third US Army, Lieutenant-General George S. Patton Jr

Allied Expeditionary Air Force, Air Chief Marshal Sir Trafford Leigh-Mallory
RAF Second Tactical Air Force, Air Marshal Sir Arthur Coningham
US Ninth Air Force, Lieutenant-General Lewis H. Brereton (to 7 August), Major-General Joyt S. Vandenberg

Air Defence of Great Britain, Air Marshal Sir Roderick M. Hill
RAF Bomber Command, Air Chief Marshal Sir Arthur T. Harris
US Eighth Air Force, Lieutenant-General James H. Doolittle

German Commanders

Oberbefelshaber West (OB West), Field Marshal Gerd von Rundstedt (to 2 July), Field Marshal Günther von Kluge (to 18 August), Field Marshal Walther Model

Army Group B, Field Marshal Erwin Rommel (to 17 July), Field Marshal Günther von Kluge (to 18 August), Field Marshal Walther Model
Seventh Army, General Friedrich Dollmann (to 28 June), General Paul Hausser (to 20 August), Panzer General Heinrich Eberbach (to 30 August)
Panzer Group West (to 5 August)/Fifth Panzer Army, Panzer General Leo Freiherr Geyr von Schweppenburg (to 6 July), Panzer General Heinrich Eberbach (to 9 August), General Joseph 'Sepp' Dietrich

Luftflotte 3, Field Marshal Hugo Sperrle

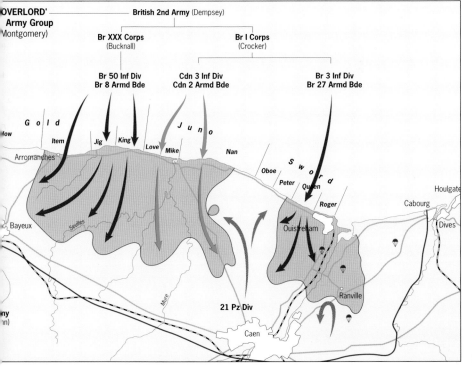

Cobra to the Falaise Pocket

Lieutenant-General George S. Patton, once it had become clear where the invasion was actually taking place, came to France, and from a small village near St-Sauveur-le-Vicomte prepared his Third Army for action. It officially came into existence on 1 August, but went into action in Operation Cobra on 25 July. On 24 July, the original date for Cobra, the 9th US Army Air Force dropped 5,000 tons of bombs on a five-mile (8 km) front west of St-Lô. They had not been informed of the delay and attacked again the next day. General Bradley had demanded that the bombers fly parallel to the road to minimize risk to his troops. The Air Force insisted on a course at right angles to the road and dropped many bombs short. Among the American dead was Lieutenant-General Leslie McNair. Among the German was the greater part of Panzer Lehr. In the east, south of Caen, the Canadians mounted Operation Spring, which the Germans misinterpreted as the principal offensive and to which they directed their main energies. On the Cotentin front the first day's infantry attack gained more than two miles, and the next another five. Modified Sherman tanks, fitted with tooth-like blades and called Rhinos, broke through the hedged banks of the *bocage*. It was on 27 July that the breakthrough came, with 2nd Armored Division roaring through towards Coutances, which VII Corps took the next day.

Avranches was taken on 30 July, and on 1 August Patton rushed four divisions through the opening at the base of the peninsula, out of the *bocage* and into the open country beyond. Bradley, with Montgomery's approval, ordered Patton to turn east,

The memorial to the meeting of Polish and American troops that closed the Falaise Gap stands beneath the walls of the ancient keep at Chambois. (Author)

detaching part of VIII Corps to head for the Brittany ports. These ports were not, in fact, taken for many weeks, and thus were denied to the Allies as supply ports. The task of opposing the breakout fell to Field Marshal von Kluge, who had replaced the wounded Rommel. His proposal to withdraw to the River Seine and establish a coherent line was vetoed by Hitler, who demanded a counter-attack to sever Patton from the rest of the Allies, cutting his supply line near Avranches. On 6 August Ultra intelligence gave warning of the attack. The remains of 1st and 2nd SS Panzer, 2 Panzer, Panzer Lehr, 116 Panzer and 17 SS Panzer Grenadier Divisions under XLVII

A wrecked German AFV and stacks of wood form a German defence position near Falaise. (Taylor Library)

The Falaise Pocket was littered with destroyed and abandoned equipment and the bodies of the slain. (Taylor Library)

Panzer Corps were to take the offensive. Between them they had only 185 tanks and eight 88 mm guns. They hit 30th Division of VII Corps late on the night of 6 August and surrounded the Americans on Hill 317 at Mortain. Here Hitler ordered them to stay, and this became known to Montgomery through Ultra. The destruction of the Germans from the air now began, with attacks by Thunderbolts and Typhoons. By 12 August the besieged 30th Division was relieved and Patton's advance had reached Sées, beyond Argentan to the south-east of Falaise.

On 7 August the Canadians had undertaken Operation Totalize, followed shortly thereafter by Tractable, strikes south towards Falaise, which they took on 17 August. To their east 1 Polish Armoured pushed forward the next day to Mont Ormel and Hill 262 overlooking Chambois down in the valley of the Dives. The Germans were now herded into a great pocket south of Falaise. Hitler appointed Field Marshal Walther Model in von Kluge's place and summoned the disgraced commander to his headquarters. Von Kluge committed suicide.

The Germans struggled to hold the rear of the pocket open as Allied aircraft bombed and strafed and Allied artillery and infantry drenched them with gunfire. During the morning of 18 August 4th Canadian Armoured took the village of Trun and attacked St-Lambert, where the Germans were still squeezing from west to east over the Dives. From the hills north of Argentan and from the height of Mont Ormel the Americans and the Poles poured fire on the fleeing enemy. On 19 August, at 19.20 hours, the Poles and the Americans met in Chambois, but the Germans still resisted. The 2nd Paratroops opened a route to Coudehard the next morning, and more men struggled out towards Camembert and Vimoutiers from St-Lambert under fire from the remaining Polish troops until, the next morning, the fight stuttered to a close. The Poles had 114 of their original 1,560 men still fit for action.

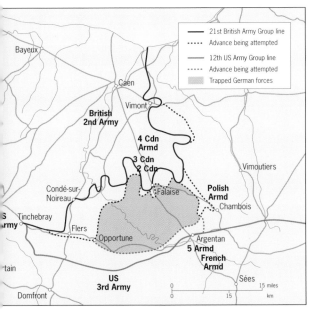

Losses in the Battle of Normandy

German:
Killed and wounded
240,000

Missing or captured
200,000

Tanks lost
1,500

Transport destroyed
20,000

Aircraft destroyed
3,600
(Total strength: approximately 1 million men)

Allies:
Killed
36,976

Other casualties
172,696

(Total strength: approximately 2 million men)

By the late summer of 1944 the Allies were victims of their own success. The victory in Normandy had inflicted serious damage on the Germans, and the subsequent advance was swift and impressive. General Eisenhower followed a strategy of a broad front but the momentum was in danger of being lost as the supply line became ever longer. In September Cherbourg had just come into operation and the temporary port at Arromanches was working to capacity, but it was not enough. The Canadians came to a halt outside Antwerp on 4 September and Lieutenant-General Brian Horrocks's XXX Corps shuffled east, seeking a way to penetrate into the Netherlands. Field Marshal Montgomery had been advocating a thrust on a narrow front – his, of course, rather than the Americans' – and on 10 September his latest idea was agreed. The First Allied Airborne Army, under Lieutenant-General Lewis Brereton, would be used to cut through the Netherlands, securing key bridges, to open a path into the Ruhr, Germany's industrial heartland.

The plan was to have 101st US Airborne land around Eindhoven, 82nd around Nijmegen and 1st British Airborne around Arnhem, and then XXX Corps would drive north from the Belgian border to pass over the bridges thus secured and proceed to wheel right into Germany. First Allied Airborne and its deputy commander, Lieutenant-General F.A.M. Browning, had just one week to organize the whole operation. The approach to the Lower Rhine at Arnhem was over largely flat land from the Belgian border up to Nijmegen. Here the hills rose to the east, around Groesbeek. Between the River Waal at Nijmegen and the bridge at Arnhem the land was completely flat. The Lower Rhine was, in 1944, a swift and turbulent river, quite unlike the tame, semi-canalized stream of today. On the northern side the land rose north of Arnhem town and a ridge curved westwards through Oosterbeek to close with the river, leaving a flood plain stretching back to Arnhem. The long road up from Belgium was flanked by polder land, drained marsh cut with a network of ditches and canals, and where the land

rose, sandy soil. The polder was unsuited to wheeled or tracked vehicles.

The German forces were the remains of Army Group B, which Field Marshal Walther Model was in the process of re-forming into an effective formation. South of Nijmegen he had General Gustav von Zangen's Fifteenth Army to the west and Colonel-General Kurt Student's First Parachute Army in the east. North of these were Lieutenant-General Willi Bittrich's II Panzer Corps with two Panzer divisions much reduced in size and reconfigured as *SS-Kampfgruppe Hohenstauffen*, under Lieutenant-Colonel Walther Harzer, and *SS-Kampfgruppe Frundsberg* under Brigadier Heinz Harmel. Two other units were available – the Hermann Göring Division Training Regiment under Lieutenant-Colonel Fritz Fullreide, and Lieutenant-General Hans von Tettau's *Kampfgruppe*. By 7 September this force could put into the field about 15,000 men and 250 tanks, and troops retiring from the Scheldt would add to them by 23 September.

The plan for Market, the airborne part of the operation, was for 101st Airborne, under Major-General Maxwell Taylor, to drop north of Eindhoven and take the bridges over the River Aa and the Willems Canal at Veghel, the bridge over the River Dommel at St-Oedenrode and the one over the Wilhelmina Canal at Son. Brigadier-General James Gavin's 82nd Airborne was to capture the Groesbeek Heights, east of Nijmegen, to forestall counter-attacks, and then take the bridges over the Maas at Grave, the Maas-Waal Canal and then the road bridge at Nijmegen. The 1st British Airborne, under Major-General R.E. Urquhart, would drop on the heathland west of Arnhem and then go six miles (9.5 km) to the road bridge over the Lower Rhine in the town, also taking the railway bridge. Then, with the support of 1st Polish Parachute Brigade under Major-General Stanislav Sosabowski, they would occupy the high ground north of Arnhem. The air plan allowed only one major drop a day, so it would take three days to move everyone into place, after which aircraft would fly in fresh supplies. XXX Corps would carry out Garden, the road approach, spearheaded by the Guards Armoured Division, and as it linked with the airborne elements it would take them under command. They had rations for four days and fuel for 250 miles (400 km).

Sunday 17 September dawned a clear, dry day. From 09.30 hours the air armada flew out, preceded by bombing missions on airfields and strongpoints. Shortly after noon the first men parachuted in at the landing zones west of Arnhem, and Field Marshal Model's lunch was spoiled by the news. He departed from Oosterbeek quickly to organize the riposte. By 02.00 hours some 20,000 troops, 511 vehicles and 330 artillery pieces had been landed in the Netherlands. At Arnhem the various parties set off along their planned routes eastwards and the first piece of bad luck was encountered. An SS

The rebuilt 'John Frost' bridge on the original piers at Arnhem. *(Author)*

battalion of 435 men commanded by Major Sepp Krafft were on a training exercise in the Wolfheze woods near the landing zones. Krafft formed a quick appreciation of the events and established a block north of the railway embankment and, as it happened, on the route that Major Freddie Gough's Reconnaissance Platoon was racing along to get to the bridge. In the centre, south of the railway, progress against light resistance was slow and not helped by the enthusiasm of the Dutch for their supposed liberators. Urquhart and Brigadier Gerald Lathbury went to hurry them up and Urquhart got cut off from his HQ. Only on the right, along the river, did things move quickly. Lieutenant-Colonel John Frost's 2nd Battalion, overcoming radio problems with calls on a hunting horn, were just too late to prevent the railway bridge being blown, but secured the northern end of the road bridge and, with about 750 men, including some from 3rd Battalion and part of Gough's unit, prepared to hold it against the inevitable counter-attack.

By the evening of 17 September XXX Corps had made fair progress at the cost of nine tanks, but it was already becoming clear that the Germans were capable of holding them back from their intended schedule. At Son the 101st Airborne were unable to prevent the bridge being blown, and the engineers had to be fed through the attacking force to throw up a temporary structure.

On 18 September in the outskirts of Arnhem a battle was in progress near the St Elisabeth hospital. 1st and 3rd Battalion were reinforced by 11th Battalion and 2nd South Staffordshire Regiment, sent forward by Brigadier P.H.W. Hicks in Urquhart's absence. The commander had become embroiled in the action nearby and had to hide in an attic, to the detriment of the command structure. At the bridge Frost was under attack but holding against it without excessive hardship and having the satisfaction of shooting up 9th SS Reconnaissance Battalion when it had tried to come north over the bridge.

Bad weather marked 19 September, preventing the arrival of the Polish Brigade, and there was no breakthrough to the bridge by the British in the west, although Urquhart was sprung from his attic. Meanwhile XXX Corps was coming on, but more slowly than needed. The 82nd attempted to take the bridge at Nijmegen but the Germans held on. General Gavin decided on a boat-crossing of the Waal to attack the bridge from the north, but the boats were with XXX Corps and he had to wait. Frost clung on at the bridge in Arnhem.

On 20 September Urquhart was forced to recognize he would not break through to Frost and he organized a defensive perimeter at Oosterbeek. At Nijmegen the 82nd, supported by the tanks of the Irish Guards, crossed the river under intense fire and took the bridge. The tanks rolled over the river and stopped, out of ammunition and, in the growing dark, without air cover. The Americans were furious at the delay. Frost was forced to surrender the next morning.

Although XXX Corps advanced enough to give 1st British Airborne artillery support on 21 September, and in spite of the arrival of the Poles at Driel, it was becoming clear that the operation would not be completed as planned. In the next days some of the Poles and the 4th Dorsets crossed the Rhine at a heavy price, but the German grip was tightening. On the night of 24/25 September 3,910 men were evacuated from the Oosterbeek enclave, leaving 1,485 dead and 6,525 as prisoners, or men still seeking to escape, 1st Airborne, glider pilots and Polish forces. Casualties on the advance up what had become known as Hell's Highway were 5,354 killed, wounded or missing, including 1,480 for XXX Corps. The German casualties are not known. Model reported 3,300, and other estimates put the figure at up to 8,000.

The possibility of further, swift advance in northern Europe in 1944, after the failure to break through the northern Netherlands from Arnhem, was severely limited by the supply problem. Although Antwerp itself had been taken in September and local resistance had prevented the destruction of harbour installations, the fight for mastery of the Scheldt estuary was long and hard. The last of the German defenders surrendered on 8 November after an amphibious assault on the island of Walcheren, but it was not until 26 November that the waterway was declared free of mines and open to Allied shipping. The danger to Germany of Allied possession of this key port was not ignored by Hitler. On 16 September he proposed to defeat the Allies by striking for and taking Antwerp once more, creating another Dunkirk, as he put it, and causing an irretrievable breakdown in relations between the Americans and the British.

The plan was for a surprise offensive through the hilly, forested region of the Ardennes, the country traversed so swiftly by the Panzers in May 1940. The long, narrow valleys, running mainly east–west, channelled the forces into predictable routes which met at a few important towns such as St-Vith and Bastogne. General Eisenhower had decided to push forward both north, via Aachen and the River Roer, and south, through Alsace, of the Ardennes, leaving the centre lightly manned with tired or inexperienced forces. The German axis of advance was intended to take them from the Eifel Mountains to the River Meuse between Namur and Liège, then both sides of Brussels to Antwerp. The movement was to be spearheaded by the new Sixth Panzer Army commanded by *Waffen-SS Oberstgruppenführer* Josep 'Sepp' Dietrich. To his left, the south, Fifth Panzer Army under Panzer General Hasso von Manteuffel was to advance alongside, taking Brussels on the way, and further south again the Seventh Army under Panzer General Erich Brandenburger would hold off any attempt by Lieutenant-General George Patton's Third Army to intervene. The two northern armies would be led respectively by the 150th SS Brigade under Otto Skorzeny, English-speakers disguised in American uniform, and *Kampfgruppe* Peiper under Colonel Joachim Peiper, these units intended to race for bridges over the Meuse.

The American forces in the area were from the US First Army, commanded by Lieutenant-General Courtney Hodges, with V Corps (2nd and 99th Infantry Divisions) under Major-General Leonard Gerow in the north, preparing to attack the Roer Dams, and VIII Corps (4th, 28th and 106th Infantry and 9th Armored Divisions) under Major-General Troy Middleton in the south, covering the Ardennes.

The attack began on 16 December, when the weather was bad and the Allied superiority in the air was neutralized for the time being. In the north, between Monschau and Losheim, 1st SS Panzer rolled forward after an opening barrage on

An Allied supply column moving up in the Battle of the Bulge in the Ardennes. (Taylor Library)

American positions where the inexperienced 99th Division held a line south of the Elsenborn Ridge at the villages of Rocherath and Krinkelt. The Americans failed to collapse, and so the Germans could not move west. The cost was high and the line became fragmented. Eventually the 99th had to fall back to positons on the Ridge itself, but there they would stand throughout the campaign, denying the Sixth Panzer Army any room on their northern flank. Immediately to the south, in the Losheim Gap, 3rd Parachute Division, Sixth Army, came up against US 14th Cavalry, and by the end of the first day had reduced them to isolated groups who were unable to resist against the Tiger tanks deployed the next day. This area was also the boundary between Sixth and Fifth Panzer Armies, and on the heights to the south of the gap, the Schnee Eifel, the US 106th Division was to be surrounded by the Germans.

In order to make progress von Manteuffel had to cross the River Our, which runs north to south along the Belgian–German border. The US 28th Division faced the advance of three German divisions and managed to hold them for the better part of the day, but were unable to man a continuous line, and it became clear that many German units were pressing on to the west, leaving their comrades to engage the Americans. This was not the swift breakthrough the Germans had planned.

In Versailles, at SHAEF headquarters, General Eisenhower took the precaution of suggesting to Lieutenant-General Omar Bradley that he move 7th Armored Division down from the north and 10th up from the south immediately. Field Marshal Montgomery, without consultation, decided to order the British 43rd Division and Guards Armoured Division to move to a position west of the Meuse.

At this stage there was no alarm, and scarcely the realization that the Germans were attempting something serious. Middleton knew better. During the night von Manteuffel kept up the pressure, and the next day was attacking Clervaux. By the middle of the day the Americans had been forced back into the ancient castle, and when a German tank smashed through the wooden doors, they had to surrender. The way was now open to Bastogne, but it had taken two full days to achieve this against resistance of unexpected courage and stubbornness. In the north Sixth Panzer Army were still battering away at the resistance of the 99th Division and Joachim Peiper was only able to make progress to the south of that conflict on the morning of 17 December, a day late. He had 100 tanks, Mark IVs and Panthers, but the traffic jams had held him up, burning precious fuel all the time. Determined to hurry on to the west as fast as possible, Peiper missed the chance to cut off the 99th Division on Elsenborn Ridge and gave them vital time to dig in. He pushed on to Malmédy, where his men were responsible for the slaughter of eighty-six American and Belgian prisoners, only one of a series of atrocities that marked their advance. As evening approached they neared Stavelot, where 291st Engineer Combat Battalion had been thrown in to make a road-block. In the gloom there was an exchange of fire and the Americans fired a bazooka, probably hitting nothing but making an impressive show. The Germans assumed that they had met a strong force and pulled back for the night. They were able to continue next day as far as La Gleize, but there, in a providential break in the bad weather, the USAAF forced Peiper to take cover, and the 30th Division arrived to block a further advance.

On the evening of 18 December units of US 10th Armored Division were scattered east of Bastogne to hold off the Germans, and 101st Airborne Division, after a dash across France in trucks with headlights blazing, were at Neffe, a village east of the city, early next day. The price to be paid would be high, but here the Americans would hold off the better part of two German divisions all day, granting an essential opportunity for the defence to be organized. The other key communications centre, St-Vith, was still in American hands, and Führer Escort Brigade was ordered to attack. Colonel Otto Remer had small stomach for this tough target and only made a gesture at it, which was strongly repulsed, so it was not until the night of 21 December that the Americans were overcome here. Then the Germans failed to exploit their success and the Americans re-formed a little way to the west.

At Bastogne the German invitation to Brigadier-General Anthony McAuliffe to surrender was rejected with the message 'Nuts!', and a stubborn defence began. In the meantime von Manteuffel passed his 2nd Panzer Division round the town, and it continued until it ran into 8th Battalion, Rifle Brigade and 3rd Royal Tank Regiment just east of Dinant on the River Meuse, just as Patton's men entered Bastogne. The US 2nd Armored Division advanced from Ciney. At Celles 2nd Panzer was surrounded and destroyed. From then on the pressure on the Germans was inexorable, although the cost to American and British troops was high. The British 53rd Division released the US 2nd Armored for action further east and moved down the centre of the salient towards Bure. The weather

American troops move forward after the recapture of St -Vith. (Taylor Library)

A restored German Panther tank at Houfalize. (Author)

improved, allowing attacks on the Germans and the improved movement of supplies. Montgomery, who had been given command of the armies north of the Ardennes salient on 20 December, used the British XXX Corps and the American VII Corps to move in. On 14 January XXX Corps linked with Patton's Third Army at La Roche, and the union with First Army took place the next day. Snow slowed the Allied progress, but the Germans had been defeated entirely. They lost about 100,000 men, a quarter of those they sent into battle. The Americans lost 10,276 killed, 47,493 wounded and 23,218 missing.

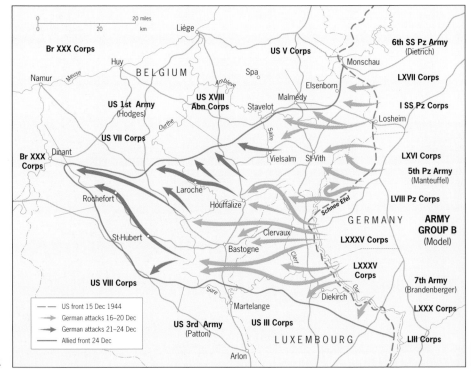

General Eisenhower's strategy remained that of advance on a broad front rather than the single penetration favoured by Montgomery, among others, so various operations were necessary to bring the Allies up to the line of the river before a crossing was attempted. General Jacob Devers's Sixth Army Group in the south had yet to deal with the German presence in the Colmar Pocket and clear the area between the Moselle and the Rhine and Montgomery's Twenty-First Army Group needed to move east from the Nijmegen position secured during Market Garden in the previous September. The Colmar Pocket was largely the business of General Jean-Marie de Lattre de Tassigny's First French Army and the rest of Devers's area was that of Patton's Third Army, and Lieutenant-General Alexander Patch's Seventh Army.

In the north the approaches to the Rhine had been flooded by the partial destruction of the Schwammenauel Dam high up the River Roer, near Monschau. In the belief that they would be able to close the discharge valves, US 309th Infantry took the dam on 9 February, but found the valves destroyed. Until the dam emptied and the Roer subsided, no attack by Lieutenant-General William H. Simpson's Ninth Army could take place, and Operation Grenade was postponed. Floods also beset the territory east of Nijmegen. Here Lieutenant-General Henry Crerar was to attack with the First Canadian Army, with XXX Corps under command. Operation Veritable, as it was called, began on 8 February without the benefit of Grenade distracting the enemy to the south. The weather, until only a few days before the operation, had been cold and the land frozen, so it was hoped that the freeze would continue. In the event the thaw set in, and mud and flood were problems as daunting as the enemy action. The trucks, tanks and Buffaloes (huge, tracked personnel-carriers) of the Canadians and the 15th Scottish Division groped their way along flooded roads towards Cleve, while the 51st Highland Division and the 52nd Lowland Division moved against the forest area of the Reichswald. Here there were defensive positions on the edge of the forest, but the chief strength of the Siegfried Line lay some three miles (5 km) beyond. The bunkers, trenches and anti-tank ditches were manned by the German 84th Infantry Division, with some 10,000 men. This serious obstacle was steadily overcome, but the rain fell, the mud deepened and the advance slowed. The breakthrough came from 13 to 17 February, when the 43rd Wessex Division stubbornly ground its way forward until, on 16 February, the 7th Duke of Cornwall's Light Infantry, in Kangaroos (turretless tanks), with the armour of 4th/7th Dragoon Guards, spearheaded a snap advance that took the British to a position dominating Goch and splitting the German forces. The battle was not yet over, but the tide had turned.

Operation Grenade was at last able to proceed on 23 February. The 84th Division created a bridgehead over the Roer at Linnich, paddling their fifteen-man assault craft across the turbulent stream. Upstream of Linnich 102nd Division crossed and 29th Division tackled Jülich with its massive citadel. In the event the Germans abandoned it before the Americans arrived. It was in the most southerly sector, that of VII Corps, that the greatest difficulty was experienced, with the great dam at Düren channelling the speeding water into veritable rapids that made the assault boats useless. Those men who did cross pressed forward and slowly suppressed resistance. It was in the north, closest to Crerar's battle, that the best progress was made, and by 3 March the Canadians and the Americans had joined forces. The Germans had lost over 90,000 men, while the Americans had lost 7,300, the Canadians 5,304 and the British 10,330.

In the centre of the broad front was General Omar Bradley's Twelfth Army Group. They attempted to advance through the Eifel Mountains after the Battle of the Bulge was over, and made no progress at all; the weather was impossible. With the crossing of the Roer by VII Corps, however, the situation improved, and Lieutenant-General Courtney Hodges was able to push his First Army towards the Rhine as a result. To his south Patton was finally making ground as the weather warmed

Canadian troops in the flooded country on the approach to the Rhine, east of Nijmegen, during Operation Veritable.
(Taylor Library)

65

British troops flushing German snipers out of houses in the suburbs of Venlo, preparatory to crossing the Maas, in December 1944. (Taylor Library)

up. As the Americans advanced, so the bridges over the rivers were blown.

During the First World War the Germans had met the problem of supplying their troops by building railways and the bridges to go with them. By 1918 at Remagen, between Koblenz and Bonn, they constructed the Ludendorff Bridge, a two-track, two-hinged trussed arch with cantilever arms. The plans for its destruction were not fully realized. Instead of the precisely calculated charges, the engineers were issued with 600 kg (1,320 lb) of TNT and told to prime the charges as late as possible to avoid the bridge blowing up by mistake, like the one at Cologne. At 14.30 hours on 7 March the newly arrived local commander, Major Scheller, gave orders to prime the detonators. Almost immediately thereafter the tanks of US 9th Armored Division were seen on the west bank. The temptation to open fire was resisted and the Americans decided to attack with infantry supported by the armour. They fought through the town, and as they came to the bridge the ramp between the bridge and the shore blew up. They made their way past that on foot, the tanks covering them, and were about to set off over the bridge itself when the main charges exploded. The bridge rocked, shifted and stayed up. The infantry, led by Sergeant Alexander

Drabik, raced over the intact walkways and took the thirty-five-man garrison with the exception of Major Scheller. He, realizing his telephone line was gone, was running back to give the news that the Americans were over the Rhine. He would have done better to be captured, as with three others, he was executed for allowing the failure.

The Germans tried to reduce the resulting bridgehead, but failed. The Americans moved men and supplies over it after some quick repairs and also built a pontoon bridge below Remagen. When Patton crossed the river near Nierstein on 23 March the effort to stem the tide here was abandoned. The taking of the bridge and the holding of it had cost the Americans about 5,500 men, and the Germans an unknown number of casualties and 11,700 prisoners. The bridge itself was closed for repairs on 13 March, but suddenly collapsed on 17 March, killing twenty-three men and injuring ninety-three. Only the towers at both ends remain.

In the north on 24 March Montgomery launched another great operation of river crossings, Plunder, with the airborne troops of Operation Varsity, to take the Rhine at Wesel and drive for Bremen and Hamburg. Patton hurled his army forward and entered Czechoslovakia. Bradley made for Leipzig. Berlin was left to the Russians.

The bridge at Remagen, photographed by an American World War I occupation unit in 1919. (USAMHI)

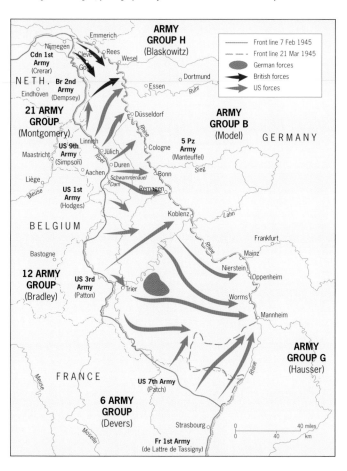

67

Operation Barbarossa

Russian artillery in woodland outside Moscow, late 1941. (Taylor Library)

Marshal Iosif Stalin, the leader of the USSR, had entered into a non-aggression treaty with Adolf Hitler in order to gain time to repair the damage he had himself done to the Soviet Army by purging vast numbers of officers in the late 1930s. The territory gained in the west, Poland, the Baltic States and parts of Romania, was occupied by Soviet troops, abandoning the strong defensive positions created along the Dvina and Dnieper rivers from the Baltic to the Crimea. Within 150 miles (240 km) of his western border Stalin had concentrated nearly two million men, 10,000 tanks and 12,000 aircraft. The front was divided by the Pripyat Marshes, an area larger than Switzerland, and north of it the two Soviet military regions, West *Front* and North-West *Front*, had thirty-six and twenty-four divisions respectively. South of the marshes the South-West *Front* had fifty-six divisions and the South sixteen.

The Germans were in confident mood. They had occupied much of Europe and they had seen the tiny army of Finland hold the massive Soviet forces at bay. Führer Directive 21, issued in December 1940, ordering Operation Barbarossa declared that the objective was to crush Soviet Russia in a swift campaign. It was also clear that the permanent occupation of the country to a line between the White Sea and the Caspian Sea was intended, including the total destruction of major cities, the execution of Soviet political officials and the eradication of Jewish peoples.

The German forces assembled to undertake the campaign were huge – some 3,360,000 men, 3,600 tanks, 7,500 guns and 2,500 aircraft. To the north of the marshes were Army Group North, under Field

Marshal Wilhelm von Leeb with twenty-six divisions and supported by *Luftflotte* 1, and Army Group Centre, under Field Marshal Fedor von Bock with fifty-one divisions and *Luftflotte* 2. To the south was Army Group South under Field Marshal Gerd von Rundstedt with fifty-nine divisions and *Luftflotte* 4.

The operation began in the early hours of Sunday 22 June with a bombardment all along the front. In the centre, at Brest-Litovsk, amphibious tanks with schnorkels crossed the river Bug. The *Luftwaffe* struck against Soviet forward airfields, and within the day destroyed more than 2,000 aircraft on the ground. Army Group Centre's Panzer Groups, Second under General Heinz Guderian and Third under General Hermann Hoth, advanced from east Poland and East Prussia respectively to envelop Minsk, Orsha and then, by 21 July, Smolensk along the highway to Moscow. By then Army Group North was within eighty miles (130 km) of Leningrad. The booty was remarkable both in men and materials of war.

In the south things were not going so well. The front was restricted to the space between the marshes in the north and the Carpathian Mountains in Romania, which put von Rundstedt's forces face-to-face with the Soviet armies of the South-West *Front*, the Kiev Special Military District. Here there were 5,580 Soviet tanks, of which nearly one-fifth were the new KVs (50-tonners) or T-34s (30-tonners with 75 mm guns). The Germans were stopped just short of Kiev. The whole German advance stalled while priorities were argued. Guderian and Hoth were keen to hurry on to Moscow in the fine, summer weather. Hitler had in mind not only the destruction of Soviet forces but also the raw materials that the Ukraine could yield. In late August the Panzers were sent south to take part in the encirclement of Kiev, where, on 12 September, 600,000 Soviet troops were trapped and forced to surrender.

German optimism was now becoming clouded by the realization that the Soviet Union was not yet approaching surrender. Stalin had moved some 3,000 factories east of the Ural Mountains, and the great mass of the Soviet armies had not, so far, been involved. The argument now hinged on whether or not to strike for Moscow. To add to the difficulty of making a decision was the growing problem of transport. The Germans had deployed a great patchwork quilt of transportation – some 200,000 trucks comprising more than 200 different types gathered up from conquered countries and all requiring different spare parts, even when the mechanics to fit them were available. As supply lines grew longer the 600,000 horses became more difficult to employ, as requirements for their feeding added to the volume of supplies to be moved. On the other hand the weather was good and the forecasts encouraging. The strike towards Moscow, Operation Typhoon, would take place.

Guderian's Second Panzer Army, for it had now been redesignated, passed to the north of Kursk to take Orel on 2 October. The tankmen had the curious experience of receiving cheerful waves from passengers in the trams, being mistaken for Russians, so swiftly had they advanced. By the end of the month they were at Tula, only 120 miles (200

km) south of Moscow. In the centre General Höpner's Fourth Panzer Group on the Moscow Highway was only fifty miles (80 km) from the Soviet capital, and in the north Hoth was in Kalinin, just twice that distance from the final objective. By that time it had been raining for ten days. They had stopped, not because of Russian resistance, but on account of the mud. This time of year is known in Moscow as *rasputitsa*, the time without roads. Meanwhile, in Moscow itself, panic threatened. Lenin's mummified corpse was removed to an underground hiding place. On 10 October Marshal Georgi Zhukov was given the command. By 1 November he was already disposing of more than a million troops and ten thousand guns. To those he could also add troops from the Far East, where intelligence revealed the Soviets were safe, for Japan was planning to attack the Americans, British and Dutch. By mid-November he had another 100,000 men and 2,000 guns, and the total of his tanks had grown to 1,150. The weather then became cold.

Over the frozen land the Germans moved once more. Here, close to the capital, the landscape was tighter, enclosed by forest, and the Panzers were channelled into predictable lines of advance. Supplies of all kinds were short. Winter clothing was lacking for the German soldiers and in December over 100,000 cases of frostbite were recorded. Hoth was ordered to circle clockwise around Moscow to meet Guderian enveloping the city from the south in an anticlockwise movement, but progress of any kind was difficult in the conditions. The Panzers were losing tanks to mechanical failure as often as to enemy action. Hitler's dissatisfaction made itself felt. The commander of Army Group South, von Rundstedt, was required to countermand an order he had given for a unit to withdraw, declined to do so and was sacked. On 18 December von Bock of Army Group Centre was relieved of his command, allegedly on health grounds. Guderian was sacked after a fierce argument, and Höpner as well.

On 3 December the Soviet counter-attack came, filtering through the German front, pressing on the flanks chipping away at their positions and rolling the line away from Moscow. Kalinin was retaken, as was Tula, and the Soviets pushed halfway back to Smolensk in the centre and further on the flanks. The Germans, ordered to stand, gathered themselves into defensive groups called hedgehogs and held on as best they could. The destruction of the Soviet Army had not been achieved.

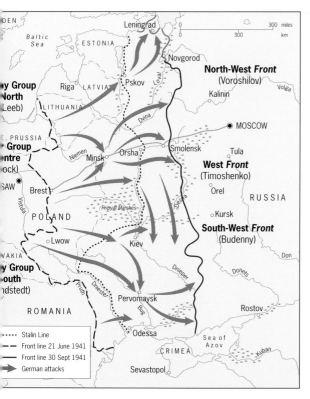

The winter counter-attack by the Soviet Army left Germany with a line roughly from Leningrad on the border with Finland to Rostov on the River Don near the shores of the Sea of Azov. The northern city of Leningrad was virtually isolated by the German advance. In September and November 1941 the land south and east of the city had been taken by the Germans, and the border with Finland to the north-west was blocked by the Finns in December. Only Lake Ladoga to the north-east provided any route in and out of the Soviet enclave, and the boats of summer and ice-crossing trucks of winter could not move sufficient supplies to sustain the populace. The siege of Leningrad lasted for 900 days, and in that time a million people starved to death. Relief was not to come until 24 January 1944.

Hitler's attention in 1942 was on the south of the Soviet Union. In the Crimea the naval base of Sevastopol was still held by Soviet forces against the German Eleventh Army under General Erich von Manstein, the originator of the concept of the Ardennes campaign of 1940 that defeated the Allies in France. He first, on 8 May, threw his strength against the bridgehead around Kerch in the eastern Crimea, smashing through three lines of fortification, and in ten days inflicting losses of 350 tanks, 3,500 guns and 176,000 casualties on the Soviets. This left Sevastopol completely isolated. Against the huge steel-reinforced concrete forts that protected the port, Fort Stalin, Fort Molotov, Fort Siberia and Fort Maxim Gorky, von Manstein brought to bear artillery of immense calibre. The 60 cm (24 in) mortar called Karl was big, but the railway gun Gustav was the largest ever built, at 80 cm (31 in), and was capable of firing armour-piercing shells of seven tonnes and high explosive of ten tonnes. The *Luftwaffe* support was also vast, with as great a tonnage of bombs dropped here in three weeks as fell on Britain during the 1941 Blitz. The city and port were steadily and relentlessly reduced to rubble. A few managed to escape by sea as destroyers came in by night and submarines brought ammunition in and took wounded out, but most of the garrison of 106,000 were killed. The city fell early in July. Some 30,000 civilians had survived the battle only to find that two-thirds of their number were deported or killed thereafter. A field marshal's baton was von Manstein's reward.

The major undertaking for the new fighting season was Hitler's Operation Blue, a three-phase effort to push far to the south-east and seize the oil-rich territory of the Caucasus. On the left flank Stalingrad would be taken to deny the River Volga to the Soviets, while on the right Rostov would be secured and a thrust beyond would take the oilfields at Maikop, Grozny and Baku, this last 745 miles (1,200 km) from Rostov. In order to do this Army Group South was divided into two parts, Army Group B on the left, northern, flank under the recalled Field Marshal von Bock, and Army Group A under Field Marshal Wilhelm List. Bock disposed of the Second, Sixth, Fourth Panzer and Hungarian Second Armies. List was given First Panzer, Seventeenth, Eleventh and Romanian Third Armies, with Eighth Italian and Fourth Romanian in reserve. The Italians of the expeditionary force sent by Mussolini in 1941 had had a tough time through the winter, being inadequately clothed and equipped, but had now been expanded to 229,000 men and 1,100 guns. During the summer an Alpine Corps complete with 20,000 mules would be added for operations in the Caucasus Mountains. In opposition Stalin had five and a half million troops in the field and more in reserve, but was in error in assuming that Moscow would again be the objective, and had taken positions accordingly.

The first phase of Operation Blue began on 28 June, and by 6 July Fourth Panzer took Voronezh and Sixth Army was on the River Don. A pincer movement was then attempted as the next phase, with Fourth Panzer striking south and First Panzer east towards Millerovo on the way to Stalingrad, but few Russians fell into their hands as the Soviet forces seemed to fragment before them. Hitler accused von Bock of poor deployment of the tanks and fired him again, putting General Maximilian von Weichs in command. Rostov fell next and part of Hoth's Panzer Group headed for the River Chir and Stalingrad. General Friedrich Paulus was ordered to take his Sixth Army forward to Stalingrad. He reached the suburbs of Stalingrad on 23 August, and 79th Panzer Grenadiers took Spartanovka that night to reach the Volga.

At the same time Operation Edelweiss was going for the oilfields with its strength depleted by the demands of Operation Heron, the Stalingrad drive. A reduction in fuel and ammunition supplies to Army Group A had been imposed just as it was meeting resistance. It pushed on with smoke rising from the oilfields as the retreating Soviets carried out the requirements of the scorched earth policy. They took Maikop on 9 August, and First Panzer turned towards the Caspian Sea while the Seventeenth Army went south towards the Black Sea. By early September First Panzer had virtually come to a halt and the Seventeenth Army was slowed by snow in the mountains. Meanwhile progress at Stalingrad was poor and there were not the resources to maintain both operations. List was sacked from the command of Army Group A, leaving Hitler in direct command, and the resources that he had were to be devoted to the more northerly front, now attracting world-wide attention. Both Grozny and Baku, on the Caspian, remained in Soviet hands, and the oilfields were denied to Germany.

As the pressure on the Soviet Union increased and their oil supply was threatened by German operations in the Caucasus, the importance of the Arctic convoys redoubled. In Hvaifjord Royal Navy escorts prepare for the departure of a convoy.
(Taylor Library)

Russian troops examining the remains of a downed Messerschmitt Bf 109.

In the depressing atmosphere of August 1942, with the Soviet losses of the previous May on the front at Kharkov to the north contributing to what seemed the irresistible progress of the German Sixth Army under General Friedrich Paulus, the commander of the Soviet Sixty-second Army in Stalingrad, General Alexander Lopatin, foresaw nothing but defeat. On 12 September, on the orders of Nikita Khruschev, he was replaced by Lieutenant-General Vasili Chuikov, a tough and determined man whose task was to secure Stalingrad against the Germans without fail.

The River Volga rises north-west of Moscow and curves round in a huge loop to the east, through Gorky and south by way of what has been known at various times as Tsaritsyn, Volgograd and Stalingrad to enter the Caspian Sea. It thus offers a crucial line of supply from the oilfields bordering the Caspian and the heartland of Russia. The German attempt to sever this line could not be tolerated, quite apart from the symbolic importance of the place which now bore the Soviet ruler's name. The city itself lay along the western bank of the river, about four miles (6.5 km) wide and fifteen miles (24 km) long. It was an important industrial centre with substantial factories – the Red October steelworks, the Barrikady ordnance factory and the tractor factory.

Chuikov's Sixty-fourth Army had some 54,000 men, 900 guns and mortars and 110 tanks, while Paulus had twenty-five divisions with over 100,000 men, 2,000 guns, 500 tanks and *Luftwaffe* support in the shape of VIII *Fliegerkorps* capable of flying over 1,000 sorties a day. The German force was well suited to fast-moving fighting in open country, and it was clear to Chuikov that he had to constrain the Germans to fight by his rules. This was to be city fighting. The Soviet troops had to stay close to their enemies to prevent attack from the air which could hit Germans by mistake. They had to prevent tanks moving freely in the shattered streets and force the infantry to fight at close quarters with bayonet and dagger as much as by bullet or

explosive, and thus compensate for the imbalance of numbers. It was going to be a very nasty business indeed.

The first German attack, on 14 September, was of terrible ferocity. The objective was the main landing stage, without which the Volga could not be crossed to bring substantial supplies or support to the city. Towards the centre of the city, from north to south, 295th, 76th and 71st Divisions attacked towards the railway station, smashing their way through Chuikov's headquarters on Mamayev Kurgan on the high ground north-west of the station as they went. To the south 24 Panzer, 94th Division, 14 Panzer and 29th Motorized Division hit the suburb of Yelshanka. The railway station was taken and retaken four times before night, but ended in Soviet hands. To the south the Soviets were almost back to the river, and that night, in spite of the exposure to fire, Major-General Alexander Rodimstev's 13th Guards Division was ferried over from the east. They lost 1,000 men in coming, but were ready to face the renewed German onslaught next morning. By the end of another three days' fighting the Germans had the station. A great grain elevator in the south was manned by a mere fifty Soviet soldiers, but it took three German divisions to take it. The 10,000 men of the 13th Guards were now down to a quarter of their strength, but the city had held from the railway station northwards.

On 27 September the next attack came further north. The *Luftwaffe* threw caution to the winds and, risking the lives of their own men, bombed heavily. The German 76th Division threw the Soviet 95th off Mamayev Kurgan, which they had reoccupied, and further north the defences were driven in for a mile. The next day the fighting continued, but Chuikov sensed that the Germans were shaken. He was correct, for their losses of junior officers and section leaders had been very heavy. The emphasis shifted north again, and by 2 October the Orlovka area had fallen. The Soviets now held an irregular ribbon along the riverside. On 4 October the Germans went for the tractor factory and suffered for it, losing four battalions in two hours to the Soviet 37th Guards Division. A further effort four days later saw the attackers thrown back.

A frenzied attack took place on 14 October when the Germans hurled 90,000 men and 300 tanks into the fray. Three divisions, 94th, 389th and 100th Jäger, were supported by 14 and 24 Panzer Divisions in their assault on Chuikov's 55,000 remaining men. The Soviets were thrust back to the river. The tractor factory was surrounded and fighting continued through the night and the next day. If ammunition ran out, hand-to-hand fighting took place. The conflict was not merely house to house but room to room. By 23 October the Germans had got into all the major factories, but they could not get the Soviet defenders out of them. These places were to remain small, foul battlefields until the end of the fight for the city. By the end of

The fight for Stalingrad became an intense struggle for the possession of ruins. (Taylor Library)

The Red Flag is raised over Stalingrad after the German surrender. The photograph is from a Soviet news film. (Taylor Library)

the month the greater part of the city was in German hands, but still a small sliver of riverbank belonged to the Soviets, supplied nightly from the eastern bank of the Volga, now a frozen highway.

Paulus's men were no longer in control. While they might have reduced the Soviets to a finger-hold on Stalingrad, they themselves were surrounded. On 19 November General Zhukov started Operation Uranus to sever the salient the Germans had created. German intelligence had reported the massing of the Soviets opposite the Hungarian, Romanian and Italian forces to Hitler on 12 November, to no avail. Those counselling withdrawal from Stalingrad were dismissed by the Führer. The Soviets brushed through the Romanian Third and Fourth Armies, north and south of the German Sixth Army, and met at Kalaisch on 23 November. Hitler believed that his men, cut off though they were, could be supplied by air, but there were some 300,000 men in the trap, needing every possible thing, including winter clothing. On 22 November Paulus estimated his supplies of fuel as almost gone, ammunition low and food for six days. His commanders demanded to be allowed to fight their way out. Permission denied; Göring undertook to supply them by air.

The attempted airlift was unsuccessful. The piercing cold prevented many aircraft flying at all, iced up, engines impossible to start. Of those that flew, the Soviet fighters took their toll. Altogether 488 aircraft were lost. Something in the region of 100 tons of supplies a day arrived, about one-sixth of the minimum requirement. Erich von Manstein mounted Operation Winter Storm to relieve Paulus. With 6, 17 and 23 Panzer Divisions and Fourth Romanian Army, he drove forward from the south-west on 12 December. He was stopped still thirty miles (50 km) from the Sixth Army's perimeter by 23 December. On 10 January 1943 General

Konstantin Rokossovsky set Operation Koltso in motion, the final reduction of the Sixth Army. Paulus had declined an offer to surrender two days earlier. He finally surrendered, in spite of being promoted Field Marshal and thus becoming the first German soldier of that rank to do so, on 31 January. Of 250,000 troops in the enclave, 150,000 died, and of those taken prisoner – 91,000 of them – only 5,000 ever saw their homeland again. For the Soviet Union and for the rest of the Allies, it was a victory beyond price.

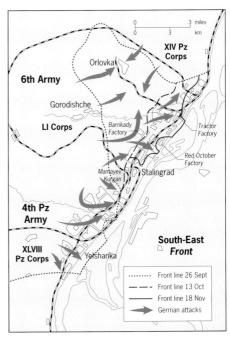

The Battle of Kursk

The shattering defeat of the Germans at Stalingrad was followed by a vigorous Soviet campaign in the south, sweeping into the eastern Ukraine, crossing the Donets River and thrusting on towards the Dnieper before the spring thaw reduced the land and roads to mud once more. Kursk was taken on 8 February and Kharkov was liberated by the Soviets on 15 February. By the end of that month the Germans had fallen back some 300 miles (480 km) at a cost that, though minimized by the skill of Field Marshal Erich von Manstein, was still great. In the pause initiated by the warmer weather the Germans struck back. Colonel-General Hermann Hoth used two Panzer divisions to retake Kharkov on 11 March and another two to capture Belgorod on 18 March. In the meantime Hitler approved the withdrawal of the Ninth Army from the salient formerly intended to threaten Moscow, which had become irrelevant. This allowed the Germans to rationalize their line and made the Ninth Army available for use in the coming summer operations.

In the European theatre of war the Germans faced threats both in the east, on the Soviet front, and in the south, where, in the Mediterranean, American and British forces could be expected to attack in the Italian or Greek regions. The most immediate was the Soviet problem, and ways of removing significant numbers of Russian troops from the scene were considered. The line had stabilized leaving one or two salients, depending on which side one viewed the scene from. The Soviets held a salient centred on Kursk, and north and south of it the Germans held salients based on Orel and on Kharkov. The Germans produced a plan for Operation Citadel to encircle the Soviets in their salient, while the Soviets made plans for Operation Kutuzov for the Orel salient and Rumyantsev for the Kharkov salient.

The thoughts of STAVKA, the Soviet High Command, were influenced by intelligence received. They were provided with the information generated as Ultra, but they also had an excellent source of their own, dubbed Lucy. The Lucy Ring was a network run by a German communist called Rudolf Rössler, a map publisher in Lucerne, Switzerland, with four agents. The information was not always precise or accurate, but in this instance it gave STAVKA invaluable data on almost the whole plan for Citadel. Marshal Zhukov decided to reinforce the Kursk salient and muster his forces on the shoulders of the German salients, so that, once the German attack had been held and turned back, he would be in a position to deliver a decisive counter-attack.

The Kursk position was defended by two Soviet *fronts*, formations equivalent to, but smaller than, a German Army Group. In the north of the salient was General K.K. Rokossovsky with his Central *Front*, and in the south General N.F. Vatutin with the Voronezh *Front*. Their strength was some 900,000 men, 5,700 anti-tank guns (in the event the key to their success), 19,500 field guns and mortars and more than 3,000 tanks and self-propelled guns. With the help of civilians they fortified the salient with eight defence lines over 100 miles (160 km) deep. Three defence zones were established, and each was planted with carefully positioned strongpoints for a company of infantry supported by anti-tank guns and tanks. Minefields were laid to channel attackers into positions of disadvantage, using more than half a million mines, both anti-tank and anti-personnel.

The German plan depended, as usual, on speed to penetrate the flanks of the salient and trap their enemies within it. To keep their schedule they would have to get through a defence zone a day. In the north was Colonel-General Walther Model's

The wide plains of central Russia invited the use of Armoured Fighting Vehicles. (Taylor Library)

Ninth Army with XX and XXIII Army Corps and XLVI, XLVII and XLI Panzer Corps, supported by *Luftflotte* 6, and in the south Army Group South (now reconstituted) under Field Marshal Erich von Manstein. He had Colonel-General Hoth's Fourth Panzer Army with II SS and XLVIII Panzer Corps, LII Army Corps and *Luftflotte* 4, as well as Panzer General Franz Werner Kempf's Army Detachment with XI and XLII Army Corps and III Panzer Corps. The original plan was for the operation to begin in April, but it was delayed as Model called for reinforcements, and then as the new German tank, the Panzer V Panther with heavier armour, was being introduced. Colonel-General Heinz Guderian, Inspector-General of Armoured Forces, protested that it was untried and unproved, to no avail. Ninth Army's most powerful tank was the Panther, with its 75 mm gun, while Army Group South was able to put over a hundred 88 mm-gunned Tigers in the field. It was some compensation that the Ninth Army was able to make use, for the first time, of sixty-six *Brummbär* self-propelled 150 mm howitzers. The Germans had 2,700 armoured fighting vehicles to use at Kursk, compared with 3,332 on the entire front in Operation Barbarossa. It would not be enough.

The Soviet intelligence system told them that Citadel would begin at 03.30 hours on 5 July, and they put down a heavy barrage on the German front lines to disrupt their assembly. Their information was two hours out, however, as 05.30 was the correct time and the Germans were still under cover. Model's attack reached the Olkhovatka Ridge and the town of Ponyri, about six miles (10 km) forward, by the evening, but got no further in the next two days. On 9 July a further massive effort was made, but the Soviets had brought up more field guns and a number of rocket launchers, known as *Katuysha*, Little Katie, to the Russians and Stalin's Organ to the Germans. The attack failed, and fruitless, bloody fighting continued there for another two days.

In the south, on the left of the German attack, Hoth's Panzers struck at Lieutenant-General I.M. Chistyakov's Sixth Guards Army in an armoured wedge led by the Tigers. The heavy guns of these Panzers knocked out the Soviet artillery and opened a gap through which the lighter tanks could rush, and by the end of the day the front line had been well penetrated. To the right Army Detachment Kempf failed to get through the first line of defence. On 6 July II SS Panzer Corps broke through the Sixth Guards' second line, causing Vatutin to move his reserves and STAVKA to send in 2nd and 10th Tank Corps. Over the next three days the Germans continued their advance towards Oboyan, but lacking Kempf to cover the right flank, Lieutenant-General Paul Hausser had to employ II SS Panzer's 3rd Panzer Grenadier 'Totenkopf' Division for that purpose instead of pushing forward. That was remedied by Kempf turning northward, and on 10 July 3rd SS 'Totenkopf' crossed the river Psel into the third defence line north-west of the village of Prokhorovka, while on their right 1st SS Panzer '*Liebstandarte* Adolf Hitler' got through the line in front of the village itself. To the right again,

Kempf's III Panzer Corps broke through into open country. Manstein sensed his opportunity to outflank the defence in front of Oboyan, and ordered all three to attack next day. He was not aware that STAVKA had allocated Vatutin the Fifth Guards Army and Fifth Guards Tank Army on 6 July and that they had moved to positions north of Prokhorovka.

On 12 July the Germans pressed forward with 450 tanks and ran into 800 Soviet vehicles. The biggest tank battle of the war began under grey, showery skies that limited what aircraft could do. Prokhorovka was entered by 1st SS Panzer, but 2nd Tank Corps ejected them by the end of the day. East of the village 2nd SS Panzer Grenadiers 'Das Reich' took on other elements of 2nd Tank Corps in a wild, confusing free-for-all. On the flanks 3rd SS Panzer Grenadiers and III Panzer Corps were also engaged in heavy fighting. As night fell it became clear that the Germans had been stopped, with the loss of over 100 tanks against Soviet casualties of 450 vehicles. On 13 July, as the British and Americans broke out of the beachheads of Sicily, Hitler demanded II SS Panzer Corps for use there and cancelled Citadel. On 12 July Operation Kutuzov was launched to the north, and Rumyantsev began five days later. The initiative now lay with the Soviet armies.

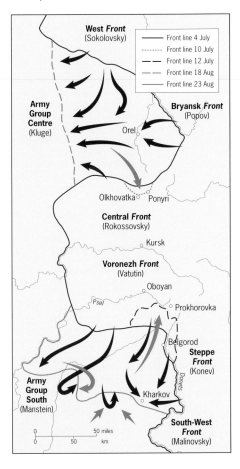

Mainstay of the Russian armoured forces was the heavily armoured and gunned T-34, a design kept unmodified in order to ensure availability of spares and efficiency of maintenance. (Taylor Library)

It was clear to Hitler that, in 1944, the Americans and British would invade northern Europe, probably around Calais, and he made provision for that rather than reinforcing his eastern front because, in the east, there was territory that could be sacrificed without risking defeat. In the early months of the year the Soviet armies had pounded the Germans in the Ukraine, liberating Kiev and, by April, establishing the front line west of the Pripyat Marshes and Pinsk, to run south to the Carpathian Mountains and thence to Odessa on the Black Sea. North of the marshes the line ran in a great curve centred on Minsk that took it east to turn north, partly along the River Dnieper, and then the Sozh, east of Orsha (on the Minsk–Smolensk–Moscow road), until it bent west again around Vitebsk before finally going due north to the Baltic Sea through Pskov. South of the marshes the country, though constricted by marsh and mountain, was open and tempting to tanks, while north of them it was a land of marsh and forest, unsuited to a war of swift movement in the eyes of many theorists. It appeared evident to the Germans that the southern sector would be the Soviet objective.

The territory around Minsk was the responsibility of Army Group Centre, commanded by Field Marshal Ernest Busch, with 800,000 men, of whom only half were experienced combat troops. There were thirty-four infantry divisions, two *Luftwaffe* field divisions, seven security divisions, two Panzer Grenadier divisions in reasonable shape and another badly depleted, and, finally, one Panzer division. Busch thus had few armoured units, nine-tenths of his tanks having gone to Army Group North Ukraine, but his largely infantry force had been in place for some time and had the opportunity to prepare defensive positions. Busch had, in accordance with Hitler's ideas, set up so-called fortresses at Vitebsk in the valley of the Dvina in the north, Orsha and Mogilev on the Dnieper on the east of the salient and Bobruisk on the River Berezina facing the south-east. The south was secured by the Pripyat Marshes. The rim of his territory was defended, but he did not hold it in depth, nor did it seem necessary to do so. The Vitebsk sector was held by the Third Panzer Army, the Orsha/Mogilev sector by the Fourth Army and the Bobruisk sector by the Ninth Army, while the Second Army was on the southern flank.

The Soviet armies constituted four *fronts* with 118 rifle divisions, eight tank and mechanized corps, six cavalry divisions, thirteen artillery and four air defence divisions – some 1,700,000 men. They were able to put 2,715 tanks, 10,563 artillery pieces, 2,306 rocket launchers, 11,514 82 mm and 120 mm mortars and 1,355 assault guns in the field. The cavalry divisions were by no means an anachronism for they gave mobility in terrain so wet and broken that armour could not manoeuvre. In addition the Soviets now had overwhelming air superiority. The plan was to encircle the Germans by taking Minsk, using Third Belorussian *Front* under Colonel-General I.D. Chernyakhovsky from the north and First Belorussian under Colonel-General K.K. Rokossovsky from the south. First Baltic *Front* would guard the northern flank, and the marshes secured the southern flank, while Second Belorussian under Colonel-General G.F. Zakharov was to confront the eastern side of the German enclave to keep the troops there distracted and to help clean up at the end of the operation. In preparation for all this, partisans behind the lines collected intelligence for the Russians, and an elaborate exercise in *maskirovka*, the masking of their intentions, was undertaken. The effectiveness of this was shown by the transfer of LVI Panzer Corps to Army Group North Ukraine and the departure of Busch to see Hitler on the day before the operation began.

At daybreak on 23 June a massive artillery bombardment fell on German positions, but because of mist the airstrikes were relatively few. Vitebsk was attacked by both First Baltic and Third Belorussian *Front*s and by the next day the Sixth Guards Army had broken through the German IX Corps north-west of the city, while the Thirty-Ninth Army was coming round the south. Colonel-General Georg-Hans Reinhardt, commanding the Third Panzer Army, sought permission from Hitler to withdraw, but by the time he had it, with conditions, it was already too late: LIII Corps had been surrounded in Vitebsk by the evening of 26 June. To their south, on the Minsk–Moscow road, General Kurt Tippelskirch's Fourth Army had the 14th Infantry, 78th Sturm and 25th Panzer Grenadier Divisions in place to cover Orsha. The boundary between the two German armies was to the 78th's left, the north, and when the Germans on the road had held against the Soviet attack on 23 June, a patrol of the Soviet 1st Guards Rifle Division managed to find a space between the enemy armies. This opportunity was eagerly seized by Soviet II Guards Tank Corps and the 11th Guards Army. By 25 June the line had been broken here as well. Tippelskirch started to withdraw, the II Guards Tank Corps swung round Orsha by the north and the town itself was taken early on 27 June. The advance now swung south-west towards Borisov, two-thirds of the way to Minsk. The Red Air Force was pounding Tippelskirch's retreating troops, and 5th Panzer Division was rushed up from the Ukraine to cover the bridgehead over the Berezina River at Borisov. They held off the direct attack, but Soviet forces soon crossed the river north-west of the town, and by 29 June the route west had been closed. South of the town the commander of 35th Guards Tank Brigade

made his own bridge by driving tanks into the river and crossing on top of them. On 30 June the majority of the German Fourth Army was trapped to the east of the River Berezina.

Soviet progress towards Minsk from the southeast was, by contrast, slow on the first day, encouraging General Hans Jordan of the Ninth Army to send his main reserve, 20 Panzer Division, forward to take part in the rout of the Soviet 48th Army. Rokossovsky countered by ordering his 65th Army to come up from the south, and I Guards Tank Corps exploited the gap they made, threatening Ninth Army's flank. When Jordan diverted 20 Panzer to deal with this, the 48th Army, supported by the Soviet 3rd Army, began to surge forward. By the morning of 27 June the Soviet IX Tank Corps was over the Berezina north-east of Bobruisk and was met by I Guards Tank Corps coming up from the south-west, trapping 40,000 Germans east of the river. The Soviets then converged on Berezino, on the river between Borisov and Bobruisk, and caught the rest of the Fourth Army. Hitler sent 12 Panzer Division to effect a rescue, but it was intercepted on 28 June west of Bobruisk. Meanwhile the Germans in the pocket were subjected to incessant fire from air and land. A breakout was attempted and about 15,000 men got out, but by 29 June, in flame and shell-burst, the enclave fell to the Soviets.

Field Marshal Walther Model now took command and tried to hold open a way to the west for his troops. Although they fought valiantly, 5 Panzer Division was finally broken by II Guards Tank Corps on 3 July and they entered Minsk from the north-east to meet I Guards Tank Corps coming from the south the next day, trapping 105,000 German troops. Operation Bagration was finished in two weeks. They had inflicted 350,000 casualties on, and taken 150,000 prisoners of, the German forces at a cost of 178,501 of their own men. It was the greatest Soviet victory of the war.

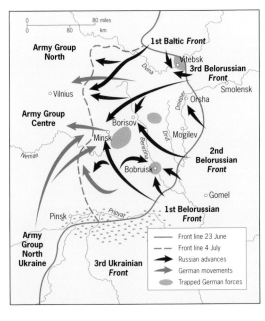

The close of 1944, satisfactory although events had been for the Allies, left Germany's adversaries a long way from Berlin and victory. In the west the British and American forces occupied France and most of the Low Countries, but had failed to break out from the Arnhem bridgehead into Germany and had been given a severe set-back in the Ardennes. In the east Soviet armies were on the River Vistula at Warsaw, on the borders of East Prussia on the Baltic coast and had taken Budapest and the greater part of Hungary. Early in 1945 the Soviet onslaught on the Germans resumed with a campaign on the northern front, Poland and East Prussia. Marshal Georgi Zhukov was removed from the high command, STAVKA, and given First Belorussian *Front*, the formation earmarked for the conquest of Berlin. Zhukov and Marshal Ivan Konev of First Ukranian *Front*, on Zhukov's left, had about 2,200,000 men with which to oppose Army Group A's 400,000 in Poland, while Second and Third Belorussian had 1,600,000 against Army Group Centre in East Prussia.

On 12 January the assault was unleashed and more than twenty thrusts were made into German lines, the most powerful being from the River Vistula, where Zhukov and Konev's superiority was of the order of ten to one. On 23 January Hitler put Reichsführer-SS Heinrich Himmler in command of the new Army Group Vistula in the north, so desperate had the position become. A thaw in late January slowed the advance, but by 3 February the line of the River Oder from the Baltic to the Czechoslovak border had been attained, and Army Group Centre was left clinging to a few pockets of territory on the coast. By 24 February Pomerania and Silesia had been taken to solidify the Oder Front. At this point Marshal Stalin's eagerness for advance in the north seemed to wane. The melting of the ice on the Oder certainly hampered supply and reinforcement of troops crossing the river, and pockets of German troops to the rear needed mopping up, and the fighting in central Europe was a distraction. In March Hitler ordered an offensive

Soviet artillerymen of the Second Ukranian Front *in action before Budapest.* (Taylor Library)

by Sixth SS Panzer Army in Hungary, but on 16 March First and Third Ukranian *Front*s attacked on both sides of the Danube towards Vienna, and the campaign ended before mid-April.

By that time the plans for the conquest of Berlin were made. Numerous small actions had consolidated Zhukov's bridgehead west of the Oder to some six miles (10 km) deep and thirty miles (50 km) wide. To his south Konev was on the River Neisse, so the Soviet front ran north to south almost in a straight line. Stalin was worried that the Allies, now across the Rhine and advancing through Germany, might not hold to their undertaking to leave Berlin to the Soviet armies, and he set 16 April as the start date for the attack. The plan approved was for First Ukranian *Front* from the south and First Belorussian from the north to mount a huge pincer movement to meet at Potsdam, west of Berlin, for the Soviets to attack in Hungary and Czechoslovakia to prevent the Germans sending reinforcements, and finally for Second Belorussian *Front* to overrun northern Germany. The strength of the three *front*s facing Berlin and northern Germany was 2,500,000 men, 41,000 guns, 6,250 Armoured Fighting Vehicles (AFVs) and 7,500 aircraft.

The German defence was in the hands of Colonel-General Gotthardt Heinrici, now of Army Group Vistula in Himmler's place at the instigation of Guderian. Heinrici had, between October and December 1943, conducted the successful defence of the front shattered later by Operation Bagration by putting the mass of his troops at Orsha and circulating the battalions in the most contested position to spread the strain. The situation he had to deal with around Berlin was distinctly unhopeful, but he did his best, organizing successive lines of defence exploiting the terrain to hold up the Russians and, with luck, allow the Americans and British to arrive first. General Theodore Busse's Ninth Army was intended to prevent a breakthrough on the main highway from the east through Seelow. The Third Panzer Army was north of the city and the Fourth Panzer Army to the south. The German forces on the Oder–Neisse line amounted to only 700,000 men, 9,000 guns and 1,500 AFVs. Of aircraft there were virtually none. It was not the intention to fight in the streets of the city, as command and control could not be exercised and the local defence force, the Volkssturm and the Hitler Youth, were made up of old men and children, numbering about 70,000 in all.

The attack began at 03.00 hours on 16 April. A bombardment of greater density than the Soviets had ever before attempted fell on German positions. The positions were empty; Heinrici had pulled his men back to the second line of defence on the hills overlooking the flood-plain of the Oder. Half an hour later the men of First Belorussian blundered into the ditches and drains, part blinded by their own searchlights and under fire from their enemies. As the day drew on, Zhukov threw in his First and

Soviet soldiers and armour leave a burning German tank behind in their advance. (Taylor Library)

Second Guards Tank Armies, but they became entangled with the infantry and presented yet tastier targets to the Germans. Here, on the main road to Seelow, the attack was bogged down. A little to the north, at Wriezen, an advance of six miles (10 km) was achieved, and on the other flank the Eighth Guards Army reached the hills. On the Neisse the Germans held Konev's attack only by committing much of their Fourth Panzer Army. The resistance shown by the Germans on this first day was impressive, but while the Soviets could sustain losses, the Germans could not.

The fighting continued with consistent ferocity over the next two days, but the German weakness soon led to gaps appearing in their lines. Busse called for reinforcements, which were supplied by the Third Panzer Army in the so-far quiet north. At Wriezen on 18 April First Belorussian broke through CI Corps's lines and LVI Panzer Corps was pushed back along the Seelow highway. On Konev's front the Soviet tanks were already heading for Berlin. The Oder–Neisse defence line was history by 20 April, and on that day the Third Panzer Army, which might have threatened Zhukov's flank as First Belorussian went forward, was itself attacked by the Second Belorussian *Front* and was falling back. From Berlin and the countryside north and south of the capital refugees were pouring westwards, all fleeing the Soviet embrace and seeking safe haven with the Americans and British. On 25 April the Fourth Guards Tank Army from the northern flank met the Forty-seventh Army from the southern side at Ketzin, north-west of Potsdam on the River Havel, and Soviet troops were entering the suburbs of Berlin. On the same day, north-east of Leipzig at Torgau on the River Elbe, men of the American First Army met men of First Ukranian *Front*.

General Karl Weidling's LVI Panzer Corps had fallen back into Berlin, and he was charged with the organization of the resistance of the city. His unit still had some 1,500 men and 60 tanks to contribute. The Soviet forces were now short of infantry support for their armour, which otherwise was vulnerable to well-placed defenders with anti-tank weapons. The final week was therefore a long, hard grind rather than a dramatic, swift dash to conquer the city. Artillery reduced the houses to rubble, and sewers permitted infiltration of the German lines. They closed in on the central defence zone by 27 April, and on 29 April the gunfire rose to a new height of violence. Eva Braun married Adolf Hitler, and on the afternoon of 30 April, they killed themselves by taking cyanide. The Red Flag was flown from the Reichstag in a carefully staged photo-shoot on 1 May.

From the west General Walther Wenck brought the German Twelfth Army to the suburbs and held the door open for soldiers and civilians to flee from the city. They were joined by the remains of Busse's Ninth Army, so that some 300,000 people managed to get out to the joys of being captured by the Americans. On 2 May, at 06.00 hours, General Weidling surrendered Berlin to General Vasili Chuikov. The victory had cost the Soviet armies 304,887 killed, wounded and missing.

Map legend:

— Russian front line 15 April
--- Russian front line 18 April
— British & US front line 24 April
➤ Russian attacks
➤ German movements
▨ German forces

Wismar

3 Pz Army

21 Army

Stettin

2nd
Belorussian
Front

Army Group
Weichsel

Schwedt

1st
Belorussian
Front

Elbe

Oder

Wriezen

Havel

Ketzin

Berlin

Seelow

Potsdam

Spree

12 Army

9 Army

1st
Ukrainian
Front

Elbe

Torgau

4 Pz Army

Neisse

Leipzig

Army Group
Mitte

40 miles
40 km

Colditz

Dresden

Relations between Japan and the United States of America, which had been in steady decline for years, reached a new low when, as a result of Japanese occupation of French Indo-China on 24 July 1941, an oil embargo was imposed by America. The British and colonial Dutch governments followed suit, and to the Japanese, with no petroleum resources of their own, this was tantamount to a declaration of war.

The possibility of having to fight the USA had been considered by the Japanese, and the benefits of destroying the American Navy at its base in Pearl Harbor, on the island of Oahu in the Hawaiian Islands, had been studied. Admiral Yamamoto Isoroku, Commander-in-Chief of the Combined Fleet, conceived the Hawaii Operation and placed the detailed planning in the hands of Rear-Admiral Onishi Takajire, who had Commander Genda Minoru produce the operational scheme. The success of the British attack on Taranto on 12 November 1940 was influential, but various technical problems had to be overcome: torpedoes that could be used in shallow water had to be devised, bombs capable of rupturing armoured flight decks created and hitherto unknown levels of accuracy achieved by bomber aircraft flying a level, horizontal course. All these were done. The operation itself was to be carried out by the First Air Fleet, under the command of Vice-Admiral Nagumo Chuichi, consisting of six aircraft-carriers with defence provided by two battleships, two heavy cruisers, one light cruiser and nine destroyers, sailing with eight fuel tankers. The Sixth Fleet of twenty-five submarines and five two-man midget submarines would support the action, the two-man vessels entering the harbour and the conventional submarines seeking targets of opportunity. In the event they were ineffectual.

Surprise was of the essence, and the need for pin-point accuracy demanded a daylight operation. The fleet would therefore approach in secret, under radio silence, from the north. Its targets were to be the aircraft and airfields of the USAAF and US Marines and the ships of the Pacific Fleet, especially the aircraft-carriers. By this means American maritime power in the Pacific was to be crippled and the US brought to a negotiated peace. Such was the theory. Other counsels feared that the Americans would react with irresistible fury if the plan succeeded or inflict terrible losses on the Japanese if it did not.

The defence of Pearl Harbor was a shared responsibility between the US Navy Pacific Fleet commander, Admiral Husband E. Kimmel, and the Army commander, Lieutenant-General Walter C. Short. Their relationship was cordial but distant, an instance of inter-service rivalry here on a scale decidedly modest compared to the extreme lack of communication prevailing in Washington, DC. The Army was responsible for air defence and for opposing an invasion of the islands themselves and the Navy for its own installations against attack by

An undamaged PBY Catalina amphibious aircraft survives amongst the mayhem caused by the Japanese attack on shore installations at Pearl Harbor. (Taylor Library)

sea or air and for the long-range protection, not only of the Hawaiian Islands, but of islands further west, such as Wake.

The Japanese intelligence relating to Pearl Harbor was supplied by agents at the Japanese Consulate in Honolulu, principally Ensign Takeo Yoshikawa, who communicated using the low-grade consular code, J-19. This had been broken by the Allies, but as Kimmel's people were working to crack the naval code, JN-25, the consular material was sent by mail to the mainland for transcription when the people there could fit the job into their workload. Full details of the locations of warships in Pearl Harbor were thus passed to Tokyo without Kimmel's headquarters knowing of it. Japanese diplomatic traffic was conveyed using code Purple, read by a decoding machine, but product of this source known as Magic, was known only in Washington and only irregularly passed to Kimmel. Enough intelligence to predict the attack was available to the Americans, but scattered about between a number of non-communicating bodies and thus useless to them; the Central Intelligence Agency's foundation resulted directly from an appreciation of this failure later.

Commander William E.G. Taylor, US Naval Reserve, had spent a year with the RAF in Britain learning about radar before coming to the Hawaiian Islands in late 1941 to introduce the Army to its use. Five mobile radar sets equipped the Air Warning Service. General Short was concerned not to wear them out, and their time of use was restricted to 04.00 to 07.00 hours, training time included. At the time of the attack the system was still a novelty, the operators inexperienced and the exploitation of the data they could provide undeveloped, in spite of Taylor's having called a meeting to address the problems on 24 November. The United States had been slow to appreciate radar's usefulness.

By 22 November the First Air Fleet had assembled at Etorofu in the Kurile Islands, and it sailed four days later, using a weather front as cover. On 27 November a warning message was sent from Washington to both commanders on Oahu. Admiral H.R. Stark, Chief of Naval Operations, told Kimmel that a Japanese attack on the Philippines and other South-east Asian locations was imminent and that precautions should be taken at Pearl Harbor. Kimmel sent the aircraft-carriers *Enterprise* and *Lexington* to take reinforcements to Wake and Midway repectively. The carrier *Yorktown* had been transferred to the Atlantic Fleet the previous April, and *Saratoga* was on the west coast of the mainland, undergoing repairs. There were thus no aircraft-carriers at Pearl Harbor. Kimmel also put the Navy on sabotage alert lest the large numbers of ethnic Japanese, known as *nisei*, harboured fifth-columnists. The message received by Short from War Department Chief of Staff General George C. Marshall prompted a similar reaction, sabotage precautions, and so he reported back that they had been put into effect. The most prominent action was the grouping together of aircraft at the air stations to permit their being guarded against clandestine ground attack; it made them easy bulk targets from the air.

From a position 275 miles (450 km) north of Pearl Harbor, at 06.00 hours on 7 December the First Air Fleet began to launch its first wave of strike aircraft. They were led by Commander Fuchida Mitsuo in a Nakajima B5N2 'Kate' (a type used either for torpedo or horizontal bombing), and approached Oahu, where they were seen on radar at 07.35. The radar signal was misconstrued as being that of incoming American B-17 bombers. First Group of the wave went down the western shore, while Second and Third Groups, fighters and dive-bombers, went down the middle of the island. At 07.49 the attack on Pearl Harbor began. It was a complete surprise. A second wave arrived over the island at about 08.40 and flew down the east coast, the fighters of Third Group escorting the two others until Second Group turned over Kaneohe Bay to head for Pearl Harbor, while First Group attacked the Kaneohe Naval Air Station and Hickam Field. This wave was opposed by American fighters from Haleiwa Field and Wheeler Field and a good deal of ground fire.

The American installations at Pearl Harbor and on the various airfields had been hard hit, indeed so hard that the Japanese decided a third attack was not needed and turned their fleet for home. The obvious damage and billows of smoke and fire concealed the reality: no fuel supplies had been destroyed, no repair facilities put out of action and the majority of ships had sustained either only superficial damage or none at all. Casualties were serious, but not disastrous. There was nothing that could not be put right or compensated for in a matter of weeks, but a mighty nation had been roused to war against Japan, a war that Japan could not win.

Losses at Pearl Harbor

American:

Service	Killed	Wounded
Navy	2,008	710
Marine	109	69
Army	218	364
Civilian	68	35
Total	2,403	1,178

Japanese:

Service	Killed	Prisoner
Airmen	55	0
Submariners	c.65	0
Midget subs	9	1
Total	c.129	1

Note: No figures for wounded.

American ships and aircraft
Ships lost: *Arizona* and *Oklahoma*, battleships. *Utah*, target vessel. Ships seriously damaged: *California*, *Nevada* and *West Virginia*, battleships. *Helena* and *Raleigh*, light cruisers. *Cassin*, *Downes* and *Shaw*, destroyers. *Curtiss*, seaplane tender. *Vestal*, repair ship. *Ogalala*, minelayer. *Sotoyomo*, tug. *YFD2*, floating dock.
Moderately or lightly damaged: *Maryland*, *Tennessee* and *Pennsylvania*, battleships. *Honolulu*, light cruiser. *Helm*, destroyer.

Aircraft: Army, 64; Navy, 98. Total: 162.

Japanese ships and aircraft
Submarines: I-70 and five midget submarines.
Aircraft: Torpedo-bombers, 5; Dive-bombers, 15; Fighters, 9. Total, 29.

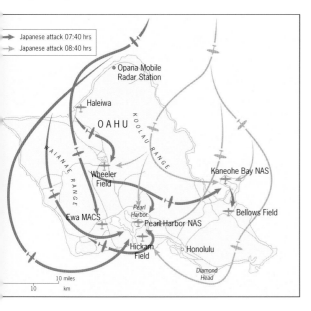

Japanese attack 07:40 hrs
Japanese attack 08:40 hrs

Opana Mobile Radar Station
Haleiwa
OAHU
KOOLAU RANGE
WAIANAE RANGE
Wheeler Field
Kaneohe Bay NAS
Ewa MACS
Pearl Harbor
Pearl Harbor NAS
Bellows Field
Hickam Field
Honolulu
Diamond Head
10 miles
10 km

The Fall of Malaya and Singapore

Oil storage installations burning after a Japanese bombing raid on Singapore Island. (Source: Soldiering On, Canberra, 1942)

The name Malaya designated the states in the Malay Peninsula including the island of Singapore, when they were part of the British Commonwealth as colonies or protectorates. The port of Singapore was important as a link in trading routes, and the peninsula produced thirty-eight per cent of the world's rubber and fifty-eight per cent of the world's tin, and were thus of much interest to the Japanese. In 1940 they were lightly defended and without conscription lest that interfered with raw material production.

The defence of Malaya was the responsibility of the British Commander-in-Chief Far East, Air Chief Marshal Sir Robert Brooke-Popham, whose 88,500 troops were commanded by Lieutenant-General Arthur Percival. The north was garrisoned by III Corps under Lieutenant-General Lewis Heath, and consisted of 9th and 12th Indian Divisions, new formations rather than the seasoned soldiers who fought so gallantly in North Africa, with inexperienced officers speaking only English, and 28th Independent Infantry Brigade. Johor, the southernmost state on the peninsula, was garrisoned by 8th Australian Division under Major-General Henry Gordon Bennett. There were no tanks and only 158 aircraft, the best that could be done given the immediate needs of the war in the Western European theatre. The possibility of war with Japan was recognized, and the idea was, if it did come about, to seize the Isthmus of Kra, where, at the border with Siam (Thailand), the peninsula narrowed near the towns of Singora and Patani.

Japanese plans for the invasion were devised by Lieutenant-General Yamashita Tomoyuki of the Twenty-Fifth Army. He had three divisions with 60,000 men, 158 naval aircraft and 459 aircraft of the 3rd Air Division, 80 tanks, 40 armoured cars and adequate artillery. A fourth division available to him was considered superfluous to his purpose – the conquest of Malaya. The invasion began on the night of 7/8 December 1941 with the bombardment at 01.15 hours of Kota Baharu on the east coast by

ships of Malaya Force under Vice-Admiral Ozawa Jisaburo. The intention was to time this to coincide with the strike on Pearl Harbor. It should be noted that the international date line intervenes between Malaya and Hawaii, and so 8 December here is the same as 7 December in Hawaii, and in addition, there is a seven-hour time difference. Takumi Force, to be joined by Koba Detachment three weeks later, parts of 18th Division landed at Kota Baharu while the 5th Division came ashore at Singora and Patani, which the British had failed to occupy. The 5th Division swept forward in two main columns to the west coast, meeting trivial resistance from the 11th Indian Division. From the three airfields abandoned undamaged by the British, Japanese aircraft harried the retreat. On the east Takumi Force made short work of the 9th Indian Division and was as far south as Kuantan by the end of the month.

The Royal Navy attempted to attack the Japanese naval support for the action. On the first day, 8 December, Force Z, consisting of the battleships HMS *Prince of Wales* and HMS *Repulse* and four destroyers, was sent north from Singapore, sailing at 17.35 hours. At 13.45 on 9 December, having passed east of the Anambas Islands, the force was sighted by Japanese submarine *I-65* and reported to base. On 10 December at 08.15 hours Admiral Tom Phillips, about to turn west to attack the Japanese fleet, realized that they had been observed from the air and, lacking any air cover himself, decided to return to Singapore. As Force Z sailed south once more, erroneous reports were received of landings at Kuantan, halfway between Singapore and Kota Baharu, and Phillips went to intervene. A second submarine, *I-58*, saw the force, and as they turned away from their futile mission, having seen nothing ashore, the British ships were attacked. The Japanese 22nd Air Flotilla had been flown off from Saigon at 07.30 on 10 December and were seen on the radar on *Repulse* at 11.00 hours. They attacked with high-level bombing, but although *Repulse* was hit, no serious damage was done. The next attack was by torpedo-bombers at 11.30 and *Prince of Wales* was hit astern, jamming her rudders in the same way as *Bismarck* was disabled. Three more torpedo-bombers attacked her, and six went for *Repulse*, achieving four hits. She sank at 12.33 hours, and *Prince of Wales* went down at 13.20. Admiral Phillips was among the few killed. The irrelevance of capital ships without air cover had been clearly demonstrated.

The progress of the Japanese land forces was swift. The automobiles and trucks left behind by the British were used to speed them south. Small boats were used to outflank defensive positions hastily improvised on the roads, and forays into surrounding jungle took the invaders past intended strongpoints. Where no motor vehicles were available, bicycles were pressed into service to hurry the Japanese along the excellent roads created to nurture commerce. By 14 December the north had been lost on both sides of the peninsula, Penang fell two days later and by the end of December the Japanese were facing the line based on the River Slim, sixty miles (100 km) north of Kuala Lumpur. The Japanese Imperial Guards Division joined the Twenty-fifth Army on 24 December and with their help Yamashita's men took Kuala Lumpur on 11 January.

Percival reorganized his forces in an attempt to stem the tide, giving Bennett the command over 'Westforce', consisting of elements from 8th Australian and 9th Indian Divisions, and shortly afterwards 'Eastforce' was set up under Heath with 22nd Australian Brigade and others to halt the incursion on the other side. The Japanese advance continued, none the less. Few units had been trained to fight in this environment, although many were courageous and some effective. The 2nd Argyll and Sutherland Highlanders, for example, had been exercised in extending their defensive lines into the jungle on either side of the road to be held, and now proved that it worked. But most units were commanded by men who had no idea how to fight here. By 31 January the last of the British and Commonwealth forces had been forced back onto Singapore Island itself.

Here reinforcements in the shape of the British 18th Division had arrived, giving Percival parity, and perhaps superiority, of numbers. The island was accessed from the mainland by a single causeway to Johor Baharu, and the straits were overlooked by concrete pillboxes and heavy gun positions facing, contrary to subsequent rumour, north, but the guns lacked high-explosive shells suitable for use against infantry. The shoreline was long and divided by inlets running south, which constrained the road system to radiate from Singapore city on the southern shore, restricting lateral movement. Percival therefore spread his men along the full thirty-mile (50 km) shoreline. On the evening of 7 February the Japanese Guards Division made a feint attack at the north-eastern corner of the island, near Changi, and on the night of 8/9 February the 5th and 18th Divisions attacked in force on the north-west, reinforced by the Guards to their immediate left the next night. The defending Australian 22nd and 27th Brigades could not hold them back. Counter-attacks by the reserves slowed, but did not halt, Japanese progress. By 15 February the reservoirs that were the city's only source of water were in Japanese hands.

Frantic attempts were made to evacuate the wounded, the colonial rulers, and their families, and all manner of vessels were hired, requisitioned and stolen for the purpose. On the evening of 15 February, in the belief that he had been defeated by a much larger force than actually he faced, and fearful of the outcome should the refugee-swollen populace of Singapore be deprived of water, General Percival surrendered. The Japanese campaign had cost them fewer than 10,000 casualties. The killed, wounded and captured of the British totalled 38,496, of the Australians 18,490 and of the Indians 67,340. Local volunteer units lost 14,382. Of these the prisoners numbered over 130,000. Although the territory would eventually be regained, the defeat spelt the end of the British Empire in South-east Asia.

Singora
Patani
Kota Baharu

Japanese
25th Army
(Yamashita)

South
China Sea

MALAYA

Ipoh

Slim

Kuantan

Repulse
sunk

Prince of
Wales sunk

Takumi
detachment

Kuala
Lumpur

Strait of
Malacca

100 miles
100 km

Malacca

Johor Baharu

→ Route of 'Force Z'

Singapore

Australian troops pose for their photograph to be taken in a rubber plantation. (Source: Soldiering On, Canberra, 1942)

The Philippine Islands lie south of Formosa (Taiwan) and between Japan and the islands of the Dutch East Indies (Indonesia), rich in oil, rubber and other raw materials, which the Japanese were fighting to include in their empire. They had been released from the colonial rule of the Spanish at the end of the nineteenth century by the Americans, who stayed there. In 1934 an Act of Congress gave the islands provisional independence, but allowed for the armed forces to be taken under American command in time of crisis. This was done on 26 July 1941, so that the ten Filipino divisions became part of the US Army, but under their existing commander, General Douglas MacArthur, who was placed in command of the US Forces in the Far East (USAFFE). In fact only the 12,000-strong Philippine Scouts Division was operationally effective at the time. The American forces present were some 16,000 strong and there were 150 aircraft. The US Navy had sixteen surface ships and twenty-nine submarines based there.

MacArthur made what hasty preparations he could against the expected attack. Reinforcements from the USA raised the number of American soldiers to 30,000, and 90,000 Filipino troops were given intensive training. The USAAF had, by early December, thirty-five B-17 bombers at Clark Field, north-west of Manila, the capital city, on Luzon and over 200 other aircraft at various locations, half of them Curtiss P-40 Warhawk (or Tomahawk) fighters. At the same time a convoy was on its way from Hawaii to bring seventy warplanes, forty-eight 74 mm guns, aviation fuel and ammunition. It did not arrive before the Japanese attack on 8 December, not quite coinciding with the Pearl Harbor attack on the other side of the international date line.

At 03.00 Manila time MacArthur received news of the strike at Pearl Harbor. At 07.00 Washington instructed him that they were at war and to commence operations against Japan. Major-General Lewis H. Brereton, USAAF, asked for clearance to launch bomber strikes against Formosan airfields, but it seems MacArthur was slow in granting it, for Brereton's warplanes were still on the ground, parked wingtip to wingtip in case of saboteurs, when the Japanese struck. Over fifty Japanese bombers, with three dozen fighters covering them, hit Clark Field, and another attack group encountered an American fighter patrol over Iba, on the coast to the west, and was destroyed bar only two aircraft. Half of the American air force had been neutralized. Lacking air cover, Admiral Thomas Hart pulled the fighting ships out of the Philippines.

Troop landings began on the northern tip of Luzon on 10 December. General Homma Masaharu's Fourteenth Army came ashore at Vigan and Aparri, and two days later a force landed at Legaspi on the south of Luzon. Their first task was to secure airfields for their supporting warplanes.

Major-General Jonathan M. Wainwright, commander of the Philippine Division, resisted in northern Luzon, but MacArthur soon realized that Homma was attempting to draw forces towards the invaders in order to reduce them piecemeal, and he determined to create a defensible enclave to oppose them within which he could await relief. Manila was declared an open city on 28 December, by which time the Japanese 48th Division, which had landed at San Fernando on 22 December, had been delayed by a succession of defensive lines behind which Wainwright brought his forces south.

Manila Bay is protected on the western side by the Bataan Peninsula, a feature about thirty miles (50 km) long and fifteen miles (25 km) wide, and in the narrows through which the sheltered bay is entered is the island of Corregidor. It was to the island fortress that MacArthur moved his headquarters and the government of the Philippines, and on the peninsula that he concentrated his troops, some 83,000 soldiers, with whom were mingled about 26,000 civilian refugees. The Bataan Peninsula is characterized by the two mountain groups in the north and the south of the area. The initial defence lines, established on 7 January 1942 either side of Mount Natib, had the same weakness as the deployments being used in Malaya: they failed to extend into the jungle, in this case up the mountainside. On the east, between 16 and 22 January, the newly arrived Japanese 65 Brigade outflanked the positions of the 51st and 41st Divisions, and between 19 and 24 January the Kimura Detachment did the same on the west, forcing the retreat of the 1st Division. The Reserve Battle Position, along the west–east road between Bagac and Orion, was continuous, and here the Americans and Filipinos held. Flanking attacks were attempted. A Japanese battalion tried to land on the south-western corner of the peninsula on the night of 22/23 January, and another attempted it four nights later. Both were destroyed.

MacArthur was robust in his calls to Washington for support, supplies and rescue, but none came. President Roosevelt adhered to his undertaking to give the European war priority, and although some supplies were slipped in by submarine, the response was an order for MacArthur to surrender the Filipino troops first and resist with American forces until surrender was inevitable. The defenders and refugees went on half rations. On 12 March MacArthur, as ordered, handed over the command to Wainwright and left for Australia. The besieged went on one-third rations. Japanese progress was slowed by disease amongst their troops, and the defenders were yet more troubled; by the end most would be suffering from one deficiency disease, beriberi perhaps, or another. On 3 April a fresh offensive, stiffened by the newly arrived 4th Division, was launched against the eastern end of the line. By 9 April the incursion had reached Kabacan at the south-eastern corner of the peninsula, and General Wainwright had to surrender. There were about 9,300 Americans and 45,000 Filipinos taken prisoner. They were marched off in what became known as the Bataan Death March. Weakness and disease killed some of them. Others died of the brutal treatment meted out by their guards should they delay or fall behind. Some 25,000 of them died at Japanese hands after they had surrendered.

On the island of Corregidor the Americans were still holding out. Between 14 April and 6 May they were subjected to a torrent of shellfire. On 4 May alone more than 16,000 rounds were fired upon them. On 5 May, at 23.30 hours, the Japanese got ashore at Cavalry Point north of the airfield at the eastern end of the island. On 6 May, at 01.30, they overcame the first line of defence as they moved to the west, and the final line fell at 10.30 that day. The last resistance was over.

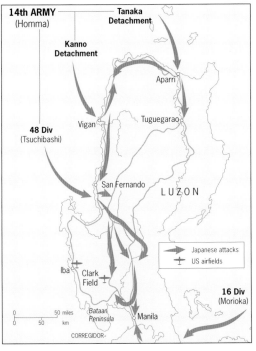

The Mitsubishi A6M 'Zeke' – better known as the Zero.

Brigadier-General Douglas MacArthur had seen action in World War I. This photograph was taken after the battle of St-Mihiel, close to the front-line troops between Beney and St-Benoit, 15 September 1918. (USAMHI)

The outbreak of war in the Pacific led to the establishment of a joint command to defend Singapore, Malaya and Burma in the north, the Dutch East Indies, the South China Sea and the coasts of Australia. The American-British-Dutch-Australian (ABDA) Command became operational on 15 January 1942, with General Archibald Wavell in command from a headquarters at Lembang on the island of Java. The naval forces were under the command of the American Admiral Thomas Hart, who had withdrawn his ships from the Philippines and now added to them, from British and Australian forces, one heavy and one light cruiser and three destroyers and, from the Netherlands naval forces of Rear-Admiral Karel Doorman, three light cruisers, seven destroyers and thirteen submarines. Hart retired at the age of sixty-five in mid-February and was succeeded by Vice-Admiral C. Helfrich as commander of ABDAFloat, as it was known.

The Japanese Navy was pushing into the complex of islands from the north-east, and on 23/24 January an American destroyer squadron sank four invasion transports in use against Borneo at Balikpapan. After the fall of Singapore the Japanese invaded Sumatra, where they took Palembang and secured nearly half the region's oil reserves. Java, they calculated, could not be taken while northern Australia was capable of sending support, and so a task force of four aircraft-carriers under Vice-Admiral Nagumo Chuichi, *Akagi*, *Kaga*, *Soryu* and *Hiryu*, with two battleships and three heavy cruisers as escort, sailed into the Timor Sea. Timor itself was scheduled to be invaded on 20 February.

At 08.00 hours on 19 February thirty-six Mitsubishi Zero fighters, seventy-one Aiichi D3A1 Type 99 'Val' dive-bombers and eighty-one Nakajima B5N2 Type 97 'Kate' horizontal bombers were launched from the carriers. They were sighted over Bathurst Island at 09.35 and approached Darwin from the south-east at 09.55. They were thought to be either American reinforcements which were expected or a returning flight of P-40s. This flight did return just as the attack was starting and was half on the ground and half still in the air. Pilot Robert Oestreicher recognised the enemy and shot down two Japanese bombers, but all the other P-40s were destroyed. Anti-aircraft fire made little impact on the raiders, and the harbour and wharves, as well as parts of the town, were set on fire. A second wave of fifty-four bombers flown from Ambon and from Kendari in the Celebes attacked the air base and wiped it out. Australian casualties amounted to about 550, of which 243 were fatal. Of the forty-seven ships in the harbour, eight were sunk, one was beached and lost, three were beached and refloated and eleven were damaged. Japanese losses were probably three bombers and two fighters. This was only the first of a series of air-raids that continued until the wet season restricted flying.

As the invasion of Java began, the sea-routes to the island came into dispute. On 27 February a convoy of forty-one transports approached, escorted by Vice-Admiral Takagi Takeo's four cruisers, including the heavy cruisers *Nachi* and *Haguro*, and fourteen destroyers. To oppose them Doorman led two heavy cruisers, *Houston* and *Exeter*, and three light cruisers, *Java*, *Perth* and *De Ruyter*, together with nine destroyers out of Surabaya. The Japanese saw them at 16.16 hours and their heavy cruisers opened fire at extreme range before closing with them. Forty-three Japanese torpedoes were fired but evaded. Doorman was inexperienced as far as fleet engagements were concerned and he had assumed that a night action would take place, so had left his observer aircraft ashore. Added to this were the difficulties of controlling so disparate a fleet, entirely lacking the training and operational exercises needed to mould it into a coherent force. At 17.08 HMS *Exeter* was hit and forced to withdraw. Soon *Houston*, *Java* and *Perth* followed suit. *Perth* made a sweep to lay smoke to cover *Exeter*, and the British destroyers *Encounter*, *Jupiter* and *Electra* were ordered to attack through the smoke. As she emerged from the cover it gave, *Electra* ran full into a Japanese barrage and, at 17.10, sank. American destroyers hastened to cover the withdrawal of the ABDAFloat force and kept the Japanese at a distance, while the Dutch destroyer *Witte de With* escorted the crippled *Exeter*. The other Dutch destroyer *Kortenear* had already been sunk.

In the dark the Japanese seaplanes followed with flares to mark the Allies' positions. *Jupiter* hit a mine and sank. At 23.00 the Japanese heavy cruisers were seen and Takeo's ships launched torpedoes. *De Ruyter* was hit and caught fire, *Perth* scraped through and *Java* was then set afire by a torpedo and sank. Doorman lost his life and the Allied squadron was shattered. They headed for the Indian Ocean by way of the Sunda Strait between Sumatra and Java. Unaware that a Japanese convoy was landing troops at Banten Bay on the north-eastern extreme of Java, and that it was covered by a force of four heavy cruisers and about twelve destroyers, they hurried westwards. Just before turning south to enter the Sunda Strait, at 23.00 on 28 February, they saw the convoy. They opened fire and sank four transports, but immediately came under withering fire from shells and torpedoes. HMAS *Perth* ran out of six-inch ammunition and resorted to firing star-shell before she was finally torpedoed at 00.25 on 1 March. USS *Houston* fought determinedly, long after her number 3 turret was put out of action, but finally sank at 00.46 hours. *Exeter*, with two destroyers, *Encounter* and *Pope*, were sunk before the end of the day as they also attempted to make a friendly port.

At sea the Japanese continued to press west. Nagumo's Western Attack Group entered the Indian Ocean and raided Colombo, Ceylon (Sri Lanka), on 5 April. The heavy cruisers *Dorsetshire* and *Cornwall* were sunk by dive-bombers, and on 9

April the carrier *Hermes* was sunk. The Japanese now had command of the eastern half of the Indian Ocean, a fine protection for the flank of their land forces making their way towards India. Nagumo's ships had accounted for five battleships, an aircraft-carrier, seven cruisers and seven destroyers. Many other ships had been damaged, numerous transport and supply vessels destroyed and many shore installations put out of action. All this without a single important vessel of his own being sunk or even sustaining serious damage. The vice-admiral had good reason to be satisfied.

On land the Japanese Fifteenth Army invaded Burma (Myanmar) on 15 January against totally inadequate British forces, of which two brigades, one Indian and one Burmese, took the first shock. In spite of support from Major Claire Chennault's 'Flying Tigers' Rangoon fell on 8 March. General Joseph Stilwell brought his Chinese Fifth and Sixth Armies to assist, but they could not stem the tide, and by mid-May the British had been pushed back to the Indian border, and the Japanese were in control of Burma. Their victories had reached their high tide.

An anti-aircraft gun and crew during the raids on Darwin. (*Source:* Soldiering On, *Canberra, 1942*)

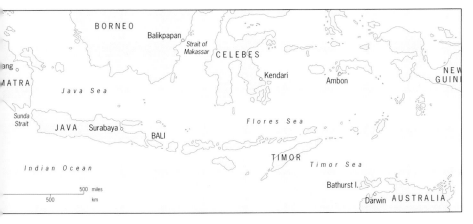

The Battle of the Coral Sea

Fumes from leaking aviation fuel pipelines ignite and the huge explosion rips through the carrier Lexington. *After a ten-hour battle to save her, in which only 216 men of her crew of 2,951 were lost, American destroyers were obliged to sink the vessel. (Derrick Wright Collection)*

As much as a propaganda and morale-boosting exercise as anything else, the United States mounted an air attack on the Japanese mainland in April 1942. Mitchell B-25s, medium bombers, had sufficient range if they could be launched from an aircraft-carrier, overflew Tokyo, bombed the city, and then carried on to land in that part of China as yet unconquered by the Japanese. The carriers *Hornet* and *Enterprise* were used on this mission, which was led by Colonel James Doolittle. On 18 April Kobe, Nagoya, Yokosuka Naval Yard and Yokohama were bombed, and twelve aircraft hit Tokyo. Of the eighty crew involved, nine did not survive the raid, and of those who did, some landed in Japanese-occupied territory. As civilian casualties had occurred, three were executed and one died in prison. The effect on the populace of Japan was minimal, and the raid recruited support for the military government. Retaliatory attacks in China inflicted serious damage, and the mission left the two carriers back in Pearl Harbor just when they were needed in the Coral Sea.

Admiral Nimitz was well aware that the Japanese were seeking to consolidate their grip on the islands and seas north of Australia as a result of Ultra intelligence. This showed that they intended to invade Port Moresby on the south-western coast of Papua and to set up airfields in the Louisiades, the islands running south-east of Papua New Guinea, and on Tulagi, an island off the northern coast of Guadalcanal in the Solomon Islands. The effect of these moves would be to close the western side of the Pacific Ocean to the Allies and to bring

Australia within range of land-based bombers. The plan to achieve this was complicated, suggesting that no significant resistance was expected. The main fighting force under Vice-Admiral Takagi Takeo would sail from Truk Atoll in the Caroline Islands, a major Japanese base some distance to the north of Papua New Guinea, while the bulk of the invasion force would start from Rabaul in New Britain and sail round the eastern end of Papua through the Jomard Passage, protected by a covering force under Rear-Admiral Goto Aritomo.

To oppose these forces Nimitz had Task Forces 11, 17 and 44, two formed around the fleet aircraft-carriers *Lexington* and *Yorktown*, and the third assembled under British Rear-Admiral John Crace and consisting of one American and two Australian cruisers, with two destroyers hurrying from Australia to join them. In the event only one of these arrived in time to take part in the action. The Allied forces were to rendezvous in the Coral Sea, between Australia and the territories targeted by the Japanese, to come under the command of Rear-Admiral Frank 'Black Jack' Fletcher, a man whose buccaneering nickname was belied by the caution that informed his decision-making. Fletcher was in the area by 3 May and the others joined him on 6 May.

The Japanese expedition to Tulagi landed there on 3 May, and Fletcher's aircraft attacked at 08.15 on the next day, without significant effect. Task Force 17 then circled southwards to meet Fitch and Crace about 400 miles (640 km) south of Guadalcanal. The weather was overcast and showers of rain reduced visibility. On 7 May the Japanese invasion fleet was sighted by a reconnaissance aircraft, and Crace was detached to intercept it south of the Jomard Passage, while Fletcher took the rest of his force northward. Meanwhile the American oiler *Neosho* and destroyer *Sims* had been seen by Japanese aircraft and sunk.

The Japanese Striking Force had passed around the most eastern of the Solomon Islands, San Cristobal, and turned west, then south and west again, seeking the Americans. The Americans were pushing westwards, seeking the Japanese. An aircraft from *Yorktown* then reported the presence of the two Japanese carriers and the four cruisers to the north, but the air strike undertaken by both the American carriers found instead the covering force of Admiral Goto and sank the light carrier *Shoho*. A strike by twenty-seven aircraft from *Shokaku* and *Zuikaku* was attacked by American aircraft, which left only seven of their enemy able to return to their mother ships. Meanwhile the presence of the Allied vessels led the Japanese to order their invasion ships to return to port until the sea had been cleared of danger.

The morning of 8 May was bright and clear in the western Coral Sea but still overcast to the east. Thus the Americans were in bright sunlight and the Japanese under cloud. Each side searched for the other. At 08.30 hours the Americans located the Japanese, and Fletcher sent out a large strike mission of Dauntless dive-bombers, Devastator torpedo-bombers and Wildcat fighters as escorts. The torpedoes were launched at too great a distance and the Japanese had time to manoeuvre to avoid them, but *Shokaku* was hit by three bombs and disabled. Only the skill of her damage control parties kept her afloat. A squall of rain enabled *Zuikaku* to take cover from view and escape.

The defence of the American fleet was now much depleted by the absence of the Wildcats, so that, when the Japanese struck in their turn, small resistance was possible. In the clear weather the advantage lay with the attackers, and two torpedo strikes were made on *Lexington* by Japanese Kates. The great carrier listed and three boilers were put out of action, as well as the aircraft elevators, but she was flying aircraft again within the hour. A bomb hit *Yorktown* in the middle of the flight deck, doing severe damage and lighting fires on four decks, but they were controlled and the ship remained operational. On *Lexington* the damage had been worse than at first thought, for the aviation fuel supply system had been compromised. Fumes gathered and at 12.47 hours a great explosion ripped through her. Two hours later the fire-fighters' gallant work was set at nought when a second detonation tore through the ship. *Lexington* sank at 20.00 hours. Through the whole action, over two days, none of the surface ships had seen their enemy's vessels – the first time a major action had been fought in this way.

The American losses outstripped those of the Japanese by a small margin, but the Japanese finished with two fleet carriers out of action for the time being, one because of damage to the vessel and the other because of the number of aircraft she had lost, and a light carrier sunk, losses they would regret at the Battle of Midway. Moreover, they had been forced, for the first time in this war, to abandon an invasion.

Allied forces
Commander-in-Chief: Admiral Chester Nimitz
Task Force 17:
Rear-Admiral Frank (Jack) Fletcher
Fleet carrier *Yorktown*, three cruisers and six destroyers
Task Force 11:
Rear-Admiral Aubrey Fitch
Fleet carrier *Lexington*, two cruisers and five destroyers
Task Force 44:
Rear-Admiral John Crace
Three cruisers and two destroyers

Japanese Forces
Commander-in-Chief:
Vice-Admiral Inoue Shigeyoshi
Invasion forces: from Turk to Tugali and from Rabaul to Port Moresby and Louisiades Archipelago
Covering Force:
Rear-Admiral Goto Aritomo
Light carrier *Shoto*, four heavy cruisers and one destroyer
Striking Force:
Vice-Admiral Takagi Takeo
Fleet carriers *Shokaku* and *Zuikaku*, heavy cruisers *Myoko* and *Haguro* and six destroyers

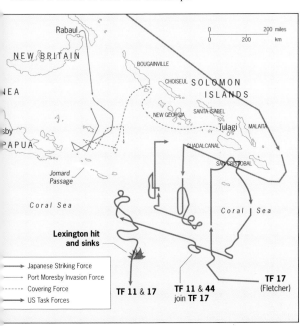

89

The Battle of Midway

Midway Island is a minute patch of land, about two square miles (5 sq km) in area, some 1,135 miles (1,815 km) west of Pearl Harbor in the Hawaiian Islands. It was, in 1942, the most westerly base of the United States in the Pacific Ocean, and its capture, in the view of Admiral Yamamoto, was a necessary stage in the advance on Hawaii, which now appeared more important than the Coral Sea venture. There was still hope of forcing the United States to a negotiated peace. He therefore devised a plan of such complexity that his staff implored him to allow more time for them and the commanders to master it. There was to be a diversionary attack on the Aleutian Islands in the North Pacific to draw part of the US Pacific Fleet away, and then three fleets, an invasion fleet, a carrier fleet and a battlefleet would be sent towards Midway. The Americans would be forced to attack in their own defence, when the superior Japanese strength would overwhelm them.

Admiral Nimitz was well informed. Not only had the Japanese naval code JN-25 been broken and intelligence, to be known as Ultra, derived, but also the Japanese diplomatic code was being read, producing the intelligence flow called Magic. The situation as far as decrypting enemy messages was never stable because codes were constantly being changed or modified, but at this time the Americans were doing very well. The Navy's radio intelligence unit at Pearl Harbor, under Commander Joseph Rochefort, became aware that a major operation was planned. The signal traffic was full of references to charts, meetings and the approaching campaign, using AF as the target and another designator as the source of the attack. Rochefort thought AF meant Midway and that the force would emanate from Saipan. A secure message, by the undersea cable link, was sent to Midway ordering them to report by radio that their water-supply system had broken down. Shortly afterwards the Japanese signalled that AF's water supply was out of commission. The timing was then revealed of a combined fleet's departure from Saipan on 27 May, which would give 2 or 3 June for the attack, but more work uncovered the plan for two days of bombing to precede the landings, and 6 June emerged as the intended landing day. The probable location of the Japanese carrier fleet on 4 June to launch the bombers could then be predicted. Within the week JN-25 was changed again and became unreadable for the time being. What American intelligence did not discover was that the carrier force was to be followed by a battlefleet.

Yamamoto was by no means so well briefed. He thought the carrier Yorktown had been sunk in the Coral Sea and, as a result of American deception, that Hornet and Enterprise were nowhere near Midway. He was therefore in no hurry to get his submarines into a screening position along the French Frigate Shoals. He sent two carriers, four battleships and a number of cruisers and destroyers

to the Aleutians to land Japanese forces on Kiska and Attu, and although the Americans failed to stop them, it was of small importance.

On 27 May Yorktown arrived in Pearl Harbor from the Coral Sea. The damage she had sustained in that battle was severe, but the ship was repaired and back in service on 31 May. Nimitz now lost the commander of Task Force 16, Vice-Admiral William Halsey, through illness, and he gave the command to Halsey's commander of cruisers, Vice-Admiral Raymond Spruance. Spruance had the carriers Hornet and Enterprise, with five heavy and one anti-aircraft cruiser and nine destroyers. The overall command of the operation passed from Halsey to Vice-Admiral Fletcher of Task Force 17, with the carrier Yorktown, two heavy cruisers and six destroyers. They had between them seventy fighter aircraft, one hundred and eleven dive-bombers and forty-two torpedo-bombers. These task forces took position north-east of Midway. To the west of Midway was a screen of US submarines. On Midway itself were various aircraft. The Navy had twenty-eight fighters, thirty-four dive-bombers, six torpedo-bombers and, vitally, thirty PBY Catalina reconnaissance planes.

Vice-Admiral Nagumo Chuichi was in command of Carrier Divisions 1 and 2 with Akagi, Kaga, Soryu and Hiryu, and of two battleships, two heavy cruisers and twelve destroyers. He had eighty-four fighter aircraft, ninety dive-bombers and ninety-three torpedo-bombers, all of which could out-perform the semi-obsolete American aircraft.

A PBY from Midway first saw the invasion fleet on 3 June, and an attack on that in the afternoon was not successful. Then, at 05.34 hours on 4 June, another PBY observed not only the carrier force, but also 'many planes' heading for Midway. The reconnaissance aircraft was not itself seen. These were the 108 aircraft being sent to wipe out American forces and installations on Midway itself. Buffalo fighters did their best to oppose them, but from twenty-six only eleven returned. The airstrip was bombed but was still usable and there had been few casualties as a result of the early warning. The ten American torpedo-bombers that set out in retaliation were intercepted, and only three of them, all severely damaged, made it back. At 07.15 Nagumo, unaware of the proximity of Task Forces 17 and 16, decided to rearm the ninety-three torpedo-bombers he had in readiness to deal with enemy ships, and to make a second attack on Midway Island instead. So those aircraft were being struck down and the decks also kept clear for planes returning from Midway. At 07.30 Nagumo received a report from an aircraft flown from the cruiser Tone that 'what appear to be ten enemy surface ships' had been sighted, but it said nothing of aircraft carriers. The first news Nagumo got of carriers was at 08.20. He cancelled the rearming order so that his planes could attack ships, but still had to keep his decks clear for returning aircraft.

Spruance had received reports of the attack on Midway, and at 07.00, two hours earlier than planned, he ordered the launch of his aircraft. His torpedo-bombers had a range of only 175 miles (280 km) so this was risky. Further, he opted to put his whole force in the air, retaining only enough fighters for air cover for his carriers. Between Spruance and Nagumo was a weather front, laying its curtain of cloud low across the sky with clear weather on each side, so long-distance observation was impossible. The aircraft had no radar, and so flew to a given location, the last-known position of the enemy. At 09.05 Nagumo changed course. The dive-bombers from *Hornet* and their escorting fighters found no target and had to make for Midway, some being forced to ditch. The torpedo-bombers from the same carrier entered the cloud, while their fighter escorts flew above it. At that moment radio contact between them failed, so when the attack planes came out of the cloud and saw the Japanese carriers they were unescorted. As they swooped towards their targets the Japanese fighters closed in and all the aircraft were shot down. All of *Hornet*'s attack planes were out of action. The torpedo-bombers from *Enterprise* suffered in much the same way as their comrades, but four of the fourteen survived.

The strike from *Yorktown* was ordered to take off at 08.30, and half of the available dive-bombers and all of the torpedo-bombers were sent. Only two of the torpedo-bombers came back. Things looked very bad for the Americans. Now luck took a hand. The *Enterprise*'s dive-bombers missed because of the course change, but then saw a lone Japanese destroyer making top speed north-eastwards. Guessing she was rejoining the fleet, they followed her and saw the carriers below, their decks thronged with aircraft about to be launched or just retrieved. The Japanese fighters had been drawn down in pursuit of the ill-fated torpedo-bombers, and the dive-bombers had an unopposed opportunity which they seized with enthusiasm. *Yorktown*'s dive-bombers arrived at much the same time, and between them they smashed *Akagi*, *Kaga* and *Soryu* into masses of twisted metal and fire. All three sank.

Admiral Nagumo moved his command to the cruiser *Nagara* and ordered the carrier *Hiryu* to go into the attack on the American carriers. At 12.15 her aircraft bombed *Yorktown* but she was operational again by 14.00. At 14.40 another attack with the last of the Japanese aircraft scored two torpedo hits. At the same time her dive-bombers were inflicting fatal damage on *Hiryu*. As night fell both sides pulled back.

Yorktown was still afloat the next day and a destroyer escort was thrown round her. Nagumo sent the submarine *I-168* to finish the job, and with great skill she did so, sinking the destroyer *Hammann* and hitting the carrier again. At dawn on 7 June *Yorktown* sank. Although American losses were grievous, the Japanese dominance of the western Pacific had been broken for ever.

The Douglas SBD Dauntless dive-bomber sank more tonnage of Japanese shipping than any other type.

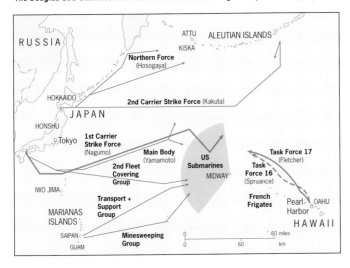

The Solomon Islands; Rendova. US Marines going ashore on 30 June 1943. (Taylor Library)

The Battle of Midway had done severe damage to Japan's position in the Pacific Ocean by sinking four of her aircraft carriers, but the Japanese Navy was still an immense force. Air cover had been reduced although not eliminated, for there were other carriers, but the immediate needs were to establish airfields on appropriate islands to support naval operations and also to develop effectiveness in night actions when air cover was not needed. In mid-1942 the Japanese began the construction of an airfield on the island of Guadalcanal, at the south-eastern end of the Solomon Islands, to supplement their existing base at Tulagi off Florida Island to the north. The Solomons lie east of Papua New Guinea and consist of two chains of islands divided by New Georgia Sound, a waterway that the Americans called the Slot. At the north-west the sound is terminated by the large, single island of Bougainville, and San Cristobal performs a similar function at the south-east. Bases on these islands could compromise Allied operations in both the western Pacific and the crucial supply lines across the South Pacific between Australia and the USA.

The American operation was mounted with all possible speed, and suffered from the haste, but immediate intervention on Guadalcanal was vital. Under the overall command of Vice-Admiral Robert L. Ghormley and the tactical command of Vice-Admiral Fletcher, the invasion force gathered at a rendezvous some 400 miles (650 km) south of Fiji on 27 July. Rear-Admiral Richmond Kelly Turner's Amphibious Force, the first of many that he was to command with distinction, put 12,000 men of Major-General Alexander Vandegrift's 1st Marine Division ashore at Lunga Point on Guadalcanal on 7 August, and 6,000 on the islands of Tulagi, Gavutu and Tananbogo off Florida Islands the next day. Only the latter landing met serious resistance, but that was soon overcome. The Japanese reaction was immediate. Troop reinforcements left Rabaul in six

transport vessels, but they were intercepted by the American submarine *S-38*, which sank one of them, and the others turned back. Meanwhile Vice-Admiral Mikawa Gunichi had put to sea with a force including the heavy cruisers *Chokai*, *Aoba*, *Kako*, *Kinugasa* and *Furutaka*, together with two light cruisers and a destroyer. The approach of this force was observed by a Coast Watcher, one of the numerous Royal Australian Navy operatives behind Japanese lines in the islands, but American air reconnaissance failed to supplement the report with precise course and speed data so Turner was forced to speculate. He decided to cover the Slot north and south of the small island of Savo with scouting destroyers in front, cruisers covering the approaches to the flocks of transports off Guadalcanal and Florida on either side and another two cruisers off Florida further south. Mikawa sent aircraft to spy out the channel, and they, unopposed, gave him a detailed appreciation of the defences. He attacked during the night, illuminating the area with flares from aircraft. In the space of two hours the Japanese sped down the southern side of the Slot and turned to leave by the northern route. In the fight they sank the heavy cruisers *Canberra*, *Astoria*, *Quincy* and *Vincennes*, and left *Chicago* badly damaged. The boldness of the attack and the effectiveness of their Long Lance torpedoes had caught the Allies off balance and given these waters the name of Ironbottom Sound. It was small comfort that the US submarine *S-44* sank the heavy cruiser *Kako* as she made her way back to base. The consequences for the Marines were serious. Fletcher pulled back his carrier force, unwilling to put his major asset at risk, and lacking air cover, Turner was obliged to withdraw the transports. This left the Marines isolated and without air protection until the first elements of 23rd Marine Air Group could bring their few fighters and torpedo-bombers in to the newly serviceable Henderson Field on 20 August.

The airfield, named after a Marine Corps officer killed at Midway, had been rebuilt by SeaBees, the men of the Naval Construction Battalion (CB), nicknamed after the unit initials.

The Japanese were able to land men of the Seventeenth Army under Colonel Ichiki at Taivu, twelve miles (20 km) east of Henderson Field, on 18 August, but the small force, under 1,000 men, was not enough to oust the Marines. At a battle known as the Tenaru River, although fought on the Ilu River, they were wiped out. The American invasion had been flawed in its support and protection arrangements, but this was a new form of warfare which, in time and at a cost of blood, the Americans would learn. In the meantime the Japanese ferried in men and supplies down the Slot in a system of convoys the Americans called the Tokyo Express, and the two navies fought for domination of the sea supply lanes. On 24 August Admiral Fletcher was drawn towards an elaborate trap by Admiral Tanaka, who hoped to destroy the American carrier force. Fletcher, however, had not concentrated his fleet, and although *Enterprise* was damaged, the Japanese lost the light carrier *Ryujo* and the Battle of the Eastern Solomons left neither side with the advantage, and both continued to supply their land forces.

In September the rest of the Ichiki Detachment, together with Major-General Kiyotake Kawaguchi's Brigade, landed at Taivu and began an advance on the south-eastern flank of Henderson Field, which was protected by a ridge where one of the strong-points Vandegrift had laid out to hold the area with his limited manpower, was situated. Colonel M.A. Edson went to hold this ridge with 1st Raider Regiment and three companies of the Parachute Battalion, US Marine Corps, on the night of Saturday 12 September. The Japanese attacked after dark on Sunday with a superiority of two to one, and the fight went on all night. The Japanese used mortars to isolate Marine foxholes and the Marines countered with their mortars, aiming perilously close to their own men. The Marines were driven back into a tight perimeter and held grimly against repeated waves of attacks. The 2nd Marine Battalion was sent to support them and American artillery joined in, despite their inadequate maps. At dawn the Japanese withdrew from what became known as Edson's, or Bloody, Ridge, leaving half their number, about 1,700 men, behind them. The Marines engaged that night suffered twenty per cent losses.

The Americans enjoyed greater success in the Battle of Cape Esperance, when a Japanese bombardment force under Rear-Admiral Goto Aritomo was to be the forerunner of another Japanese landing. He was preparing to commence his shelling to cover the activities of the landing when his flotilla was observed on the new radar of Rear-Admiral Norman Scott's force, which was patrolling off Cape Esperance to cover an American landing. By chance Scott crossed Goto's 'T', that is, was at right angles to his enemy's course and thus could optimize his firepower. Goto was killed and two of his ships sunk. The landings, however, took place all the same.

Reinforcements, 3,000 men of the Americal Division, arrived in mid-October in time to resist the Sendai Division, which had landed to the west around the mouth of the Matanikau River. Henderson Field was subjected to more bombardment, and the next big effort was made in November. In the three-day Battle of Guadalcanal the Americans lost six ships against the Japanese loss of three in a night action of 12/13 November, but the flyers of the US Marines did great damage to the enemy the next day. Another night action saw further American losses, but the Japanese were losing their ability to maintain forces on the island. Off Tassafaronga on 30 November Admiral Tanaka inflicted further losses on the Americans but again failed to resupply the land forces. Meanwhile the Americans relieved the exhausted Marines with the 25th Infantry Division, and Major-General Alexander Patch took over the command. With their grip on the sea lanes slipping, the Japanese eventually had to withdraw, and in a brilliant evacuation operation, took some 13,000 men off the island to continue the fight on islands further north.

The American losses amounted to 1,752 killed and 4,359 wounded. The gain was the first forced retreat of the Japanese land forces, but it would take another year to clear them from the Solomon Islands.

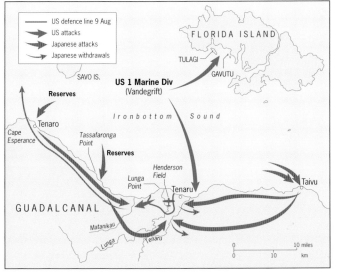

US defence line 9 Aug
US attacks
Japanese attacks
Japanese withdrawals

FLORIDA ISLAND

TULAGI
GAVUTU

SAVO IS.
US 1 Marine Div
(Vandegrift)

Reserves

Ironbottom   *Sound*

Tenaro
Cape Esperance
Tassafaronga Point

Reserves

Henderson Field

Lunga Point
Tenaru
Taivu

GUADALCANAL

Matanikau

Lunga   Tenaru

0   10 miles
0   10   km

At the time of the war the island of New Guinea was divided into Dutch New Guinea (now Irian Jaya), and Papua (the southern half of the eastern part) and New Guinea (the northern half). Both of the latter were Australian territories. The island is characterized by the high, mountainous, jungle-clad spine and the numerous rivers that run through swampy lowlands to the sea. The tropical wetness of the climate encourages disease, notably malaria. As campaigning country it is almost intolerable. It was, however, suitable for airfields, and the Japanese had only been prevented from seizing Port Moresby on the south-west coast of Papua by their reverse at the Battle of the Coral Sea.

On 12 July 1942 the Japanese South Seas Detachment under Major-General Horii Tomitaro landed at Buna on the north-eastern coast, directly across the Owen Stanley Range of mountains from Port Moresby. This frustrated the plan of General Douglas MacArthur, commander of the South-West Pacific Area, to have his Australian forces occupy the place, moving from Port Moresby by way of Ioribaiwa, the Gap (a pass in the mountains) and Kokoda. General Sir Thomas Blamey, commander of the Australian Military Forces and ground commander under MacArthur, was sadly ignorant of the conditions in Papua and sent more men in, poorly equipped, over-loaded and badly supported and supplied. They were driven back from Isurava by Horii, who had taken personal command of the Japanese. The conflict degenerated into a miserable hunt and clash contest in the jungle in which the

Australians were eventually thrust off the mountains down to Ioribaiwa. At the end of August the Japanese tried to open a new front at Milne Bay in the extreme south-east, but Ultra intelligence gave the Allies news of the plan and they were able to reinforce the island and eject the Japanese Special Naval Landing Forces. The Kokoda Trail remained a problem, and an impatient MacArthur suggested Blamey take personal command from Lieutenant-General Sydney Powell. It was irrelevant, for Horii, constantly harrassed by the Fifth US Army Air Force under Lieutenant-General George C. Kenny, had already started to withdraw to his beachhead.

The Allies now established their own beachhead east of Buna with the US 32nd Division, and while they attacked from the coast the 25th and 16th Australian Brigades of 7th Division threw the Japanese out of the mountains and struck towards the west end of the Buna beachhead on 19 November. The campaign quickly lost impetus, and MacArthur sent Lieutenant-General Robert L. Eichelberger to get things moving with the remark that he should take the place or not come back alive. Eichelberger found that neither the officers on the ground nor the commanders back at headquarters understood or knew how to deal with the vile conditions. Men's uniforms had rotted to rags, disease had reduced the force to a shadow of its theoretical strength and supplies were entirely insufficient. Officers were relieved of command and reinforcements brought in, and the village was taken on 14 December, although the area was not fully secured until 2 January 1943.

Japanese resistance continued until 24 February 1944 in the island of New Britain, north of Papua. This US Marine machine-gunner is returning to base after nineteen days' continuous combat at Cape Gloucester. (Taylor Library)

The 32nd Division had experienced 9,688 casualties out of a total strength of 10,825 men. Of these, 7,125 men were sick. From then on the attention given to the logistics of supply and support increased markedly. Those killed in action in the first part of the New Guinea campaign were 930 Americans and 2,165 Australians, but the number of casualties by cause of illness were 8,659 Americans and 9,249 Australians. Guadalcanal casualties seem light by comparison. Of the 20,000 Japanese engaged, some 12,000 had perished of one cause or another.

An Australian soldier's impression of jungle conditions: 'Playing Tarzan in New Guinea.'

The Japanese then landed men of Lieutenant-General Adachi Hatazo's Eighteenth Army further west in the Huon Gulf, south of the mountainous Huon Peninsula and north of the central range that formed the spine of the island. More men were landed at Wewak, on the north coast yet further west. Then, on 28 February 1943, destined for Lae on the Huon Gulf, 7,000 men of 51st Division, Eighteenth Army, sailed from Rabaul in New Britain on eight transports, escorted by eight destroyers. The Americans knew they were coming – Ultra intelligence once again. The convoy was located precisely at 08.30 hours on 2 March at the western end of New Britain. The Fifth USAAF made its first attack with B-17 Flying Fortresses from 5,000 feet (1,500 m) and sank one transport, damaging two more. Destroyers picked up 950 men and raced for Lae. As they rejoined the convoy the next day, B-25 Mitchell bombers, modified to carry six machine-guns in the nose and 500 pound (225 kg) bombs with delayed-action fuses, escorted by fighters, attacked. They flew in, machine-gunning the crowded decks and released their bombs, which exploded under water. They were followed by Beaufighters of the Royal Australian Air Force, strafing the ships and rafts. The four surviving destroyers gathered up whom they could, 2,734 men, and made for base. After dark ten American PT (Patrol Craft Torpedo) boats swept the area, and the next morning aircraft and PT boats were back to ensure that there were no more survivors. More than 3,600 troops died in the water in the Battle of the Bismarck Sea, and the Japanese abandoned reinforcing their army with surface transport.

American air power had inflicted a terrible defeat on the Japanese, and they determined to counter the power of Kenny's forces. To this end their Fourth Air Army built up its strength at Wewak on the north coast of New Guinea, beyond the range of the fighters with which the Americans could operate their bombers with safety. Once again Ultra informed Kenny of the Japanese plans, and he built a forward airstrip sixty miles (95 km) west of Lae which the Japanese did not detect until too late. On 17 August some two hundred American aircraft attacked Wewak's four airstrips. The Japanese had no radar and their observation arrangements were faulty. The strike came as a complete surprise. When it was over a mere thirty-five Japanese aircraft were operational and only one runway could be used. Air power now showed its uses. The US 503rd Parachute Regiment dropped to take Nadzab airfield, into which 7th Australian Division were airlifted to close the trap which 9th Australian's seaborne attack had set around the Japanese beachhead on Huon Gulf. Operation Cartwheel was under way.

It was MacArthur's plan to bypass the Japanese at Rabaul in New Britain, leaving them isolated as he advanced towards the Philippines. To this end, having lost confidence in the Australian General Blamey, he created Alamo Force under Lieutenant-General Walter Kreuger, including his Sixth Army, and had Kreuger report direct to him. New Guinea Force, comprising Australian and American units, continued to chew its way west through New Guinea in a series of coast-hopping operations to which the intelligence reports contributed vitally, revealing, as they did, where the Japanese were concentrating their troops. None the less the island was not secured by the Allies before the end of the war, and many years later lone Japanese soldiers were still emerging from the jungle finally to surrender.

The Battle of Tarawa

While General MacArthur's forces of South-West Pacific Area were thrusting along the northern coast of New Guinea, Admiral Halsey's campaign in the South Pacific Area to the east was rolling up the Solomon Islands, and the two appeared to be converging in an approach to the Philippines. The US Navy was, by now, rebuilding its power after the disaster of Pearl Harbor, especially in battleships and aircraft carriers. The possibility of mounting devastating bombardments of shore installations and providing curtains of anti-aircraft fire to shield aircraft carriers was a real one. At the Washington Conference of May 1943 the Allies agreed that the Pacific campaign could be enlarged, and in July Admiral Nimitz was authorized to plan for landings in the Gilbert and the Marshall Islands.

This decision brought with it a change in the nature of the war that they were fighting. In New Guinea and the Solomon Islands the campaigns were fought on land and the battles in support took place at sea. The land masses in the western Pacific are numerous but very small and the stretches of sea between them very large indeed. South of Wake Island a string of island groups stretched away towards Fiji: the Marshall Islands, and south of them the Gilberts (Kiribati) and then the Ellice islands (Tuvalu). To the west the Marshalls scatter onwards towards the Caroline Islands, and to their north the Marianas. To their west are the Philippines and to their north Iwo Jima and Japan itself. The new American Navy was equipped for this with fast battleships and even fleet carriers capable of thirty knots and carrying enough gunnery to defend themselves against all known styles of attack. These would be the core of the Fast Carrier Task Forces which would work with the fast transports and swift escorts to push west towards the Philippines.

Tarawa, in the Gilbert Islands, like so many of the objectives the Americans would face in the coming months, is an atoll, a ring of coral reefs, some exposed at low tide and others covered, and of islands around a lagoon. The main island, Betio, is

two and a half miles (4 km) long and half a mile (800 m) wide, about the size of London's Hyde Park or Central Park in New York. In the middle of the island was an airstrip that made it worthy of invasion. The majority of the 4,500 Japanese garrison were concentrated here, while the balance were on Makin and Apamama. The limitation of size meant that defence could not rely on manoeuvre but had to be based on the quality and design of fixed emplacements of concrete, wood and steel and on their inter-relationships in terms of interlocking fields of fire. The Japanese commander, Vice-Admiral Shibasaki Keiji, was so satisfied with his arrangements that he said the island could not be taken by a million men in a hundred years.

The American force was under the overall command of Vice-Admiral Raymond A. Spruance, who had distinguished himself at Midway. The strength he had to deliver to the Gilbert Islands amounted to 27,600 assault troops, 7,600 garrison troops, and 6,000 vehicles. The Tarawa assault would make use of twenty-two transport ships carrying the 2nd Marine and 27th Infantry Divisions. The naval assault force consisted of seven battleships, eight cruisers, thirty-four destroyers and eight escort carriers, with two hundred and eighteen aircraft. The covering escort, Task Force 50, had five battleships and eleven carriers, with more that eight hundred aircraft.

The airfields in the Gilberts were quickly subdued by American bombing, and Tarawa was subjected to a bombardment of 3,000 tons of naval shells as well as air strikes. The assault by 2nd Marine Division under Major-General Julian Smith was slow to go in because wind and sea conditions were rough. The men were packed into the 100 LVTs available. The LVT, Landing Vehicle Tracked, also known as Amtrac, was a development of a rescue vehicle used in the Florida swamps, with armour and armament added. The LVTs followed two minesweepers through the lagoon entrance and

US Marines on Red Beach, Tarawa. (Taylor Library)

The heavy cost of landing on Red Beaches 1 and 2: damaged Amtracs and the bodies of American troops strew the shoreline and drift in the shallow waters of the lagoon. (Derrick Wright Collection)

some cover from the anti-boat guns that caused most damage; the heavier guns could not be brought to bear on small vessels and men. The Marines worked their way inland. They had too few flame-throwers to use against bunkers, but support fire from the Navy helped them as long as their radios remained serviceable. Offshore the follow-up supply-carrying landing craft gathered, unable to run in to a beach that was still barely taken, and there they became targets for Japanese guns. By the end of the day about 5,000 Marines had come ashore, of whom some 1,500 had become casualties. The Americans clung on to what ground they could hold, from the centre of Red 2 to the centre of Red 3 and the western part of Red 1, and waited for dark and a higher tide. That night the artillery and eleven Sherman tanks were brought ashore, and in the dark the Marines filtered silently onto Green Beach, the western end of the island.

The night provided welcome respite for the Japanese. Admiral Shibasaki had been cut off from his troops for much of the day and unable to organize a counter-attack on the Marines' flanks. Half of his force had been lost and the other half had to use their own initiative in fighting the invaders. With daylight came more Americans; the divisional reserves assaulted the eastern end of Red 1 and suffered as severely as their comrades had the day before. Marines landed on Green Beach, and artillery was put ashore on neighbouring Bairiki Island to provide support fire and prevent a Japanese withdrawal. The tanks rumbled about from pillbox to pillbox, firing at point-blank range to silence them. By the end of the day a front line across Betio at the eastern end of the airstrip had been established. The fourth and last day saw desperate and suicidal counter attacks by the Japanese. They were futile. The soldiers who finally surrendered were all wounded. There were seventeen of them. The Americans had lost 1,009 killed and 2,101 wounded out of the 18,313 men who had come ashore. The mistakes made at Tarawa would be rectified, but it was clear that advancing against defenders of this bravery and commitment was going to be very expensive in blood and lives.

turned south for their run in to the beach. Enough time had elapsed for the Japanese to concentrate their manpower against the beaches, and a fierce fire met the marines. Following the first wave came more marines in ordinary, untracked, landing craft. They could not, once grounded on the off-shore reef, propel themselves forward, crawling over it, so they had to dump their men into the water to wade the last six hundred yards (540 m) in the face of bitter defensive gunfire.

The landing beaches had been designated Red 1, 2 and 3 from west to east, and between Red 2 and Red 3 a pier stretched out into the lagoon. This gave

In February 1944 Spruance attacked the Marshall Islands, having destroyed Japanese air power there with carrier-borne and Tarawa-based aircraft. The atolls of Majuro, Kwajalein and Roi-Namur were quickly taken, and well ahead of the planned schedule Eniwetok at the extreme west of the group fell and Truk in the Carolines was neutralized by a carrier force. The Marianas, from where the new American B-29 bomber would be able to attack the Japanese homeland, were to be the next objective.

The Battles of Imphal and Kohima

At the end of May 1942 the British forces had been ejected from Burma (Myanmar) by the Japanese, and the front line lay along the border with India. Burma is essentially a long valley down which, from north to south, the great River Irrawaddy (Ayeyarwady) runs with its tributary in the northwest, the Chindwin. The mountains to the east border China and Siam (Thailand), and in the west the Indian border is marked by the mountains that run from Nagaland in the north and become the Chin Hills before dwindling into the Arakan Yoma. The western coast alongside these hills, facing the Bay of Bengal, is a region known as the Arakan at that time and where, at Akyab, there was a useful airfield. The country was largely tropical forest which covered the hills and was cut through by numerous small streams.

During 1942 and 1943 the British Indian forces attempted to retake the Arakan, but ended back where they had started. In the north Major-General Orde Wingate's Chindits made their first foray behind Japanese lines in February 1943, taking heavy losses and achieving little other than valuable lessons in the problems of air supply and jungle combat. In 1943 both the Japanese and the British reorganized their armies in the region. The Japanese created the Burma Area Army under Lieutenant-General Kawabe Masakazu and declared Burma's

A British mule train threads through the Arakan jungle.
(Taylor Library)

independence in August. In September the Allies' South East Asia Command was formed and Lieutenant-General William Slim took command of the new Fourteenth Army. One of his first acts was to enforce strict medical discipline to combat malaria. A counter-offensive was now planned in which XV Corps, commanded by Lieutenant-General Philip Christison, was to attack in the Arakan, Slim's right flank, and on the left flank Lieutenant-General Joseph Stilwell's Northern Combat Area Command's Galahad force, known to journalists as Merrill's Marauders, but in fact 5307 Composite Unit (Provisional) under Brigadier-General Frank D. Merrill, would co-operate with Chiang-Kai-shek's army to take northern Burma and open the way for a supply road from Assam to China. A second Chindit expedition would be airlifted into Burma to interfere with north–south lines of Japanese communication and supply. In the centre IV Corps, 17th and 20th Indian Divisions, under Lieutenant-General Geoffrey Scoones, would amass supplies for a future advance towards the Chindwin and push forward immediately with patrols through Tiddim and Tamu. His base was the Imphal Plain, an isolated area of level ground of about 800 square miles (2,000 sq km) on the main route, by way of Dimapur and Kohima, through the mountains from India.

The Japanese response was an ambitious campaign. They created the Twenty-eighth Army under Lieutenant-General Sakurai Shozo to fight in the Arakan and Thirty-third Army under Lieutenant-General Honda Masaki to meet Stilwell in the north. In the centre the Fifteenth Army under Lieutenant-General Mutaguchi Renya was to take Imphal preparatory to invading India. The fight in the Arakan was intended to pin down the British so that they could not support the defence of Imphal, but it failed because Christison had set up an administration and supply centre which, when he was attacked, formed a fine defensive position against which the Japanese, lacking air power, broke. The British had been taken by surprise but were not overwhelmed when surrounded as they had tanks to oppose ground attacks and aircraft to supply them. Reinforcements then arrived to enfold and destroy the Japanese. The British success at the Battle of the Admin Box was to allow Slim to reinforce Imphal.

Slim himself described the country around Imphal as 'a chaos of jungle-matted, knife-edged ridges, running up to peaks of over eight thousand feet [2,440 m], split by precipitous valleys and pierced from the Indian side only by that fantastic road from Imphal the troops themselves had built.' That the Japanese were preparing to attack was evident from intelligence gathered by patrols, from captured documents and from the evidence of log rafts being readied on the Chindwin. Scoones and Slim agreed that the battle should be fought at Imphal and that the 17th Indian Division should be withdrawn from Tiddim, where it was too exposed. Kohima, it was thought, would be a Japanese objective but the difficulties of the terrain would slow the Japanese progress. When, on 7 March, Mutaguchi had his 33rd Division attack Tiddim, the speed with which they moved came close to preventing the Indians' planned withdrawal and turned it into a fighting retreat, though retreat they did to the pre-appointed positions. To the north of that action Yamamoto Force struck at the 20th Indian Division around Tamu but were halted at Shenam Saddle. North again, the Japanese 15th Division crossed the Chindwin to invest Imphal on the north, and 31st Division crossed to make for Kohima in much greater numbers than expected. Not that their progress was entirely smooth. South of Ukhrul, some seventy-five miles (120 km) south and east of Kohima, the 50th Indian Parachute Brigade, together with a battalion of the 23rd Division, dug in and held for two full days before being pushed back to Sangshak, nine miles (14 km) to the south. Here, with supply drops by the RAF, they stood from 21 to 26 March until loss of a water source and casualties forced them to break out and make for Imphal. By 30 March the Imphal–Kohima road was blocked, and Kohima was surrounded on 4 April.

Kohima was occupied by three battalions, 4th Royal West Kents, one Nepalese and one of the Assam Rifles, and commanded by Colonel H.U.

Richards. On 6 April a company of Rajputs got in, and a platoon brought out some two hundred wounded, but then the investment by the Japanese became complete. The defenders were squashed into a tiny space, the possession of a tennis court became a vital issue, trenches were literally only a few paces apart and any movement by a soldier brought down enemy fire. Water was in short supply and severely rationed. This force held out, with some reinforcement by 5 Brigade, until relieved by the 161st Indian Brigade on 20 April. These relief forces of XXXIII Corps, under Lieutenant-General Sir Montague Stopford, had fought their way up from Dimapur. Then fierce battles ensued as the Japanese struggled to take the town, notwithstanding the strength of the new arrivals. Slowly the British and Indian troops gained ground until, in early June, the Japanese began to withdraw.

At Imphal the 5th and 7th Indian Divisions were arriving from the Arakan to reinforce the position. The fighting here was dominated by the roads which emanated from the town like spokes of a wheel with thick jungle in between. A continuous series of attacks on all sides was met with continuous counter-attack, forces being moved quickly to crisis spots. The business of aerial supply proved to be much more demanding than anticipated, but the RAF Third Tactical Air Force moved, during the four months of the battle, a mass of supplies, including a million gallons (4.5 million litres) of fuel and 14 million pounds (6.35 million kg) of rations. It evacuated 13,000 casualties and brought in 12,000 reinforcements.

The Japanese were in yet more difficult circumstances where supplies were concerned, running stores up over mountain roads or trekking mule trains through the jungle. The quick capture of Imphal was intended to furnish the fresh supplies they needed for the advance. The Japanese forces fought with amazing courage and determination, but the Gandhi Brigade of their allies, the Indian National Army, was a dismal failure. The plea for reinforcements from Sato's 31st Division fell on deaf ears and when it withdrew on Sato's orders alone on 31 May, Mutaguchi's position became impossible. It was not until 22 June that the Japanese grip fell loose and Imphal received supplies by road. On 18 July the Japanese finally abandoned the fight. They had suffered 53,000 casualties of which 30,000 were fatal. They had lost 17,000 mules and pack ponies. They brought back none of their guns or tanks. It was the largest defeat inflicted on the Japanese Army in the entire war.

The Allies had 17,000 casualties, no trivial cost, but the way was opened for an advance into Burma, and the supply route to China was secure.

General Slim's objectives in 1944 were twofold. First, he wanted to degrade Japanese strength sufficiently to make the retaking of Burma a practical proposition. Second, the problem of supplying Chiang Kai-shek and his army, who were fighting the Japanese in China, had become a considerable burden. After the Chinese coast had been sealed off, the roads through Burma were used until lost with the invasion of the country, when airlift became the only method possible. The route flown by the China Wing of US Air Transport Command went over a series of mountain ridges, some as high as 15,000 feet (4,500 m), between Dinjan, Assam and Kunming, a distance of some 500 miles (800 km). It was known as the Hump, and involved significant danger, including icing up and adverse weather conditions at the aircraft's ceiling altitude. In April 1944 the system worked in reverse to bring 18,000 Chinese troops to take part in Lieutenant-General Joseph Stilwell's planned advance, and in July 1944 supplies for the Chinese going the other way amounted to some 18,975 tons. It was the possibility of building a road and oil pipeline from Ledo in Assam to Kunming that excited American interest in the Burma campaign, and when that was done, in January 1945, their support ceased. In April 1944 the motivation for the attack by Stilwell's Chinese forces, Galahad formation and the Chindit incursion, Operation Thursday, was to clear the way for the making of the road.

Major-General Orde Wingate was experienced in irregular warfare in Palestine, Ethiopia and Burma, and especially interested in Long Range Penetration (LRP) operations behind enemy lines. His unconventional ideas and attitudes attracted Winston Churchill and horrified many others. However, his tactics, which called for supply by air, made the Japanese approach of infiltration, encirclement and denial of supply lines irrelevant, for there were no supply lines if the Allies had air superiority. The mission was intended to be integrated with some larger purpose and to tie up enemy troops and disrupt communications and supplies. A first operation, Longcloth, was undertaken in February 1943 with Wingate's 77th Infantry Brigade (13th King's Liverpool Regt, 3/2 Gurkha Rifles, No. 142 Commando Company and 2nd Burma Rifles) in northern Burma. The force was known as the Chindits, a name derived from the Burmese for lion. The mission involved long marches and resulted in high casualties and doubtful achievements, but proved it could be done. It granted Wingate the chance to build a yet larger force, including Galahad from the USA, although he had to hand this unit over to Stilwell before undertaking the penetration in support of the American's campaign against the 18th Japanese Division.

Operation Thursday was to set up strongholds, fortified, air-supplied encampments, from which Japanese communication centres at Mogaung and Indaw on the rail route to Myitkyina airfield could

4 February 1945: a convoy of trucks crosses the Irrawaddy on a pontoon bridge, part of the completed Stilwell Road supply route. (Taylor Library)

be attacked, and to support Stilwell's advance on the airfield itself. This last was the prime objective, but the progress of the Nationalist Chinese Yunnan Armies coming from the east could be assisted, as well as a general causing of mayhem and confusion in enemy lines. This required the establishment of outposts north of Mandalay around the headwaters of the Irrawaddy's tributaries, and four flat clearings were selected in the jungle, well clear of the roads and with water available. They were named Aberdeen, Piccadilly, Broadway and Chowringhee. The 16th Brigade was to march in from Ledo towards Indaw, and then 77th would go in by glider to Broadway and Piccadilly, with 111th coming in later by the same means. The three remaining brigades would have to go later as there were not enough aircraft to take them in the first wave. On Sunday 5 March, with eighty-three RAF and USAAF C-47 Dakotas and eighty gliders ready for take-off, aerial reconnaissance showed tree trunks dumped on Piccadilly. Was the operation known to the Japanese? They decided to go anyhow, and found regular wood extraction was taking place.

Within days 12,000 men, 2,000 mules and other supplies and ammunition had been taken in to Broadway and Piccadilly. Lentaigne's 111th Brigade landed at Chowringhee on 10 March and fought off a Japanese attack successfully. Spitfire fighters of 211 Group RAF, newly arrived on this front, destroyed half the Japanese fighter strength. The move was then made to set up White City between the road and the railway north of Mawlu. This was not achieved without a fight, and was followed by a concerted Japanese attempt to break the Chindits, which was also fought off, American P-51 Mustangs giving support. Aberdeen was next to be set up when 16th Brigade arrived after a fifty-day march on 10 March. Wingate ordered them to attack Indaw, a deviation from his own rule against LRP missions attempting to take prepared positions. Two events changed the picture entirely. On 15

March the attacks on Imphal and Kohima began. On 27 March Wingate was killed in an aircraft crash. The former concentrated Slim's attention on the Indian border battle, and the latter led to Lentaigne assuming command and Brigadier John Masters taking over 111th Brigade. The interference with supply lines they were suffering, particularly in their 31st Division's sector in the north, stimulated the Japanese to organize their 56th Division to reduce these damaging Allied enclaves. On 9 April the plan was changed by Slim, Lentaigne and South East Asia Command's Supreme Commander, Admiral Lord Louis Mountbatten. The Chindits, acting as a conventional force, were to attack Mogaung from the south to aid Stilwell's advance.

White City was now subjected to continuous attack, at terrible cost to the Japanese. They died in futile charges against the barbed wire

and minefields, and approaching aircraft were able to identify their location by the stench of rotting corpses. On 10 May, after a month's siege, White City was abandoned and Masters set up a new stronghold north along the railway and south of Mogaung. Blackpool, as it was called, was not a

A silk scarf, with messages of friendship in various languages, for use by troops behind enemy lines attempting to establish contact with local people. (Lyster/Turrall collection)

well-chosen position. The Japanese 53rd Infantry Division enjoyed an easy approach from the south, and their garrison at Mogaung rained shellfire on it. It was evacuated after two weeks, a mire of dead men remaining after the dying, who could not be moved, had been shot by their comrades.

Stilwell took the Chindits under command on 17 May and used them as part of his plan to capture Mogaung and other towns, but was without understanding of the nature or strength of the unit or, indeed, its weaknesses. On 26 June Calvert delivered Stilwell Mogaung as required, by which time 77th Brigade had 150 men fit to fight. They had no artillery or tank support in achieving this, nor were they adequately supplied. Although they had been too long in action, it was not until 26 August that the last of the Chindits was evacuated.

Wingate's theories and the performance of the formation he brought into being have been much criticized, but there is no doubt that they played a crucial role in denying supplies to the Japanese 31st Division in its attack on Kohima and seriously disrupted Japanese opposition to Stilwell. It is estimated that one sixth of Fifteenth Army's 30,000 casualties were attributable to Chindit action. The Chindits themselves lost 3,628 killed, wounded or missing in this campaign, and although they went into training for new operations, they were disbanded in February 1945.

Chindit Order of Battle in North Burma

14th Infantry Brigade, Brigadier Tom Brodie: 1st Bedfordshire and Hertfordshire Regiment, 7th Leicestershire Regt, 2nd Black Watch, 2nd York and Lancaster Regt.
16th Infantry Brigade, Brigadier Bernard Fergusson: 51st 69th Field Regt, RA (as infantry), 2nd Queen's Royal Regt (West Surrey), 2nd Leicestershire Regt.
77th Indian Infantry Brigade, Brigadier Michael Calvert: 1st King's (Liverpool) Regt, 1st Lancashire Fusiliers, 1st South Staffordshire Regt, 3/6 Gurkha Rifles, 3/9 Gurkha Rifles, 4/9 Gurkha Rifles, part 3/4 Gurkha Rifles.
111th Indian Infantry Brigade, Brigadier Walter Lentaigne: 1st Cameronians, 2nd King's Own Royal Regt, part 3/4 Gurkha Rifles. 3rd
West African Brigade, Brigadier Gillmore: 6th Nigeria Regt, 7th Nigeria Regt, 12th Nigeria Regt.
In the initial force for Operation Thursday: Four troops, 160th Field Regiment, Royal Artillery with eight 25-pounders, four troops, 69th Light Anti-Aircraft Regt, RA with twenty-four Bofors guns and three Royal Army Service Corps air-supply companies, as well as medical and other units.

Brigadier Wingate (right) and George Bromhead his Brigade Major, plan 77 Brigade's expedition into Burma in early 1943.

The Battle of the Philippine Sea

The Mariana Islands run north and south some 1,600 miles (2,600 km) east of Manila in the Philippines, and the largest of them, Guam, is the same distance south of Tokyo in Japan. With the exception of Guam, an American territory, the islands had been a Japanese mandate for over forty years, and all had been occupied by Japanese troops since 1941. The strategic importance of the main island, Saipan, and its neighbours for the planned liberation of the Philippines and for the fight against mainland Japan was evident, for from here the new B-29 bombers could strike targets in both of these enemy territories.

Saipan is fourteen miles (22 km) long, and was then a major administrative centre for the Japanese, with a large civilian population. It is a substantial island and had well-built fortifications and shelters in the limestone caves, although work on these was incomplete. The defence was under the command of Lieutenant-General Saito Yoshitsugu with 32,000 men of the Thirty-First Army. The challenge of taking the island was massive. It is 3,500 miles (5,600 km) from the American base at Pearl Harbor from which the invasion force of 127,000 men was to embark. Over 700 ships were needed, and they would be devoted to this operation alone for three months. The overall command was in the hands of Admiral Spruance, and the Joint Expeditionary Force itself under Vice-Admiral Kelly Turner.

The landings began after attacks had been made on airfields from which the Japanese might have flown in support of the Saipan garrison. Bombardments of Saipan and the neighbouring island of Tinian on 13 June were made by new battleships which achieved little. The next day the old hands joined in: *Maryland*, *Colorado*, *Pennsylvania* and others shelled the shore installations. They did better, but the damage was still relatively slight. Frogmen explored the coral

reefs, blasting ways through them and gathering what information they could for the guidance of the landing craft. On 15 June the landings began with the 2nd and 4th Marine Divisions of Lieutenant-General Holland Smith's 5th Amphibious Corps. The 700 LVTs carried 8,000 Marines ashore in the first wave. The fire they met was devastating; the defenders' guns had been left untouched by the barrage. The Marines crept inland, unsupported by naval artillery because the radio contact was lost. By the end of the day 20,000 men had landed, of whom ten per cent had already become casualties, and only half the intended beachhead had been taken. Fighting went on through the night, and only the arrival of five Sherman tanks turned the tide in the Americans' favour.

Towards evening the following day the 27th Division landed, bringing supplies and all its artillery. At 03.00 hours next morning a strong Japanese attack was made, supported by forty-four Japanese light tanks. The US Navy lit the scene with star shell, and a desperate defence of the beachhead started. Crucial in their success were the Marines' 75 mm guns mounted on their half-track vehicles. With the coming of morning on 17 June the landing grounds were secure in American hands, but the battle for the island had only just begun.

General Saito wanted to hold on long enough for rescue to come, for he knew that the Japanese Mobile Fleet under Vice-Admiral Ozawa Jisaburo was on its way from Tawi Tawi in North Borneo. Admiral Ozawa was concerned not only with the relief of Saipan but, more importantly, with the destruction of the American fleet. The new Yokosuka D4Y 'Judy' dive-bombers and Nakajima B6N 'Jill' torpedo-bombers and an updated Zero fighter were now available, although their pilots were not fully trained and lacked experience. Ozawa deployed about twenty-five submarines to scout and harass American shipping, but signal intercepts revealed their positions, and seventeen of them were sunk without an American ship being damaged. The Japanese also relied on their land-based aircraft, unaware that the Americans had already attacked their airfields and destroyed their planes. Admiral Spruance made matters worse for them by sending a task force to attack the Bonin Island air bases of Iwo Jima, Chichi Jima and Haha Jima on 17 June. Spruance also had a numerical advantage with seven carriers to Ozawa's five, eight light carriers to four, seven battleships to five, thirteen light cruisers to two and sixty-nine destroyers to twenty-eight. Only in heavy cruisers, at eleven to eight, did the Japanese have the edge. In aircraft the 475 Japanese machines were outnumbered twice over, but had significantly greater range. However, Spruance had only a hazy notion of Ozawa's whereabouts, while the Japanese reconnaissance had, on 18 June at 15.14 hours, located the Americans precisely.

Spruance took no risks. He pulled back towards

US Marines come to the assistance of a wounded comrade during the Guam invasion, June/August 1944. (Taylor Library)

Saipan and prepared American Task Force 58, under Vice-Admiral Mark Mitscher, for action. Mitscher arranged his forces in four carrier groups and a battleship group, each available to support the others. The Japanese advanced with a vanguard of three light carriers, four battleships, four cruisers and nine destroyers. A hundred miles (160 km) astern followed the main battlefleet of one light and five fleet carriers, a battleship, two cruisers and nineteen destroyers. At 10.00 hours on 19 June the Americans observed a Japanese airstrike on radar at a distance of 150 miles (240 km). Mitscher flew off a massive fighter force and many of his bombers, clearing the decks of aircraft and stationing them to his east. The air cover, 140 Hellcats flying to meet the enemy and another 82 patrolling above, met the 69 Japanese raiders and shot down 42 of them. One bomb hit *South Dakota* but did not affect her operational status. Four American flyers were killed.

Rearmed and ready to take off when the next raid was spotted at 11.07, the Hellcats had time to get in

US Marines dash through Garapan, capital of Saipan, July 1944. (Taylor Library)

position to meet the eighty bombers and torpedo-bombers and their forty-eight escorting fighters. Ninety-seven of these aircraft failed to return to their carriers. Meanwhile the Japanese fleet was attacked by the American submarine *Albacore*, and torpedoes sped towards Admiral Ozawa's flagship, the carrier *Taiho*. One of her aircraft, taking off, saw the tracks and dived on a torpedo, blowing himself and it to pieces, but another hit the ship. Fuel leaked within her, and when fans, switched on in error, spread the fumes, an explosion lifted off the flight deck and fire engulfed the carrier. The Admiral moved his flag to the cruiser *Haguro*, and *Taiho* sank at 1830 with the loss of 1,650 of her 2,150 crew. At noon the submarine *Cavalla* made four torpedo hits on the veteran carrier *Shokaku* and she sank with a similar loss of life.

A third air raid on the American fleet failed, and a fourth failed to find targets and headed for Japanese-held Guam. Such a move was anticipated and they were destroyed. Evening was approaching. The 'Great Marianas Turkey Shoot' was over. Of the 475 aircraft he had at dawn on 19 June, Ozawa had 120 left. The Americans lost twenty-three shot down, nine from other causes and twenty-seven aircrew.

On Saipan the Americans had taken the key Aslito airfield on 18 June, but the Japanese then withdrew progressively into the hilly central area and onto the jungle-clad Mount Tapotchau. The 27th Division battled against an escarpment that became known as Purple Heart Ridge, after the decoration awarded to those wounded in action. Naval shellfire supported the hard-won progress, and Japanese losses mounted. On 6 July General Saito issued his last order, for a last attack, and killed himself. Vice-Admiral Nagumo did likewise. At 04.45 hours on 7 July some 2,500 troops hurled themselves forward in the largest *banzai* charge of the war. They hit the 27th and smashed through, along the railway line and under the guns of the Marines, who feared to fire towards the men of 27th Infantry. Then they came into the sights of Battery H of the 3/10th. The gunners set their fuses to four-tenths of a second and the shells exploded only seventy-five yards (70 m) ahead of their positions. In the hand-to-hand fighting that followed, the last of the Japanese were killed. Some pockets of resistance held out for another two days, and, at the last, soldiers and civilians threw their children off the cliff at Marpi Point, at the north of the island, and then jumped after them to their deaths. Of the 32,000 defenders fewer than a thousand lived to be taken prisoner. The Americans lost 3,426 killed and 13,099 wounded; of these casualties 78 per cent were Marines.

The Grumman F-6F Hellcat played a vital role in defending the US fleet. (Gordon Bain)

The Battle of Leyte Gulf

A Japanese destroyer under attack in Ormoc Bay, off Leyte. A Mitchell bomber had already scored one hit, and the circle shows where another bomb is on the point of striking its target. (Taylor Library)

There was a strong school of thought that the Philippines should not be reconquered, but bypassed, isolated to be cleaned up once the Japanese homeland had been taken. The American Admiral Ernest King, Chief of Naval Operations, was keen to move against Formosa (Taiwan), but General MacArthur pointed out the strategic importance of the Philippines as well as the moral duty to liberate their allies and long-time dependants, the Filipinos. The argument was won by the general, in part because he had forces available to undertake the task. The Philippines is made up of numerous islands, of which Luzon, in the north, was the most important politically. Leyte, beyond Samar to the south, had tactically valuable airfields, and Mindanao, to the south-west, was simply large, but also mountainous and heavily forested. MacArthur originally considered starting with the latter and working north, but then decided to bypass it and take Leyte first.

On 20 October the invasion began. Some 700 ships and 130,000 men of Lieutenant-General Walter Kreuger's Sixth Army faced a defence some 20,000 strong. The Japanese, however, saw this as an opportunity to smash the American Navy. They had long sought to draw them into a decisive battle, and plans had been made, Operation *Sho*, for a number of possible locations. Land-based aircraft and naval gunfire were to be combined to achieve the result. The Third US Fleet under Vice-Admiral William Halsey was to be decoyed northwards by Vice-Admiral Ozawa, leaving Vice-Admiral Thomas Kinkaid's Seventh US Fleet at the mercy of

a pincer movement to be carried out by Vice-Admiral Kurita Takeo of 1st Striking Force going north around Leyte and Vice-Admiral Shima Kiyohide of 2nd Striking Force going south, supported by Vice-Admiral Nishimura Shojo with elements of 1st Striking Force. It was a complicated plan which called for close co-ordination and timing.

On 18 October the order to proceed was given by Admiral Toyoda Soemu, Commander-in-Chief of the Combined Navy. The JN-25 code had recently been changed, and this fact, together with strict radio silence, concealed the plan from the Americans. Ozawa left the Japanese Inland Sea with his Northern Force, the decoy fleet, consisting of the old battleships *Ise* and *Hyuga*, the veteran carrier *Zuikaku* and the light carriers *Zuiho*, *Chitose* and *Chiyoda*. There were three light cruisers and eight destroyers as escort, but this formation had no air capability; the Marianas Turkey Shoot had ended that role for them. The Japanese air power was now landbased, with about 600 machines flown in to Luzon. Ozawa made for the eastern side of Luzon in order to tempt Halsey away from the invasion fleet. Kurita's Centre Force of 1st Striking Force refuelled in Brunei and moved north-east. He had the two new, massive battleships *Yamato* and *Musashi*, as well as the older battleships *Nagato*, *Kongo* and *Haruna*, ten heavy cruisers, two light cruisers and fifteen destroyers. They made course for the Sibuyan Sea, the island-enclosed sea south of Luzon, and the San Bernadino Strait north of Samar island. The Southern Force under Nishimura sailed for the Surigao Strait south of Leyte with the battleships *Yamashiro* and *Fuso*, a heavy cruiser and four destroyers. From the north-west came Shima's Second Striking Force with three heavy cruisers, two light cruisers, twelve destroyers and transports carrying troops to the Philippines.

The first contact between the opposing forces was made by the American submarines *Dace* and *Darter*, when Kurita's flotilla was seen off the island of Palawan, and at 06.32 hours on 23 October *Darter* torpedoed the Admiral's flagship, the cruiser *Atago*, and sank her. The submarine immediately used her stern torpedoes to do the same for the next cruiser, *Takao*. Halsey now knew Kurita's force was coming, and the next day he received the news of Shima's and Nishimura's forces, but still knew nothing of the decoy force. Halsey sent part of his Task Force 38 under Vice-Admiral Marc Mitscher closer to Luzon, and it was attacked by land-based aircraft that hit the light carrier *Princeton*. In the act of coming to her aid 600 men of the cruiser *Birmingham* were caught in an explosion. The carrier could not be saved and was sunk. This did not delay operations against Kurita's ships. In successive waves 226 American aircraft attacked, and the giant battleship *Musashi* was hit by seventeen bombs and nineteen torpedoes and sank, while the cruiser *Myoko* was also torpedoed and had to return to base. Eighteen American planes were lost. Kurita pulled back, and it was reported to Halsey that he was retiring altogether.

As, late on 24 October, Kurita was given his set-back, Ozawa's Decoy Force was seen, and knowing that Kinkaid had the Surigao Strait covered, Halsey sent Task Force 38 north to destroy it. It was a decision he held to even when night reconnaissance showed that Kurita had resumed his approach to the San Bernadino Strait. In the south, intending to burst into the open sea beyond the Surigao Strait by dawn on 25 October, Nishimura's force was steaming in line through the narrows, with Shima some forty miles (65 km) astern. Kinkaid was, indeed, ready for him.

The classic tactical manoeuvre in naval surface warfare is to cross the enemy's 'T': that is, to have all your ships in a line able to bring all their guns to bear to one side on a column coming head-on from that side, and thus able to use only their forward gun turrets. Kinkaid had seven cruisers going back and forth across the mouth of the strait, and behind them six experienced bombarding battleships. At 23.00 on 24 October PT boats opened the action, but over the next three hours made no hits. At about 03.00 hours five destroyers of First Squadron attacked. The battlleship *Fuso* was hit and slowed. At 03.23 a second attack was aided by the explosion of the destroyer *Yamagumo*, which must also have been hit, and two more Japanese destroyers were

hit, as well as the flagship, the battleship *Yamashiro*. At 03.53 the heavy shelling from the battleships and cruisers began. At 04.19 *Yamashiro* came to a stop, capsized and sank. Of Nishimura's ships only a destroyer and the badly damaged cruiser *Mogami* remained to retreat. Shima turned away at once, although one of his ships collided with a wreck from the preceding flotilla. As the ships withdrew, aircraft took up the pursuit, and *Mogami* finally went down, as did two other vessels. It was a remarkably complete defeat for the southern pincer.

Kurita, by the morning of 25 October, had returned to pass through the San Bernadino Strait and turn southwards towards the Leyte landing beaches with six heavy cruisers flanked by destroyers and followed by his four battleships two and a half miles (4 km) astern. The only American naval force in the area was escort carrier Task Group 77.4, divided into three groups called Taffy 1, 2 and 3. Taffy 3, under the command of Rear-Admiral Clifton Sprague, consisted of six carriers, three destroyers and three destroyer escorts. At 06.45 observers saw anti-aircraft fire from the north, a radar contact was made and the pilot of an Avenger reported Kurita's strength twenty miles (32 km) to the north of Taffy 3. The Japanese were equally taken by surprise. Sprague launched aircraft and his destroyers laid smoke before attacking the enemy. The confusion put Kurita off balance, and he lost control, although his ships sank two destroyers, a carrier and a destroyer escort. Another carrier, from Taffy 1, fell victim to a *kamikaze* attack. Aircraft from other units of the Task Force joined the battle and sank two of his heavy cruisers as Kurita withdrew.

Mitscher, in the meantime, had attacked Ozawa's ships. At 08.10 on 25 October American aircraft went into action, and by 09.37 one light carrier and a destroyer had been sunk. The second strike at 09.45 accounted for another light carrier, and the third, at 11.45, for the veteran fleet carrier *Zuikaku*. The fourth carrier lasted until the next day. The destruction was not complete, for Halsey was obliged to send ships south against Kurita. They arrived too late, and Ozawa managed to get his battleships away. The largest naval action ever fought had come to an end, satisfactory, if not entirely successful, for the Americans.

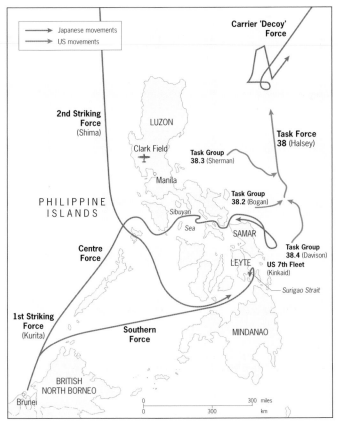

The Battle of Iwo Jima

American troops finding what cover they can on the beaches of the volcanic sand on Iwo Jima. (Derrick Wright Collection)

The island of Iwo Jima lies 650 miles (1,000 km) south-east of Tokyo, and from it the Americans knew they could fly fighter aircraft as escorts for B-29 bombers raiding the Japanese home islands from bases in the Marianas. Furthermore, it was a necessary conquest, given the intention to land on Okinawa, a similar distance west, as a preliminary to invading Japan itself. It had two operational airfields and a third under construction. The island's name, sulphur island, is testimony to its volcanic origin. It is some five miles (8 km) long and about half of that in width at its widest point. On the south-western end is Mount Suribachi, which rises to some 554 feet (169 m), and the northern half is formed of a series of ledges rising to a plateau at about 350 feet (105 m), cut with ravines and riddled with caves. Between the heights the connecting ridge is flanked with beaches covered with black volcanic ash in which a man sinks ankle deep, tracked vehicles struggle and wheeled vehicles cannot move at all. Today the vegetation is sparse, and at the time it had been blasted out of existence. It was a deeply unattractive place at any time, and worse in war.

The island was defended by Lieutenant-General Kuribayashi Tadamichi, with 26,000 army and navy men. Whereas the Japanese elsewhere had attempted to throw invaders back with counter-attacks, Kuribayashi planned to fortify the place in detail and fight a long, attritional battle to wear out the Americans. He had 361 75-mm field guns, and dug hundreds of bunkers with interlocking arcs of fire. On Mount Suribachi there were 165 concrete bunkers, and at Kita, on the north-western shore, a command bunker entered by a tunnel 500 yards (450 m) long. The innumerable caves and bunkers were connected by eleven miles (17.5 km) of tunnels to allow the Japanese to move underground, evading incoming fire. The island had been converted into a fortress.

The Americans knew that the task was formidable, but not how formidable it was to prove in the event. The plan was to subject the island to air strikes over a period of seventy-two days, and then to a naval bombardment, before landing two Marine divisions on the south-east shore. They were to advance to the opposite shore, take out the mountain to the south-west and then roll up the Japanese northwards to complete the conquest in fourteen days. In overall command was Admiral Raymond Spruance, with the amphibious operation under Vice-Admiral Richmond Kelly Turner and the troops under Lieutenant-General Holland M. 'Howling Mad' Smith, with the operational command of V Amphibious Force under Major-General Harry Schmidt. The 5th Marine Division under Major-General Keller E. Rockey was to land on the left, and the 4th under Major-General Clifton B. Cates on the right. In reserve was the 3rd Marine Division under Major-General Graves B. Erskine. The Marines numbered 70,000 men.

The pre-invasion barrage was laid down by Rear-Admiral William Blandy's Task Force 52. Schmidt had asked for ten days of shelling but was vouchsafed only three, and the first two days were dogged by bad weather. On the final day, D-Day itself, 19 February, clear weather greeted the arrival of Admiral Marc Mitscher's Task Force 58 with its sixteen carriers, eight battleships and fifteen cruisers to join the shelling. The first wave to approach the beaches at 08.30 was headed by twelve support landing craft which strafed the shore with rocket, cannon and machine-gun fire. Sixty-eight of the 482 Amtracs allocated to carry eight battalions ashore followed to land the first men, on time, at about 09.00 hours. A wave of F4U-ID Corsair fighters gave covering fire, and the Navy's bombardment began rolling forward. As they advanced up the beach the Amtracs encountered the first terrace of rising land and many failed to climb it. The Marines had to leap out and struggle forward through the deep, loose sand. After fifteen minutes, with the beaches now filling with men and machines, the Japanese opened fire.

The leading units of Marines had gone about 200 yards (180 m) inland before coming up against the front line of pillboxes, and found virtually no cover. The arrival of the first tanks at 09.44 helped only to a limited extent as they, too, churned away in the sand and baulked at the terrace; indeed, some backed off to open up a line of fire on the pillboxes. Fire poured down from emplacements on Mount Suribachi, and soon the beach was a shambles of burning vehicles and hastily dug, unstable foxholes. In spite of this, with stubborn courage, the Marines pressed on. Casualties were numerous, but by 10.35 the first objective, reaching the far shore, had been achieved. The task of holding the ground gained was made harder by the re-occupation of pillboxes already overcome by Japanese using underground tunnels. On the extreme right the 4th Division had particular difficulty near East Boat Basin, which was overlooked by cliffs. By nightfall the engineers, SeaBees, had cleared the way through minefields and bulldozed the terrace slopes for the tanks and the beachhead had been stabilized. The first day had cost 2,450 casualties, but 30,000 Marines were ashore.

The night was unpeaceful. The Navy lit the scene with flares, the Japanese kept up mortar fire and the Marines tried to consolidate their line. The next day they inched a little further up Mount Suribachi on the left and moved against the airfields on the right. By noon Airfield No.1 was taken. The next day at 08.45, in driving rain which turned the dusty soil to a sucking, sticky mud, the 28th Regiment attacked Mount Suribachi. The tanks did not arrive to flatten the barbed wire the Marines had strung for protection overnight, but when they did appear progress was made. By the afternoon of 22 February, still in foul weather, they had surrounded the mountain. The next day dawned clear, and at 08.00 3rd Platoon renewed the assault on Suribachi. Resistance was light, many defenders having crept away through the tunnels. By 10.00 they reached the rim of the crater and cleared away the remaining Japanese. At 10.20 they raised a small Stars and Stripes flag, which was replaced by a larger one at about noon, an event recorded by cameraman Joe Rosenthal in an unposed photograph that became the most famous of the war in the Pacific, and the model for the Marine Corps Memorial at Arlington Cemetery.

The rest of the Marines devoted the day to consolidation, resupply and the establishment of command posts for the divisions now ashore, which included part of the 3rd, which it had been hoped would be preserved intact for Okinawa. On the west the 5th Division faced the Japanese, with the 3rd in the centre and the 4th on the east. The next day's action took them approximately to the 0-1 line, the cross-island objective on the northern flank planned for D-Day.

The long fight continued. On the east the 4th Marine Division had to attack a complex of positions that became known as the Meatgrinder. It consisted of Hill 382, a depression called the Amphitheater, a hill called Turkey Knob and the shattered village of Minami; it was to hold out until 15 March. Hill Peter, near the end of the runway of Airfield No.2, faced the 3rd Marine Division. It was just the first of a series of tough positions they took. By 11 March, the twenty-first day of the operation, the Japanese had been driven back to an area near the village of Higashi, an enclave known as Cushman's Pocket and Kuribayashi's last redoubt in Death Valley, or Bloody Gorge, between Kita and the northern coast. On 14 March, as a public relations exercise, Iwo Jima was declared secure, but it took ten more days to finish the defenders of Death Valley. Approximately a thousand Japanese, many of them too severely wounded to kill themselves, were made prisoner. The Marines lost 5,931 killed and 17,372 wounded.

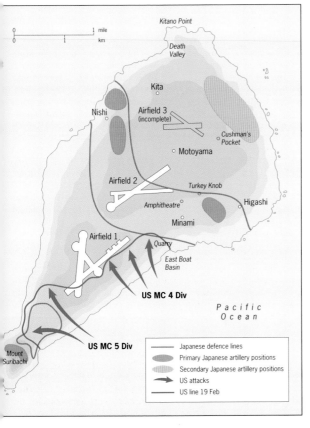

Kitano Point

Death Valley

Kita

Nishi

Airfield 3 (incomplete)

Cushman's Pocket

Motoyama

Airfield 2

Turkey Knob

Higashi

Amphitheatre

Minami

Airfield 1

Quarry

East Boat Basin

US MC 4 Div

Pacific Ocean

US MC 5 Div

Mount Suribachi

—— Japanese defence lines
Primary Japanese artillery positions
Secondary Japanese artillery positions
➤ US attacks
—— US line 19 Feb

The Battles of Luzon and Manila

The taking of the island of Leyte was not, in spite of the great victory at sea, an easy matter. General Yamashita Tomoyuki threw in an additional 50,000 troops, and by the end of 1944, when General Douglas MacArthur secured the territory, some 80,000 Japanese had been killed and fewer than 1,000 had surrendered.

The invasion and reconquest of Luzon was the obvious next step. In order to land a large number of troops only one location sufficed, the same as that used by the Japanese themselves in 1941, the Lingayen Gulf on the north-west shore. From here Yamashita was sure the Americans would head for Manila in order to secure the huge and vital harbour. Although he had about 270,000 troops, he could only put 600 aircraft up and had very few tanks. Naval support of significance was absent, and the main danger to the American fleet was *kamikaze* attack, bomb-laden aircraft flown by suicide pilots into US ships. He had, therefore, to devise a defence strategy to negate the American supremacy in the air and on the sea. He decided to permit the Americans to have the city of Manila and the one million inhabitants who needed to be fed, and to hold on to the harbour by retaining Corregidor Island and the Bataan Peninsula to its north. He therefore put Rear-Admiral Iwabuchi Sanji in command of 20,000 men to destroy vital installations in Manila and withdraw in due course. Three groups were to defend the rest of the island. The Kembu Group, some 30,000 strong, was to cover Clark Field and its surroundings north of Manila, a huge complex of airfields and support facilities. Shimbu Group, with 80,000 men, was to take position east of Manila, and the rest of the men he would have under his personal command in the north-east of Luzon.

At 10.00 hours on 9 January 1945 Lieutenant-General Walter Kreuger's Sixth Army of 200,000

men began to land, as predicted, in the Lingayen Gulf. The 6th and 43rd Divisions came ashore to the east and the 37th and 40th to the west. In the next few days contact was made with both Shobu Group and Kembu Group. Kreuger concluded that an advance would be foolhardy until his beachhead was fully established. This did not suit MacArthur. He was keen to race to Manila, a city in which he had lived for years and which, emotionally and in honour, he felt compelled to liberate as soon as possible. He was informed by his intelligence staff that the Japanese numbered only half of their actual strength, and determined that Kreuger was being too cautious. So he outflanked his own subordinate.

MacArthur ordered Lieutenant-General Robert Eichelberger of the Eighth Army to send the 11th Airborne Division to land at Nasugbu, south of Manila harbour, on 31 January. The commander of the 37th Infantry Division, Major-General Robert S. Beightler, received orders direct from MacArthur to head for Manila, as did Major-General Vernon D. Mudge of the 1st Cavalry Division. When the 11th Airborne ran into resistance on the Tagaytay Ridge, north of Nasugbu, Major-General Joseph Swing put two battalions on it by parachute. By 5 February the Americans had surrounded the city, and the next day the liberation of Manila was announced by MacArthur's headquarters. This announcement did not take account of the 20,000 Japanese within it.

Meanwhile Admiral Iwabuchi had been planning his defence, or, possibly, his last stand. He did not withdraw from Manila as Yamashita had ordered, either because he would not take orders from a soldier or because the advance was so swift that he could not get his troops out in time. The northern side of the city was provided with the natural moat of the Pasig River, and to the south a line of defence was built across Nichols Field to Fort McKinley. An

The American landing in the Lingayen Gulf was, like this on Leyte, unopposed. The huge landing craft (LSTs) give evidence of the vast resources the United States devoted to the war effort. (Taylor Library)

A Japanese cruiser off Manila attempts to avoid American bombs. Although America had almost achieved domination of the air and the sea by late 1944, the Japanese Army was to continue to offer a fanatical resistance. (Taylor Library)

attack from the east would be impeded by setting fire to the wooden houses and using the north–south avenues as fire-breaks before finally falling back to the financial district and then to the old walled city, Intramuros, which was still a fortified enclave. The troops had been reorganized into serviceable units, and the Filipino collaborators, a militia called the Makapili, lent their strength of some 5,000 men to the enterprise.

On 5 February, as the smoke from fires set by the

Japanese rose over the city, the 11th Airborne Division ran into heavy shellfire when they attempted to advance on Nichols Field. Immediately to the north the suburbs of Paco and Pandacan became a battlefield for the 149th Infantry Regiment. The Americans were obliged to use their artillery to lay down concentrated barrages and their aircraft to hit Japanese defence concentrations with napalm in order to make any progress. In the first few days American casualties amounted to more than a thousand men. They managed to isolate some of the defenders in a pocket between Nichols Field and the city centre around Rizal Stadium which fell to tank attack on 14 February. The next day Yamashita ordered Iwabuchi to break out, but the directive was rejected by the Admiral, who made a broadcast declaring his intention to fight to the death. His troops ran amok in the city, raping women and slaughtering everyone of European appearance they could find. The refugees in the German Club were attacked, and the building was set on fire with many still within. The Americans closed in, driving the Japanese back into Intramuros, reducing building after building to rubble as the only way to silence the stubborn persistence of enemy gunfire from them. MacArthur, hoping to minimize civilian casualties, forbade air attacks, so artillery breached the great walls of the old town, and on 23 February 129th and 145th Infantry fought their way into Intramuros. Iwabuchi and his staff killed themselves two days later, but it was not until 3 March that the last of the Japanese ceased fire. MacArthur's favourite city had ceased to exist. American dead numbered 1,100 and the Japanese dead actually found came to 16,650. How many civilians died is not known, but it is probably of the order of 100,000 people.

While the reduction of Manila was in hand, the Americans were fighting in Bataan and attempting to take back Corregidor. Both proved to be tough objectives, not overcome until the end of February. At Corregidor the 5,000 defenders eventually ignited ammunition and explosives in the underground tunnels, taking themselves and many Americans to their deaths. Fifteen Japanese were taken prisoner.

American operations continued to mop up the remaining Japanese in the other islands, and on Luzon Yamashita fought a long, attritional campaign as he withdrew to the north-east. The Americans were drawn into forest and valleys, into the mountains, and were forced to fight all the way. By August 1945, when the war at last ended, there were still 50,000 Japanese under arms.

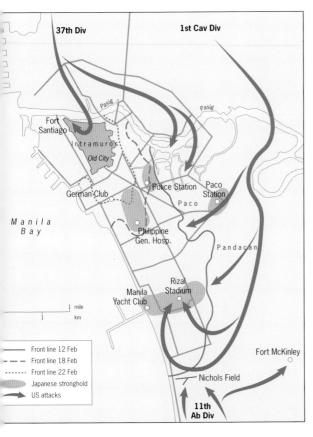

37th Div
1st Cav Div
Pasig
Pasig
Fort Santiago
Intramuros
Old City
Police Station
Paco Station
German Club
Paco
Manila Bay
Philippine Gen. Hosp.
Pandacan
Rizal Stadium
Manila Yacht Club
Fort McKinley
Nichols Field
11th Ab Div

1 mile
1 km

—— Front line 12 Feb
– – – Front line 18 Feb
········ Front line 22 Feb
Japanese stronghold
➤ US attacks

Having dealt the Japanese so considerable a set-back at Imphal and Kohima, Lieutenant-General William Slim was already deep into planning the ejection of his enemy from Burma (Myanmar) and the retaking of Rangoon (Yangon). The advance would involve crossing the Chindwin River as a preliminary to going east of the Irrawaddy (Ayeyarwady) River. This massive stream flows the length of Burma, first on the eastern flank of the country then, at Mandalay, taking a swing to the west and running south alongside the mountains called the Arakan Yoma before dividing into the myriad waterways of the delta draining into the Andaman Sea. The main line of communication runs east of the river and east of the Pegu Yoma hills to the south of Mandalay before curving westwards for Rangoon. Slim decided that the Japanese would contest the issue somewhere north of Mandalay on the Shwebo Plain, north and west of the river. However, it soon became apparent to him that he was wrong and that the new Japanese commander in Burma, Lieutenant-General Kimura Hyotaro, was not going to give him a chance to deploy his tanks in force, and a new plan had to be made at short notice.

Men of the British 36th Division move through the Burmese jungle. (Taylor Library)

The river that had to be crossed was a considerable obstacle. After flowing between hills north of Mandalay it emerged onto a broad plain and spread itself wide, up to 4,500 yards (4,100 m), with shoals alternating with deep runs and variable water levels according to the time of year. A crossing in the face of a prepared enemy would be a disaster.

The first task was to consolidate the position in the Arakan, the coastal area facing the Bay of Bengal, to avoid problems from the western flank and to secure the use of the airfields. The next job was to confuse the Japanese and to convince them that Mandalay was the objective. Operation Cloak was mounted to pass false information, and this included the setting up of a bogus headquarters making misleading radio signals. The 19th Indian Division would then make

a move upstream of Mandalay to draw off the enemy, while the Irrawaddy was approached at a variety of locations either side of Mandalay, disguising the secret approach of the IV Corps's tanks and Indian divisions along the Myittha valley to cross at Nyaungu. The implementation of the operation was made harder by the loss of three squadrons, seventy-five aircraft, of Dakotas which the Americans had to transfer to China, where Japanese attacks were threatening their support airfields.

The Japanese in the Arakan were already withdrawing, and only Lieutenant-General Sakurai Shozo's 54th Division remained to face the 3rd Royal Marine Commando Brigade and the 26th Division at the end of 1944. They were soon pushed out. Meanwhile, on 4 December 1944, the 19th Indian Division began their push from Sittaung on the Chindwin eastwards towards Indaw and made much better progress than expected. They turned south along the Irrawaddy and by 9 January were as far south as Thabeikkyin. On the other flank Messervy's men had got held up at Gangaw, and it took the support of the Strategic Air Force with highly accurate bombing to clear the way for Lushai Brigade to take the place on 10 January. The 19th Division made probing patrols across the river and cleaned up Japanese enclaves on the west bank over the next ten days. Then, on the night of 14/15 January the full divisional crossing began at Kyaukmyaung, fifty miles (80 km) north of Mandalay, with a battalion getting over undetected and being joined by another the next night. The crossings continued, and the Japanese put in their first serious counter-attack on the night of 20/21 January. The conviction that this was preparatory to an assault on Mandalay must have been growing in Japanese minds, for the 36th British Division was to the north-east and it looked as if the two were intended to join and roll southwards. Lieutenant-General Katamura moved parts of his Fifteenth Army north, but instead of building up his forces for an all-out strike he committed his forces piecemeal, and the two brigades of the 19th were thus able to absorb the blows over the next three weeks. The RAF played an essential part in repelling Japanese attacks.

On the River Chindwin the 20th Indian Division advanced to Monywa, took the town against stiff resistance by 22 January and moved on to the Irrawaddy at Myinmu, thirty miles (50 km) west of Mandalay to look for a crossing place. Kimura moved more men north and, indeed, brought a regiment of his 2nd Division up from Meiktila, Slim's intended and well-disguised objective. On 13 February the Border Regiment of 100 Brigade, 20th Division, led the way across the river west of Myinmu, virtually unopposed. Seven miles (11 km) downstream the Northamptonshire Regiment took the lead for 32 Brigade. The Japanese took two days to respond in force, and, against their resistance, the bridgehead was expanded until, a week after crossing, infantry and tank counter-attacks were attempted by them with suicidal vigour. Rocket-firing Hurricane fighters were used against the Japanese armour.

From Gangaw IV Corps made its careful advance, with the 28th East African Brigade as vanguard. Trees felled across the roads were cleared with gun-towing vehicles and elephants. By 3 February they were at Pauk, and the 7th Indian Division came through to advance towards the river, while the East Africans turned south towards Chauk as a diversionary force. Another party made for Pakokku to put on a second diversionary display, while the real crossing place was to be at Nyaungu, where the river, although 1,000 yards (900 m) wide, was at its narrowest. On the night of 13/14 February the South Lancashire Regiment's men were to cross upstream of Nyaungu while the Sikhs of 89 Brigade were to go for Pagan, six miles (10 km) downstream. The South Lancashires had difficulty in embarking, were delayed by engine failures when the outboard motors would not start and then came under heavy fire and had to withdraw. The 89 Brigade crossing failed as well, but then a boat came over to them with men of the Indian National Army who had, that very morning, been left to hold the town. Now that the Japanese had gone they wished to surrender! The Sikhs crossed and accepted their capitulation. As the day went on, IV Corps poured across the river. By 21 February the 17th Indian Division and 255 Tank Brigade were ready to strike at Meiktila. The town was quickly surrounded and was defended with the now usual bravery. It took four days for the British to take it. The counter-attack was immediate. Lieutenant-General Honda Masaaki brought the 49th Division to do the job, and for a while the 17th Indian Division were surrounded and supplied from the air. On 28 March he withdrew. A month later the British were at Pegu, having enjoyed the cover afforded by Aung San's Burma Independence Army, which had changed sides to fight against the Japanese, and only fifty miles (80 km) from Rangoon. The city was abandoned by the Japanese and reoccupied at the end of April. Slim's superb plan for the crossing of the Irrawaddy had been the key to the victory in Burma.

Indian troops on exercise with DUKWs and Alligator supply transports in preparation for the assault on the Arakan in support of Extended Capital. (Taylor Library)

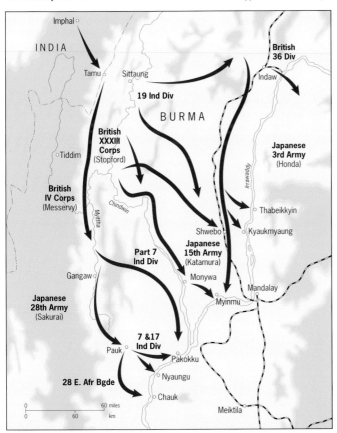

Allied Forces

IV Corps,
Lieutenant-General Frank Messervy, 7th and 17th Indian Divisions, 255 Tank Brigade (with Sherman tanks), Lushai Brigade, 28 East African Brigade.

XXXIII Corps,
Lieutenant-General Montagu Stopford, 2nd Division, 19th and 20th Indian Divisions, 254 Tank Brigade (with Lee-Grant and Stuart tanks), 268 Brigade.

111

The Battle of Okinawa

US marines await the results of an explosive charge thrown into a Japanese cave on the Shuri defence line. (Taylor Library)

In March 1945 America was preparing for the final effort in the defeat of the Japanese Empire – the invasion of the home islands of Japan itself. The fanatical resistance of Japanese soldiers, sailors and airmen suggested it would be no easy task and it was essential to establish a forward base from which to conduct operations. Okinawa, in the Ryukyu Islands, lies 340 miles (550km) from mainland Japan. It is sixty miles (96km) long, a hilly terrain rising to mountains in the south. It had a civilian population involved in agriculture and fishing before the war, and was dotted with towns and villages. For the purposes of war four airfields had been built with their attendant facilities.

The defence of the island was entrusted to Lieutenant-General Ushijima Mitsuru, who had at his disposal the Thirty-Second Army with 77,000 men. In addition there was the local Militia, some 20,000 strong, and even civilian volunteers, including children. Ushijima did not think it possible to resist an American landing without swift loss of a large number of men, and planned instead to fight a long drawn-out battle to inflict maximum casualties on the attackers. The uplands of the extreme south were therefore prepared by excavating tunnels to supplement the natural caves, building dug-outs and creating a strong, fortified line across the island from west to east through the village of Shuri. A secondary defensible area was made on the Motobu Peninsula on the north-western coast.

The American invasion force was huge. The landings were to be carried out by the Tenth Army under Lieutenant-General Simon Bolivar Buckner, son of the Confederate general of the same name who surrendered Fort Donelson to Grant. In all some 180,000 combat troops and 115,000 support troops would be landed. The first assault was to be by III Amphibious Corps (1st and 6th Marine

Divisions) under Major-General Roy Geiger on the left and XXIV Corps (7th and 96th Infantry Divisions) under Major-General John Hodge on the right. An armada of 1,213 ships was employed. The landings took place in the south of the island on the western shore, north of the capital city, Naha. Task Force 54 carried out the pre-invasion bombardment, and it was attacked by *kamikaze* pilots who achieved hits on the battleship *Nevada* and the cruisers *Biloxi* and *Indianapolis*, as well as four destroyers. Frogmen cleared underwater obstacles and, under cover of a bombardment from 06.40 to 07.35 hours on 1 April, the landing craft moved in. The carriers launched their planes in supportive strikes. The Landing Craft, Tank prepared to deliver their Shermans to the shore. On a five-mile (8 km) front the Americans moved towards the coast.

There was no response. The landings were unopposed, and by evening 50,000 men had come ashore. The Marines went north and east and the Army turned south. By 4 April the middle of the island had been secured, with 1st Marines in control of the Katchin Peninsula and 6th Marines through the Ishikawa Isthmus defence line. All the northern half of Okinawa, including the Motobu Peninsula, was in the hands of the Marines by 20 April. In the south, however, XXIV Corps had run up against Ushijima's fortress, and the advance stopped on a line south of the town of Kuba.

From the Japanese mainland support came for the beleaguered defenders. At the orders of Admiral Toyoda Soemu, Operation Ten-go went into action on 6 April. Massed attacks of *kamikaze* aircraft, attacks called *kikusui* (floating chrysanthemums) by the Japanese, were launched against the American fleet. In all, 700 aircraft, 355 of them *kamikaze*, swept into the attack. The destroyers *Newcomb* and *Leutze* were badly damaged. Picket ships some eighty-five miles (135 km) away were heavily assaulted, and the destroyers *Bush* and *Colhoun* were sunk. By nightfall another destroyer had gone, three support vessels had been sunk and a further ten ships severely hit.

Toyoda then ordered a surface attack. The 64,000-ton battleship *Yamato*, the largest in the world, was sent in company with the cruiser *Yahagi* and eight destroyers, supplied with five days' rations and fuel for only a one-way trip. They sailed from Bungo Suido on 6 April, and were seen and reported by the American submarines *Threadfin* and *Hackleback* immediately. The ships had no air cover, and American reconnaissance planes tracked them until the first American air strike at 12.10 on 7 April. Some 300 aircraft attacked the squadron. By 13.44 five torpedoes had hit *Yamato* on the port side, and she slowed. Bombs and torpedoes struck her time and again. At 14.17 she rolled over and sank, taking 2,496 men with her. *Yahagi* was also bombed and torpedoed to extinction, and four destroyers were sunk. The remaining four destroyers, or what was left of them, did make it back to port.

Air attacks on the American Navy and the supply vessels continued, and between 7 and 11 April another eleven US warships had been hit, the battleship *Maryland* included. On 12 April another *kikusui* raid took place with 150 fighters, 45 torpedo-bombers and 185 *kamikaze* planes. What was new was the *baka* bomb. The word means 'idiot' in Japanese, and was the name the Americans gave to a small, piloted, rocket aircraft that carried 1,800 pounds (816 kg) of explosive. The Japanese names were *ohka*, cherry blossom, and *jinrai*, thunderbolt. The weapon was launched from a twin-engined bomber, clumsy and easily shot down, and then flown by its suicide pilot into the target. One of the ships on picket duty, the *Mannert L. Abele*, was sunk by a *baka* on 12 April. The destroyer *Zellars* and the battleship *Tennessee* were hit by conventional *kamikaze*. By the end of June some 1,900 Japanese pilots had given their lives on such missions and a further eighty Americans ships had been hit, including the carriers *Enterprise* and *Bunker Hill*.

The lesser islands offshore had been taken, Tsugen on 11 April by the 27th Infantry Division and Ie by the 77th Infantry Division in fighting from 16 to 21 April, but in the south of Okinawa the advance had ceased. The 7th and 99th Infantry came to a halt at the Shuri defence line on 14 April. A massive bombardment of the line followed in which the Navy fired 19,000 rounds in forty minutes. This was followed by 650 Navy and Marine aircraft with bombs, napalm and rockets. When the Americans renewed the attack, the Japanese emerged from their underground bunkers, ancestral tombs and caves to fight as stubbornly as before. The 7th and 99th Infantry were relieved by the Marines and by the 77th and 29th Infantry, and the fighting went on, the Americans inching forward with rifle, machine-gun, grenade and flame-thrower against pocket after pocket of entirely dedicated Japanese infantry. On 4 May Ushijima made a substantial counter-attack which the Americans threw back. The Marines finally broke the defence line at Shuri, and on 27 May Naha was taken. The Japanese fell back to their final redoubt, the Oroku Peninsula. On 4 June the 6th Marine Division made a flanking landing on the peninsula's western shore and the bitter fighting continued. On 18 June Lieutenant-General Buckner was at a forward observation post when a salvo of shellfire landed, shattering the coral rocks and sending a shard of stone through his heart. General Stilwell was to succeed him.

By 22 June the end was near, and the Japanese commander, Lieutenant-General Ushijima, committed ritual suicide. With his death and those of the other commanders, resistance petered out, and on 2 July the fighting ceased. For the first time Japanese soldiers, some 7,400 of them, surrendered, but not only had the rest of the 97,000 defenders been killed, but perhaps as many as 25,000 civilians. Allied losses were serious. Thirty-six ships and landing craft had been sunk and 368 damaged. The Navy lost 4,900 dead and 4,824 wounded, while the Army and Marines had 7,613 killed and 31,807 wounded. The American commanders could not but consider what the price might be for the conquest of Japan itself.

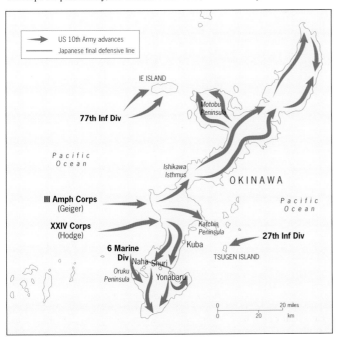

113

The Bombing Campaign on Japan

The workhorse of the American bombing campaign against the home islands of Japan, a B-29 Superfortress, takes off from Saipan. (Taylor Library)

The Doolittle Raid of April 1942 was a gesture to demonstrate that the United States could strike at the Japanese homeland, but strategic bombing was not possible until the new B-29 Superfortress bomber came into service and bases close enough to Japan could be established. The B-29 could carry a bomb-load of 20,000 lb (9,080 kg) and had a range of 1,600 miles (2,575 km). The first raid took place on 15 June 1944 when the steel mills at Yawata, Kyushu, were bombed by fifty aircraft of 20th Bomber Command from China. Operations from China were limited, and of fifty missions flown only nine hit Japan itself, and the rest were against targets in Korea, Formosa (Taiwan) and occupied China.

On 24 November 1944 the first raids were mounted from the Marianas. About eighty bombers of 21st Bomber Command under the command of Brigadier-General Haywood S. Hansell attacked the Nakajima aircraft factory in Tokyo. In December and January Hansell, who was strongly in favour of precision bombing of key industrial targets rather than of saturation bombing of cities, hit aircraft factories in Nagoya and Tokyo, but bad weather and technical problems with his bombers limited the effectiveness of these operations. General Henry Arnold, Commanding General of the US Army Air Force, was unhappy with this policy, although he had supported it in Europe, and advocated the fire-bombing of Japanese cites with their vulnerable wooden houses. Low-level flight would use less fuel, permit a greater payload and, if undertaken by night, risk fewer losses. In December Hansell was specifically ordered to carry out such a raid on Nagoya. He protested but obeyed. The attack took place on 3 January, with indeterminate results, while a precision raid on Kobe shortly afterwards destroyed an aircraft plant. Arnold made up his mind to get a more compliant subordinate and moved Major-General Curtis LeMay from 20th Bomber Command to take over the 21st.

On 25 February 1945 a force of 150 B-29s raided Tokyo with incendiary bombs. Almost a square mile (2.5 sq km) of the city was destroyed. Arnold was impressed and ordered more of the same night-time, low-level operations. LeMay increased the payloads by removing the now unwanted self-protective gunnery, leaving only a tail-gunner. On the night of 9/10 March a raid twice the size, 334 aircraft, hit the city. From altitudes of less than 9,000 feet (2,750 m) the bombs fell on Tokyo for two hours. Wind encouraged the conflagration, and fifteen and a half square miles (40 sq km), a quarter of the city area, burnt to the ground. Twenty crucial industrial sites ceased to exist, as did nearly 85,000 people. Tens of thousands were injured and yet more made homeless. In the next ten days similar raids were made on Nagoya, Kobe and Osaka, and two more raids were made on the Tokyo-Kawasaki area. A pause followed, in part because incendiary bombs were now in short supply and in part because the invasion of Okinawa required the support of 21st Bomber Command.

Air raids on Japan became yet easier to carry out in April. The P-51 Mustang fighters were now operating out of Iwo Jima to give cover to the bombers, and in mid-May operations against Japan resumed. Nine raids 500-bombers strong hit Tokyo, Nagoya, Kobe, Osaka, Yokohama and Kawasaki before the end of the month. The number of Japanese killed came to more than 100,000, and the cities were in ruins. Nagoya had more than three square miles (7.5 sq km) burnt down. On 25 May Tokyo's immolation covered an area even greater than on 10 March. In June, having run out of big city targets, the Americans turned their attention to smaller places. Sixty raids spread the destruction to more than fifty fresh locations, and the number of refugees fleeing to the countryside exceeded ten million.

All this time the military rulers of Japan held firm to their policy of fighting to the last. Their hope was that, despite the suffering of their people, the Americans might fear the possibility of yet greater suffering for their own troops if invasion went ahead. Plans had been made for Operation Olympic, the invasion of the most westerly of the home islands, Kyushu, by the Sixth Army, and preparations were already in hand, with October set for its execution. The plans for the invasion of the largest, main island, Operation Coronet by the Eighth and Tenth Armies, were in formation. The Japanese themselves expected an October attack and had reorganized their defensive forces into six self-contained, independent command zones so that the cost of success for the Americans would be as high as possible. The civilian powers in Japan were much less determined on continued resistance, but only the Emperor was in a position to overturn the military government's policy.

The conference codenamed Terminal, the last Allied conference of the war, took place in Potsdam, Germany, from 17 July to 2 August. It was attended by Marshal Stalin and, for the USA, by President Harry S. Truman, who had succeeded to the post on Roosevelt's death. In the course of the conference the result of the British elections came through, and Winston Churchill was replaced by the new Prime Minister Clement Attlee. Truman came to the meeting with the knowledge that at least one new weapon of fearful power was now available as a result of the work of the Manhattan Project – an atomic bomb called 'Little Boy' (a reference to Roosevelt), using uranium-235. Almost immediately on his arrival he was informed that the other, 'Fat Man' (a reference to Churchill), a plutonium-239-based weapon, was also operational. He shared this information with his allies, and on 26 July the Potsdam Declaration was issued, renewing the call for unconditional surrender by Japan and threatening 'prompt and utter destruction' if refusal continued. The threat was treated with contempt.

On the island of Tinian in the Marianas two B-29s of 509th Bomb Group awaited their orders. General Carl A. Spaatz had been sent from Germany to form US Strategic Air Forces in the Pacific and to run the campaign against Japan. When Truman ordered him to drop Little Boy, Spaatz insisted on having so momentous an order in writing. The B-29 'Enola Gay' arrived over Hiroshima in western Honshu and dropped the bomb at 08.15 hours on 6 August. It descended by parachute, to the puzzled interest of the city's inhabitants. It exploded with the force of 12.5 kilotons of TNT, destroying five square miles (13 sq km) of the city and causing the deaths, up to 10 August 1946, of 118,661 civilians and some 20,000 military personnel. On 9 August another B-29,

'Bock's Car', diverted from Kokura because of cloud, dropped Fat Man on Nagasaki, Kyushu, at 11.02 hours. Because of the terrain, the city sat in a valley, and two and a half square miles (6.7 sq km) was utterly flattened, 73,884 people were killed and 74,909 injured, with long-term effects from radiation disease adding to their number, as at Hiroshima.

On 14 August Emperor Hirohito directed that the Potsdam Declaration be accepted. On Sunday 2 September the official surrender documents were signed on board the battleship *Missouri* in Tokyo Bay, General Douglas MacArthur presiding.

USAAF Tonnage of Bombs and Losses

The estimated tonnage of bombs dropped by 20th Bomber Command, flying mostly from China, and 21st Bomber Command, operating mainly from the Marianas and Guam, is given, together with total losses and, in brackets, losses from causes other than enemy action.

| | 20th | | 21st | |
	Bombs	Losses	Bombs	Losses
1944				
June	547	18 (8)		
July	209	8 (5)		
August	252	19 (5)		
September	521	10 (7)		
October	1,669	21 (16)		
November	1,631	21 (2)	575	9 (5)
December	1,556	22 (6)	2,105	27 (6)
1945				
January	2,006	7 (3)	1,404	27
February	1,865	6 (2)	2,155	29 (3)
March	1,436	3 (1)	13,847	34
April			117,492	58 (1)
May			24,285	91 (3)
June			32,542	51 (7)
July			42,551	27 (5)
August			21,029	18 (7)
Totals	**11,691**	**147 (67)**	**157,985**	**371 (37)**

Colonel Paul Tibbets and his aircraft, 'Enola Gay' (named after his mother), after dropping the atom bomb on **Hiroshima**. *(Derrick Wright Collection)*

All B-29 Superfortress bombers were used during the final assault on Japan.

War Graves
American Battle Monuments Commission, Arlington, VA, USA. Tel: (703) 696-6897. In France: 1-4701-1976. In Rome: 06-4824-157. In Manila: 632-844-0212.
Commonwealth War Graves Commission, Maidenhead, Berks, UK. Tel: (01628) 34221. www.cwgc.org
Service des Sépultures de Guerre, Paris. Tel: 01 48 76 11 35.
Volksbund Deutsche Kriegsgräberfürsorge, Kassel, Germany. Tel: 05 61/ 1 98 81.

National Museums and Memorials
Australian War Memorial, Canberra, Australia. www.awm.gov.au
Canadian War Museum, Ottawa, Canada.
Imperial War Museum, London, Duxford and Manchester, UK. www.iwm.org.uk
Musée de l'Armée, Hôtel des Invalides, Paris. Tel: 1 47 05 04 10.
National Army Museum, London, UK. www.national-army-museum.ac.uk
National War Museum of Scotland, Edinburgh, UK. www.nms.ac.uk
New Zealand Memorial Museum, the Domain, Auckland, NZ.
Royal Armouries, Leeds, UK. www.armouries.org.uk
Royal Artillery Museum (Firepower), London, UK. www.firepower.org.uk
Royal Marines Museum, Southsea, Portsmouth, UK. www.royalmarinesmuseum.co.uk
Victory Memorial Museum, Messancy Handelange, Belgium (E25/E411 Autoroute service area).
Royal Museum of the Army of the Cinquantenaire, Brussels, Belgium.

Museums in the USA
Alabama: USS *Alabama* Battleship Memorial Park, Mobile. Tel: (334) 433 2703.
California: General Patton Memorial Museum, Chiriaco Summit. Tel: (619) 227 3227.
The Air Museum Planes of Fame, Chino. Tel: (909) 597 3722.
CEC/Seabee Museum, Port Hueneme. Tel: (805) 982 5163.
Connecticut: Nautilus Memorial and Museum, Naval Submarine Base, Groton. Tel: (860) 449 3174.
Washington DC: Smithsonian Museum, National Air and Space Museum. Tel: (202) 357 2700.

US Navy Museum, Washington Naval Yard. Tel: (202) 433 4882.
Florida: National Museum of Naval Aviation, Pensacola. Tel: (904) 452 3604.
Kentucky: Patton Museum of Cavalry and Armor, Fort Knox. Tel: (502) 624 3812.
Louisiana: Louisiana Naval War memorial, Baton Rouge. Tel: (504) 342 1942.
see also: D-Day and Normandy below.
Massachusetts: Battleship Cove Marine Museum, Fall River Heritage State Park. Tel: (508) 678 1100.
Michigan: Kalamazoo Air Museum and the Guadalcanal Memorial Museum, Kalamazoo. Tel: (616) 382 6555.
USS *Silversides* and Maritime Museum, Muskegon. Tel: (616) 755 1230.
Nebraska: Strategic Air Command Museum, Offutt Field, Bellevue. Tel: (402) 292 2001.
New Jersey: US Naval Museum, Hackensack. (201) 342 3268.
New Mexico: National Atomic Museum, Albuquerque. Tel: (505) 845 6670.
New York: Intrepid Sea-Air-Space Museum, Pier 86. Tel: (212) 245 0072.
North Carolina: USS *North Carolina* Battleship Memorial, Wilmington. Tel: (910) 762 1829.
82nd Airborne and US Army Special Warfare Museums, Fort Bragg, Fayetteville. Tel: (910) 432 5307 and (910) 432 4272 respectively.
Ohio: US Air Force Museum, Wright-Patterson Airforce Base, Dayton. Tel: (513) 255 3286.
Oregon: Fort Stevens Museum, Hammond. Tel: (503) 861 2000.
Texas: Iwo Jima War Memorial, Harlingen. Tel: (210) 423 6006.
USS *Lexington* Museum on the Bay, Corpus Christi. Tel: (512) 888 4873.
Silent Wings Museum, Terrell. Tel: (214) 563 0402.
Admiral Nimitz State Historical Park and Museum of the Pacific War, Fredericksburg. Tel: (512) 997 4379.
Seawolf Park, Galveston. Tel: (409) 744 5738.
Battleship *Texas* State Historical Site, La Porte. Tel: (713) 479 2411.
Utah: John M. Browning Fire Arms Museum, Ogden. Tel: (801) 629 8535.
Virginia: War Memorial Museum of Virginia, Newport News. Tel: (804) 247 8523.
US Marine Corps Air-Ground Museum, Quantico. Tel: (540) 640 2606.
Washington: Naval Undersea Museum, Keyport. Tel: (360) 396 4148.
Museum of Flight, Seattle. Tel: (206) 764 5720.

The Western Theatre, Western Front – France, 1940:
Ambleteuse, near Calais. World War II Museum.
Tel: 03 21 87 33 01.
Calais: Musée de la Guerre. Tel: 03 21 34 21 57.
Stonne, near Sedan: Circuit Historique, Mai-Juin
1940. Tel: 03 24 22 63 33.

Battle of Britain and Bombing Campaign:
Aviation Museum, Tangmere, West Sussex.
Tel: 01243 775223.
Imperial War Museum, Duxford, Cambridge.
Tel: 01223 835000. www.iwm.org.uk
RAF Museum, Hendon, London NW9. Tel: 020
8205 2266. www.rafmuseum.com

Battle of the Atlantic:
Merseyside Maritime Museum, Liverpool.
Tel: 0151 478 4499.
Royal Naval Museum, Portsmouth. Tel: 023 9272
7562. www.royalnavalmuseum.org.uk
Submarine World (RN Museum), Gosport.
Tel: 023 9252 9217.
Western Approaches, Liverpool.
Tel: 0151 227 2008.

Malta:
Aviation Museum, Ta'qali Airfield.
Lascaris War Rooms, Valletta. Tel: 234936.
War Museum, Fort St Elmo, Valletta.

North African battles:
The Tank Museum, Bovington, Dorset.
Tel: 01929 405096. www.tankmuseum.co.uk

Flying Bombs:
St-Omer, France: La Coupole. Tel: 03 21 93 07 07.
www.lacoupole.com
Éperlecques (near St-Omer): V2 Blockhouse.
Tel: 03 21 88 44 22.
Landrethun le Nord (near Calais): V3 Base,
Mimoyecques. Tel: 03 21 87 10 34.

D-Day and Normandy:
America: National D-Day Museum, New Orleans,
LA. Tel: 504 527 6012. www.ddaymuseum.org
France (select list):
Arromanches: Musée de Débarquement
Arromanches. Tel: 02 31 22 34 31.
www.normandy1944.com
Bayeux: Musée Mémorial de la Bataille de
Normandie. Tel: 02 31 92 93 41.
Caen: Mémorial. Tel: 02 31 06 06 52.
www.unicaen.fr/memorial

Falaise: Musée Août 1944 (Falaise pocket).
Tel: 02 31 90 37 19.
Ranville: Mémorial Pegasus. Tel: 02 31 78 76 08.
Sainte-Mère-Église: Airborne Troops (US)
Museum. Tel: 02 31 41 41 35.
Sainte-Marie-du-Mont: Musée du Débarquement
Utah Beach. Tel: 02 33 71 53 35.
www.utah-beach.com, www.utah-beach.org
Great Britain: D-Day Museum, Southsea,
Portsmouth. Tel: 023 9282 7261.
www.portsmouthmuseums.co.uk

Operation Market Garden:
Groesbeek: Liberation Museum and Dome of
Honour. Tel: 024 3974404.
Oosterbeek: Airborne Museum Hartenstein.
Tel: 026 3337710. www.airbornemuseum.com

Battle of the Bulge (select list):
Bastogne: Bastogne Historical Center.
Tel: 32 61 21 14 13.
Clervaux: Musée de la Bataille des Ardennes.
Tel: 352 99 72 15.
La Gleize-Stoumont: Museum December 1944.
Tel: 32 80 78 51 91.
Luxembourg: National Museum of Military
History, Diekirch. Tel: 352 80 89 08.

Battles of the Rhine:
Irrel, Germany: Westwall Museum at the
Katzenkopf (ask at Tourist Information).
Overloon, Netherlands: Nationaal Oorlogs-en
Verzetsmuseum. Tel: 04781 41820.
Remagen, Germany: Friedensmuseum Brücke von
Remagen.

The Pacific Theatre:
Pearl Harbor, Honolulu:
USS *Arizona* Memorial. Tel: (808) 422-0561/2771.
USS *Bowfin* Submarine Museum.
Tel: (808) 423-1341.
Battleship *Missouri* Memorial. Tel: (808) 973-2494.
www.ussmissouri.com

Singapore:
Battle Box, Fort Canning.
Changi Chapel and Museum. Tel: (65) 736 6622.
Fort Siloso, Sentosa Island. www.sentosa.com.sg

Australia:
East Point Military Museum, Darwin.
Tel: 8981 9702.

Book List

Reference:
The Oxford Companion to World War II, Oxford & New York, 1995.

General histories:
Craven, W.E., and L.J. Cate, *The [US] Army Air Forces in World War Two*, Chicago, 1949
Hamilton, John, *War at Sea, 1939–1945*, Poole, New York & Sydney, 1986
Jones, James, *WWII*, New York, 1975
Keegan, John, *The Second World War*, London, 1989
Lewin, Ronald, *Ultra Goes to War*, London & New York, 1978.
Roskill, S.W., *The [Royal] Navy at War 1939–1945*, London, 1960
Weinberg, Gerhard L., *A World at Arms: A Global History of World War II*, Cambridge & New York, 1994

Atlases:
Badsey, Stephen (ed), *The Hutchinson Atlas of World War II Battle Plans*, Oxford, 2000
Esposito, Vincent J., *The West Point Atlas of American Wars*, Vol. 2, New York, 1959
Natkiel, Richard, *Atlas of World War II*, London, 1985

The Western Theatre, Western Front
General:
MacDonald, Charles B., *The Mighty Endeavor*, New York, 1969
Terraine, John, *The Right of the Line: the RAF in the European War 1939–1945*, London, 1985
Wilmot, Chester, *The Struggle for Europe*, New York, 1952
Marix Evans, Martin, *Norway 1940: The Forgotten Fiasco*, Shrewsbury, 2002
France 1940:
Horne, Alistair, *To Lose a Battle*, London, 1969
Lord, Walter, *The Miracle of Dunkirk*, New York, 1982
Marix Evans, Martin, *The Fall of France: Act with Daring*, Oxford, 2000
Battle of Britain:
Deighton, Len, *Fighter – The True Story of the Battle of Britain*, London, 1977
Hough, R., and D. Richards, *The Battle of Britain: A Jubilee History*, London 1990
Ziegler, P., *London at War 1939–45*, London, 1995
Battle of the Atlantic:
Haworth, Stephen, and Derek Law, *The Battle of the Atlantic*, London, 1994
Terraine, John, *Business in Great Waters, the U-Boat Wars*, Part III, London, 1989
Mediterranean:
Mackintyre, D., *The Battle for the Mediterranean*, London, 1964
Malta:
Bradford, E., *Siege: Malta 1940–1943*, London, 1985
Bombing of Germany:
Hastings, Max, *Bomber Command*, London, 1987

North Africa:
Barnett, Corelli, *The Desert Generals*, London, 1983
Carver, Michael, *Dilemmas of the Desert War*, London, 1986
El Alamein, London, 1962
Harrison, Frank, *Tobruk*, London, 1996
Irving, David, *The Trail of the Fox*, London, 1977
Jackson, William, *The Battle for North Africa*, London, 1975
Sainsbury, K., *The North African Landings 1942*, London, 1976
Crete:
Beevor, Antony, *Crete: the Battle and the Resistance*, London, 1991
MacDonald, C., *The Lost Battle: Crete, 1941*, London, 1993
Dieppe:
Villa, B., *Unauthorized Action: Mountbatten and the Dieppe Raid*, Oxford, 1990
Italy and Sicily:
d'Este, Carlo, *Fatal Decision: Anzio and the Battle of Rome*, London, 1991
Ellis, J., *Cassino: The Hollow Victory*, London, 1984
Ford, Ken, *Cassino: The Four Battles*, Ramsbury, 2001
Graham, Dominick, and Shelford Bidwell, *The Tug of War: The Battle for Italy 1943–1945*, New York, 1986
Trevelyan, Raleigh, *Rome '44*, London, 1981
Flying Bombs:
Young, R.A., *The Flying Bomb*, Shepperton, 1978
Normandy:
Badsey, Stephen, *Normandy 1944*, Campaign No.1, London, 1990
d'Este, Carlo, *Decision in Normandy*, New York & London, 1983
Hastings, Max, *Overlord*, London, 1984
Keegan, John, *Six Armies in Normandy*, London, 1982
Ryan, Cornelius, *The Longest Day – the D-Day Story*, New York & London, 1982
Market Garden:
Badsey, Stephen, *Arnhem 1944*, Campaign No.24, London, 1993
Powell, G., *The Devil's Birthday*, London, 1984
Ryan, Cornelius, *A Bridge too Far*, New York & London, 1974
Ardennes and the Rhine:
Arnold, James R., *Ardennes 1944*, Campaign No.5, London, 1990
Ford, Ken, *The Rhineland 1945*, Campaign No.74, Oxford, 2000

The Western Theatre, Eastern Front
General:
Glantz, D.M., and J. House, *When Titans Clashed*, Lawrence, Kansas, 1995
Winchester, Charles, *Ostfront: Hitler's War on Russia, 1941–1945*, Oxford, 1998

Barbarossa:
Erickson, J., *The Road to Stalingrad*, London, 1975
Stalingrad:
Beevor, Antony, *Stalingrad*, London & New York, 1998
Kursk:
Glantz, D. M., *The Battle for Kursk 1943*, London, 1999
Healy, Mark, *Kursk 1943*, Campaign No.16, London, 1992
Bagration:
Erickson, J., *The Road to Berlin*, London, 1985
Zaluga, Steven, *Bagration 1944*, Campaign No.42, Oxford, 1996
Berlin:
Beevor, Antony, *Berlin: The Downfall*, London & New York, 2002
Ryan, Cornelius, *The Last Battle*, New York & London, 1966

The Pacific Theatre

General:
Blair, C., *Silent Victory: The US Submarine War against Japan*, New York, 1975
MacIntyre, D., *The Battle of the Pacific*, London, 1966
Spector, R., *Eagle Against the Sun: The American War with Japan*, New York, 1985
Tuchman, Barbara W., *Stilwell and the American Experience in China, 1911–1945*, New York, 1972
Vat, D. van der, *The Pacific Campaign: the US-Japanese Naval War, 1941-1945*, London, 1992
Pearl Harbor:
Prange, Gordon, *At Dawn we Slept*, New York, 1981
Slackman, Michael, *Target: Pearl Harbor*, Honolulu, 1990
Malaya and Singapore:
Allen, Louis, *Singapore, 1941-1942*, London, 1977
Philippines:
Morton, L., *The Fall of the Philippines*, Washington, DC, 1953
Java Sea:
Van Oosten, F.C., *The Battle of the Java Sea*, Annapolis, 1976
Midway:
Prange, Gordon, *Miracle at Midway*, New York, 1982
Guadalcanal:
Coggins, J., *The Campaign for Guadalcanal*, New York, 1972
Imphal and Burma:
Allen, Louis, *Burma: The Longest War, 1941–1945*, London, 1984
Calvert, Michael, *Prisoners of Hope*, London, 1971
Slim, William, *Defeat into Victory*, London, 1956
Leyte and Luzon:
Bruer, W., *Retaking the Philippines*, New York, 1986
Cannon, H., *Triumph in the Philippines*, Washington, DC, 1953
Connaughton, R., J. Pimlott and D. Anderson, *The Battle for Manila*, London, 1995
Iwo Jima:
Wheeler, R., *Iwo Jima*, New York, 1994
Wright, Derrick, *Iwo Jima 1945*, Campaign No.81, Oxford, 2001
Okinawa:
Gow, I., *Okinawa 1945*, London, 1986
Rottman, Gordon, *Okinawa 1945*, Campaign, Oxford, 2002
Bombing campaign:
LeMay, C.E., with MacMinley Kantor, *Mission with LeMay*, Garden City, NY, 1965

Guide Books, *General:*
Bookman, John T. and Stephen T. Powers, The March to Victory *(Battlefields from London to the Rhine)*, Niwot, Colorado, 1994
Marix Evans, Martin, *The Military Heritage of Britain & Ireland*, London, 1998
Osborne, Richard E., *World War II Sites in the United States*, Indianapolis, 1996

Guide Books, *Detailed:*
Cooksey, Jon, *Boulogne,* Battleground Europe, Barnsley, 2002
Calais, Battleground Europe, Barnsley, 2000
Dunphie, Christopher, and Garry Johnson, *Gold Beach,* Battleground Europe, Barnsley, 1999
Forty, George, *Channel Islands,* Battleground Europe, Barnsley, 2002
Holt, Major & Mrs, *Battlefield Guide to Market Garden*, Barnsley, 2001
Battlefield Guide to Normandy, Barnsley, 1999
Kilvert-Jones, Tim, *Sword Beach*, Battleground Europe, Barnsley, 2001
Omaha Beach, Battleground Europe, Barnsley, 1999
Saunders, Tim, *Hill 112*, Battleground Europe, Barnsley, 2001
Market-Garden, Hell's Highway, Battleground Europe, Barnsley, 2001
Market-Garden, Nijmegen, Battleground Europe, Barnsley, 2001
Market-Garden, The Island, Battleground Europe, Barnsley, 2002
Normandy – Jig Beach, Battleground Europe, Barnsley, 2002
Shiletto, Carl, *Pegasus Bridge/Merville Battery*, Battleground Europe, Barnsley, 1999
Utah Beach, Battleground Europe, Barnsley, 2001
Steer, Frank, *Market Garden – Arnhem*, Battleground Europe, Barnsley, 2002
Tolhurst, Michael, *Battle of the Bulge – Bastogne*, Battleground Europe, Barnsley, 2001
Battle of the Bulge – St Vith, Battleground Europe, Barnsley, 1999
Vickers, Philip, *Das Reich – the Drive to Normandy*, Battleground Europe, Barnsley, 2002
Whiting, Charles, *The Battle for the German Frontier*, Moreton-in-Marsh, 2000
Wilson, Patrick, *Dunkirk*, Battleground Europe, Barnsley, 2000

Index